Rewriting Crusoe

TRANSITS:
LITERATURE, THOUGHT & CULTURE, 1650-1850

Series Editors
Kathryn Parker, University of Wisconsin—La Crosse
Miriam Wallace, New College of Florida

A long running and landmark series in long eighteenth-century studies, *Transits* includes monographs and edited volumes that are timely, transformative in their approach, and global in their engagement with arts, literature, culture, and history. Books in the series have engaged with visual arts, environment, politics, material culture, travel, theater and performance, embodiment, writing and book history, sexuality, gender, disability, race, and colonialism from Britain and Europe to the Americas, the Far East, and the Middle East. Proposals should offer critical examination of artifacts and events, modes of being and forms of knowledge, material culture, or cultural practices. Works that make provocative connections across time, space, geography, or intellectual history, or that develop new modes of critical imagining are particularly welcome.

Recent titles in the *Transits* series:

Rewriting Crusoe: The Robinsonade across Languages, Cultures, and Media
Jakub Lipski, ed.

Narrative Mourning: Death and Its Relics in the Eighteenth-Century British Novel
Kathleen M. Oliver

Lothario's Corpse: Libertine Drama and the Long-Running Restoration, 1700–1832
Daniel Gustafson

Romantic Automata: Exhibitions, Figures, Organisms
Michael Demson and Christopher R. Clason, eds.

Beside the Bard: Scottish Lowland Poetry in the Age of Burns
George S. Christian

The Novel Stage: Narrative Form from the Restoration to Jane Austen
Marcie Frank

The Imprisoned Traveler: Joseph Forsyth and Napoleon's Italy
Keith Crook

Fire on the Water: Sailors, Slaves, and Insurrection in Early American Literature, 1789–1886
Lenora Warren

Community and Solitude: New Essays on Johnson's Circle
Anthony W. Lee, ed.

The Global Wordsworth: Romanticism Out of Place
Katherine Bergren

For a full list of *Transits* titles, please visit our website: www.bucknell.edu/UniversityPress.

Rewriting Crusoe

THE ROBINSONADE
ACROSS LANGUAGES,
CULTURES,
AND MEDIA

Edited by
JAKUB LIPSKI

LEWISBURG, PENNSYLVANIA

Library of Congress Cataloging-in-Publication Data

Names: Lipski, Jakub, editor.
Title: Rewriting Crusoe : the Robinsonade across languages, cultures, and media / edited by Jakub Lipski.
Description: Lewisburg, Pennsylvania : Bucknell University Press, [2020] | Series: Transits : literature, thought & culture, 1650–1850 | Includes bibliographical references and index.
Identifiers: LCCN 2020004533 | ISBN 9781684482313 (paperback ; alk. paper) | ISBN 9781684482320 (cloth ; alk. paper) | ISBN 9781684482337 (epub) | ISBN 9781684482344 (mobi) | ISBN 9781684482351 (pdf)
Subjects: LCSH: Robinsonades—History and criticism. | Voyages, Imaginary—History and criticism. | Defoe, Daniel, 1661?–1731. Robinson Crusoe. | Defoe, Daniel, 1661?–1731—Influence.
Classification: LCC PN3432 .R49 2020 | DDC 823/.5—dc23
LC record available at https://lccn.loc.gov/2020004533

A British Cataloging-in-Publication record for this book is available from the British Library.

This collection copyright © 2020 by Bucknell University Press

Individual chapters copyright © 2020 in the names of their authors

All rights reserved

No part of this book may be reproduced or utilized in any form or by any means, electronic or mechanical, or by any information storage and retrieval system, without written permission from the publisher. Please contact Bucknell University Press, Hildreth-Mirza Hall, Bucknell University, Lewisburg, PA 17837-2005. The only exception to this prohibition is "fair use" as defined by U.S. copyright law.

⊖ The paper used in this publication meets the requirements of the American National Standard for Information Sciences—Permanence of Paper for Printed Library Materials, ANSI Z39.48-1992.

www.bucknelluniversitypress.org

Distributed worldwide by Rutgers University Press

Manufactured in the United States of America

CONTENTS

Foreword by Robert Mayer   ix

Note on the Edition Used   xiii

Introduction   1
JAKUB LIPSKI

PART ONE: Exploring and Transcending the Genre

1   "Mushrooms, Capers, and Other Sorts of Pickles": Remaking Genre in Peter Longueville's *The Hermit* (1727)   9
RIVKA SWENSON

2   "If I Had . . .": Counterfactuals, Imaginary Realities, and the Poetics of the Postmodern Robinsonade   23
PATRICK GILL

PART TWO: National Contexts

3   Castaways and Colonialism: Dislocating Cultural Encounter in *The Female American* (1767)   39
PRZEMYSŁAW UŚCIŃSKI

CONTENTS

4 Setting the Scene for the Polish Robinsonade: *The Adventures of Mr. Nicholas Wisdom* (1776) by Ignacy Krasicki and the Early Reception of *Robinson Crusoe* in Poland, 1769–1775   52
Jakub Lipski

5 The Rise and Fall of Robinson Crusoe on the London Stage   65
Frederick Burwick

6 Islands in Robert Louis Stevenson's *Kidnapped* (1886): A Counter-Robinsonade   79
Márta Pellérdi

PART THREE: Ecocritical Readings

7 Stormy Weather and the Gentle Isle: Apprehending the Environment of Three Robinsonades   93
Lora E. Geriguis

8 Robinson's Becoming-Earth in Michel Tournier's *Vendredi ou les Limbes du Pacifique* (1967)   117
Krzysztof Skonieczny

PART FOUR: The Robinsonade and the Present Condition

9 "The True State of Our Condition": The Twenty-First-Century Worker as Castaway   135
Jennifer Preston Wilson

10 *Gilligan's Wake*, *Gilligan's Island*, and Historiographizing American Popular Culture   148
Ian Kinane

Coda: Rewriting the Robinsonade   165
Daniel Cook

CONTENTS

Acknowledgments	175
Bibliography	177
Notes on Contributors	189
Index	193

FOREWORD

THE ASTONISHING, SEEMINGLY INFINITE, variety of the Robinsonade—and of the critical literature associated with it—is perhaps best (if somewhat paradoxically) suggested by the fact that examples of the form antedated the appearance of the urtext in the series, Daniel Defoe's *Robinson Crusoe* (1719).[1] Anticipations of Defoe's endlessly purloined, imitated, appropriated, translated, or otherwise transformed castaway narrative appeared well before the original, both in putatively factual travel literature (such as Woodes Rogers's *A Cruising Voyage round the World*, 1712) and in fictional texts (like Henry Neville's *The Isle of Pines*, 1668).[2] The first reworkings of Defoe's text appeared within months of the book's original publication, and the genre was given a name in 1731, when Johann Gottfried Schnabel used the term in the preface to his work of fiction, *Insel Felsenburg*.[3] And this "appropriative form" that originated at the beginning of the eighteenth century has been constantly and quite variously refashioned ever since, as we can see in, to name only twenty-first-century examples discussed in this volume, the written and cinematic versions of both *Life of Pi* by Yann Martel (2001) and *The Martian* by Andy Weir (2011) as well as the British film *Moon* (2009) and the American novel *Gilligan's Wake* (2003), whose title alludes not only to James Joyce's last work of fiction and but also to an American television program of the 1960s representing farcical castaways from California.[4]

It is easier to say what the Robinsonade is—what it contains—than to specify what it reveals to us, why it is so enduring a form, and why creators and receivers of texts (written and otherwise) have for so long found it so compelling. Referring, in however attenuated a fashion, to Defoe's novel, Robinsonades can include shipwreck, adventures before and after that calamity, an island, the ordeal of isolation, the challenges (physical, technological) of a castaway existence, an encounter with alien Others, rescue and return. But as both earlier commentators and the authors of the essays in this volume make clear, the list of motifs appropriated or adapted from Defoe's text allows for endless permutations. For some, a reworking of *Robinson Crusoe* that omits "island solitude" is not an "authentic" but rather a "pseudo-Robinsonade."[5] However, for other creators of Robinsonades, the protagonist's solitude can be more psychic than geographical. Thus, the Robinson of Patrick Keiller's film trilogy—*London* (1994), *Robinson in Space* (1997), and *Robinson in Ruins* (2010)—journeys first in London and then more widely in England and finds as he moves in his homeland "shipwreck and the vision of Protestant isolation."[6] Similarly, in some Robinsonades Defoe's Friday figure looms very large; this is the case, for example, in Jack Gold's film *Man Friday* (1975), in which the encounter between Crusoe and a supposedly "benighted" Other reveals not the savagery of the non-Westerner but the destructive, exploitative nature of the Englishman who is described by Friday as "sickness itself."[7] Other films—like *Cast Away* (2000) and *The Martian* (2015)—seemingly leave Friday out, but even those works recuperate the crucial Other in such elements as a blood-stained volleyball or a human clone. In any case, awareness of Defoe's *Robinson Crusoe* gives us some sense of what we might expect to find in any specific example of a Robinsonade, but one needs also to recognize that the form is as much shaped by variations on, and departures from, the original as by adherence to it. Thus, there are examples set in a dazzling array of countries, oceans, islands, planetary bodies; juvenile and adult Robinsonades; individual castaways and surprisingly large groups stranded on islands that can seem malign, beneficent, or simply mysterious. The Robinsonade encompasses narratives that endorse the colonialist values often associated with Defoe's text (or other, similarly hegemonic, ideological constructs), but it also includes, as this collection shows, works that critique or look beyond those values.

This brings us to the question of what kind of cultural work the Robinsonade does, how it serves so many purposes, and why it has proved so attractive and useful for the last three hundred years. I have argued elsewhere—in respect to not only *Crusoe* but also other novels by Defoe like *Moll Flanders* (1722) and *A Journal of the Plague Year* (1722) as well as his *Tour thro' the Whole Island of Great Britain* (1724–1726)—that Defoe the writer and his works are what Jan Assmann describes as "figures of memory," enduring both as "fixed points . . . of the past" and as elements useful within what Klaus Poenicke describes as "a project of permanent rewriting" that is "oriented toward the future."[8] Defoe, particularly, is such a figure of memory (much more so, for example, than most other eighteenth-century British imaginative writers) because he so frequently wrote with a very specific, practical end in view. Defoe's biographer Paula Backscheider asserts of works published by him in the 1720s (including the novels) that he wrote "to set his countrymen straight, to guide them, and to help them make distinctions."[9] Defoe, that is, treated crime or disease or commerce or politics or international affairs to shape his readers' thinking and to effect change. And if one studies the afterlife of Defoe's works, one finds again and again that other writers and artists—

FOREWORD

from Defoe's day to our own—whether they were focused on epidemics, the status of women, "the *problem* of England" at the end of the twentieth century, or relations between Westerners and peoples who were formerly their colonial subjects, have seen Defoe and his texts as what Ann Rigney describes as "sites of collective significance."[10] Thus, as the essays in this volume demonstrate, a constitutive feature of the Robinsonade as a genre is that it both imaginatively reworks Defoe's most famous narrative and addresses itself to the present. Put simply, as Carl Fisher observes of the genre, "the novel and its retellings capture the values of every age."[11] So it is not surprising that the mainly young scholars from Europe and the United States contributing to this volume have much to tell us about the Robinsonade in our own day.

The genre discussed herein is, in short, something of a wonder. And, in closing, we should add that this is true in no small part because it is, in addition to so much else, a crucial illustration of how genre works. Mikhail Bakhtin observes that "elements of the *archaic*" are "always preserved in a genre." These may be hard to identify in Robinsonades like the sitcom *Gilligan's Island* or the postmodern novel *Gilligan's Wake*, but they are nevertheless present, and, what is more, they are "preserved . . . only thanks to their constant *renewal*, which is to say their contemporization." From the eighteenth century down to 2020, we see the Crusoe myth made contemporary across time and space and historical moments and ideological formations, and thus the texts discussed in this foreword and the rich sample of Robinsonades treated in this collection illustrate Bakhtin's memorable dictum: "A genre lives in the present, but always *remembers* its past"; it is "a representative of creative memory in the process of literary development." And the essays in this volume have much to teach us about (borrowing again from Bakhtin) both "the *unity* and *uninterrupted continuity*" of the Robinsonade.[12]

Robert Mayer

NOTES

1. For discussions of the Robinsonade, in addition to those named below, see, for example, Lieve Spaas and Brian Stimpson, eds., *Robinson Crusoe: Myths and Metamorphoses* (Houndmills: Macmillan, 1996), and Ian Kinane, *Theorising Literary Islands: The Island Trope in Contemporary Robinsonade Narratives* (London: Rowman & Littlefield, 2017).
2. See the appendix to Daniel Defoe, *Robinson Crusoe*, 2nd ed., ed. Michael Shinagel (New York: Norton, 1994), 230, 227; for a confirmation of the popular view of the link between *The Isle of Pines* and *Crusoe*, see John Scheckter, *The Isle of Pines, 1668: Henry Neville's Uncertain Utopia* (London: Routledge, 2016), 3, and the sources cited therein.
3. Carl Fisher, "Innovation and Imitation in the Eighteenth-Century Robinsonade," in *The Cambridge Companion to "Robinson Crusoe,"* ed. John Richetti (Cambridge: Cambridge University Press, 2018), 100–102.

[xi]

4. Daniel Cook, "On Authorship, Appropriation, and Eighteenth-Century Fiction," in *The Afterlives of Eighteenth-Century Fiction*, ed. Daniel Cook and Nicholas Seager (Cambridge: Cambridge University Press, 2015), 20. Cook observes that "the long eighteenth century abounded in appropriative texts," citing, among many other examples, Jonathan Swift's complaint (in the voice of Gulliver) about "'Libels, and Keys, and Reflections, and Memoirs, and Second Parts" of *Gulliver's Travels* (21).
5. Carl Fisher, "The Robinsonade: An Intercultural History of an Idea," in *Approaches to Teaching Defoe's* Robinson Crusoe, ed. Maximillian E. Novak and Fisher (New York: MLA, 2005), 130.
6. Patrick Keiller, dir., *London* (BFI Production; Koninck Studios, 1994).
7. Jack Gold, dir., *Man Friday* (ABC Entertainment; ITC Films, 1975); Robert Mayer, "Three Cinematic Robinsonades," in *Eighteenth-Century Fiction on Screen*, ed. Robert Mayer (Cambridge: Cambridge University Press, 2002), 42–45.
8. Jan Assmann, "Collective Memory and Cultural Identity," *New German Critique* 65 (1995): 129; Klaus Poenicke, "Engendering Cultural Memory: 'The Legend of Sleepy Hollow' as Text and Intertext," *Amerikastudien/American Studies* 43.1 (1998): 20. See Robert Mayer, "Defoe's Cultural Afterlife, Mainly on Screen," in Cook and Seager, *Afterlives of Eighteenth-Century Fiction*, 233–252.
9. Paula R. Backscheider, *Daniel Defoe: His Life* (Baltimore: Johns Hopkins University Press, 1989), 516.
10. Patrick Keiller, dir., *Robinson in Space* (BBC; Koninck Studios, 1997); Ann Rigney, *The Afterlives of Walter Scott: Memory on the Move* (Oxford: Oxford University Press, 2012), 18.
11. Fisher, "Robinsonade," 138.
12. Mikhail Bakhtin, *Problems of Dostoevsky's Poetics*, ed. and trans. Caryl Emerson (Minneapolis: University of Minnesota Press, 1984), 106.

NOTE ON THE EDITION USED

All references to Daniel Defoe's *The Life and Strange Surprizing Adventures of Robinson Crusoe* (1719) are given parenthetically and are to the following edition: Daniel Defoe, *Robinson Crusoe*, Norton Critical Edition, 2nd ed., ed. Michael Shinagel (New York: Norton, 1994).

Rewriting Crusoe

INTRODUCTION

Jakub Lipski

How does one write about the Robinsonade after three hundred years in the life of the genre? The common denominator behind the multitude of possible answers is likely to be a belief that in order to grasp its complexity, one must go beyond traditional ways of writing about literature. Indeed, how else to study a genre—if one does understand the Robinsonade as a genre—that has been continuously reworked in such disparate fields as literature, theater, television, gaming, and the visual arts? One must also go beyond national boundaries: the Robinsonade has always been a global phenomenon by virtue of both represented realities and publishing contexts. The example was set by Daniel Defoe and the three volumes of the *Robinson Crusoe* trilogy—encapsulating, as it were, the whole globe and inherently diversified in terms of form.

The present collection of tercentenary essays, while it has no pretense of offering a definitively comprehensive study of the phenomenon, is based on the conviction that one can do justice to the Robinsonade only when adopting a perspective that transcends languages, geographical boundaries, modes of expression, and theoretical preconceptions—a perspective that is reflected not only in the contents and thematic structure of the book but also in the truly international set of contributors and variety of critical standpoints they adopt. The final product offers a multifaceted account of both the transformations undergone by the genre throughout the centuries and the changing patterns of reception. Our main concern here then is studying the Robinsonade as a genre in a constant state of becoming, transcending, as it were, any formal restrictions one might impose on it, a genre, as Ian Kinane succinctly puts it, "caught in this state of never-completed-completion."[1] Accordingly, we adopt a relatively broad understanding of the form. Recent criticism of the Robinsonade has oscillated between two extremes: on the one hand, the genre has been identified with the castaway narrative;[2] on the other, it has been treated as a subcategory within this tradition, depending for its identity on the relationship with (the first volume of) Defoe's *Robinson Crusoe*. While the subsequent chapters in this collection do establish links between the studied texts and *Robinson Crusoe*, thus subscribing to the latter critical tradition, we do

[1]

not consider a specific variant of this relationship as a fundamental generic prerequisite.[3]

The book is divided into four sections, each highlighting a particular aspect of the Robinsonade's transformations. The two chapters making up the first of them—"Exploring and Transcending the Genre"—address the issues of genre and literary form. Appropriately, they juxtapose material from Defoe's time with twentieth- and twenty-first-century reworkings of the pattern, which elaborate on the possibilities that were, in a sense, projected by Defoe himself. This heterogeneous set makes it possible to ponder some more general questions about the Robinsonade as a genre. What is it exactly? Where are its limits? How does one define it? These questions will reappear throughout the volume and will be further problematized in the closing essay.

Rivka Swenson's chapter on Peter Longueville's *The Hermit* (1727) zooms in on what might be termed the Robinsonade microgenre—that is, a narrowly understood genre of the Robinsonade developing in the immediate context of *Robinson Crusoe* encompassing works following Defoe's lead and written as a direct response to him. Swenson's case study brings us back to a specific historical moment—the 1720s—and foregrounds Longueville's novel as a gem in the already rich tradition of the early transformations of Defoe's model. Indeed, Longueville himself remarks in his preface that bookshops have been "*already crowded with* Robinson Crusoe, Moll Flanders, *Colln.* Jacks."[4] It is worthwhile to note here that the first examples of the microgenre had appeared already in 1719, shortly after *Crusoe* itself: a bound edition of *The Adventures, and Surprizing Deliverances, of James Dubourdieu* and *The Adventures of Alexander Vendchurch*.[5] That year was also when the first chapbook abridgements of *Robinson Crusoe* came out: editing, adapting, and abridging Defoe's narrative have always constituted a vital part of the Robinsonade phenomenon.

Rather than reconstructing a wider panorama of the Robinsonade in the 1720s, given the fact that there have already been successful attempts at this,[6] Swenson offers a micro-scale study, which, on the one hand, establishes the significance of *The Hermit*, especially in terms of its sensually descriptive poetics, and, on the other, sheds light on the metafictional strategies determining the life of the genre in general. These are conceptualized in the metaphor of pickling, which may stand for the idea of "remaking genre."

The following essay by Patrick Gill illustrates some of the ways in which the formal possibilities contained in the Robinsonade have been employed in twentieth- and twenty-first-century fiction, in particular by such writers as Muriel Spark, J. M. Coetzee, and Yann Martel. Gill elaborates upon what is, paradoxically, both absent and implicitly present in Defoe's model, thus shedding light on the nature of Robinsonade transformations in general. He concentrates on the category of the counterfactual, understood as "an alternate version of events" suggested intradiegetically, for example, by way of the narrator's internal monologues or authorial narrative experiments. This significant element of the Robinsonade poetics, already employed by Defoe, conceptualizes the mentioned paradox of absence and presence: just as Robinson's musings about the way things might have turned out differently constitute a vital part of his frame of mind, the various forms taken by the Robinsonade genre might be seen as realizations of the implicitly contained "alternate versions."

The contemporary Robinsonade has also taught us that what is absent from Defoe's realm is meaningful on its own merit and as such is artistically and ideologically inspiring.[7] This is the premise on which counter-Robinsonades are based; works such as Coetzee's *Foe* (1986), which bestows agency on a female character and thematizes Friday's silence, or, perhaps less seriously, *The Wild Life* from 2016—a French-Belgian animated motion picture telling Crusoe's story from the perspective of a parrot named Tuesday.

The second section of the volume comprises chapters studying the Robinsonade in the varying national contexts of the eighteenth and nineteenth centuries: both geographically—from England and Scotland, to France, Poland, and America—and ideologically, by making sense of the local transformations. The contributors elaborate on the potential of the Robinsonade to adapt to changing circumstances, in terms of content and genre, and on its continuous relevance in new contexts. Collectively, the chapters account for the globalization of the pattern and show that the process itself depended on transnational mediation—with special credit given to the French—and underscored the role of Defoe himself, who was universally cherished neither as the author of *Crusoe* (promoted as "Written by Himself" on the title page) nor as a proper novelist until the late eighteenth century.

Przemysław Uściński analyzes the complexity and contradictions of colonial ideology as reflected in *The Female American*, an anonymous Robinsonade from 1767, in particular its implied tentativeness in offering a coherent critique of British imperialism. Uściński argues that while the figure of a biracial female Robinson carries an inherently subversive potential, her willing subjection to the role of a Christian missionary guided by Providence inevitably reinforces the conventional ideological message. The following chapter by Jakub Lipski traces the early steps in the development of the Robinsonade in Poland. The emergence of *Robinson Crusoe* in Polish translation is here taken as an incentive to provide more general insights into the evolution of modern print culture in Enlightenment Poland and the Rousseauvian influences in the circle of King Stanislaus August. French

[3]

mediation in the Robinsonade phenomenon is also addressed by Frederick Burwick, who traces the history of the theatrical Robinsonade in London, from the late eighteenth century to the mid-nineteenth. Burwick acknowledges the role of French adaptations as well as showing that the political context, including the French Revolution and the Napoleonic Wars, was a determining factor for the subsequent London performances. The section closes with Márta Pellérdi's discussion of Robert Louis Stevenson's *Kidnapped* (1886) as a counter-Robinsonade. Pellérdi argues that the novel's message depends on an ideological shift that deconstructs the Defoevian representation of the Others as "savages." Specifically, it problematizes the position of Scotland within the British Empire from the eighteenth century to the late Victorian period. Similar shifts in representation, ever since Jonathan Swift's *Gulliver's Travels* (1726) and its revision of the cultural encounter and its implications in book IV, have constituted an intriguing possibility in the Robinsonade tradition, and as such are also addressed elsewhere in this volume.

The two chapters constituting the third part of the book—"Ecocritical Readings"—transcend conventional disciplinary limitations in responding to Defoe's *Crusoe* and the Robinsonade. Informed by posthumanist criticism, the chapters point to new interpretative possibilities granted by a paradigmatic shift in our understanding of agency. The issue of agency, as has been touched on above, has long constituted a vital element in the history of *Crusoe*'s transformations and has appeared particularly prone to feminist and postcolonial readings.[8] This volume's "Ecocritical Readings" go even further in empowering the silenced voices and highlighting the importance of the world of nature.

Lora Geriguis concentrates on the narrative and ideological functions of representations of climate and specific environments in *Crusoe* and three seemingly dissimilar Robinsonades: *The Female American*, *Daniel Defoe's Robinson Crusoe* (1997), and *Cast Away* (2000). Geriguis shows that a shift in perspective that leads to more attention paid to such representations may become a useful critical strategy in uncovering the otherwise elusive links between a target Robinsonade and (post)colonial discourse. In the following chapter, adopting Rosi Braidotti's concept of "becoming-Earth," Krzysztof Skonieczny offers a reading of Michel Tournier's *Vendredi ou les Limbes du Pacifique* (1967), focused on Robinson's and Friday's relationship with the island Speranza, which, rather than an object of conquest, becomes an empowered subject in the novel. Skonieczny discerns an ideal of interpersonal communion with Mother Nature that is suggested in *Vendredi*, an ideal that questions the mythical story of civilization, especially in terms of Robinson's agency.

The volume closes with two chapters exploring the relevance of the Robinsonade for what might be labeled "the present condition." It is not accidental that

INTRODUCTION

in doing so they both expose the genre's protean form and transmediality: oscillating between literature and cinema, showing how literary form becomes televised and vice versa—how contemporary fiction may feed on television. One might claim that, among other reasons, the formal adaptability of the Robinsonade to new social, historical, and cultural realities—a conviction that is expressed throughout this book—is the main explanation for its enduring pertinence.

Jennifer Preston Wilson focuses on the figure of contemporary worker in three relatively recent film Robinsonades: *Cast Away*, *Moon* (2009), and *The Martian* (2015). Wilson shows how the motif of the shipwreck, taking up various forms in the films discussed, helps capitalize on the spiritual crisis evoked by contemporary workplace environments. The three Crusoe figures are here analyzed as characters whose individuality is threatened by their employers' work systems, and for whom being stranded on the island (or the Moon or Mars for that matter) constitutes an opportunity to reconsider their allegiance to the corporate world and its ideologies.

Ian Kinane's focused reading of Tom Carson's 2003 *Gilligan's Wake* traces yet another trajectory of the Robinsonade's transformations: it shows how the texts making up the tradition can feed on themselves, at times being entirely or almost entirely disconnected from Defoe's model. *Gilligan's Wake* revisions a popular TV show from the 1960s—CBS's *Gilligan's Island*—rather than Defoe's *Crusoe*, and other examples of such "secondary" Robinsonades include, for example, a number of "Young Robinsons" written in nineteenth-century Europe in the wake of Joachim Heinrich Campe's *Robinson the Younger* (1779), which followed the ideas of Jean-Jacques Rousseau, or—even more famously—William Golding's *Lord of the Flies* (1954), written as a response to R. M. Ballantyne's *The Coral Island* (1858). This confirms the status of the genre as a "body of work that further fictionalises (and is fictionalised by) its own cultural history."[9] Like *Crusoe*, the later Robinsonade tradition has also established its own mythology and iconography, gradually becoming part of the mass culture industry: Chuck Noland's Wilson in *Cast Away* and the witticisms of King Julian from the *Madagascar* series (2005–2012) are the best known examples here.

Kinane's analysis of *Gilligan's Wake* foregrounds a conviction that is expressed throughout the book—that of the enduring relevance of the Robinsonade pattern. Carson's pastiche, in its blend of the high and low, the past and the present, is here presented as a metonym of the American twentieth century, a micro-scale container of collective cultural and historical consciousness. In other words, just like Defoe's *Robinson Crusoe* in the early eighteenth century, it captures the essence of its time.

Daniel Cook's coda to the present volume begins with a provocative question of what it is like to write a Robinsonade today. The answers given make us

[5]

realize the long distance between Defoe's model and its afterlife in the twenty-first century. On the other hand, in spite of this distance, the variety of possibilities mentioned make us also realize the scale of the phenomenon—one that does not yield to conventionally systematic approaches. It is our hope that the decision to transcend national boundaries, formal and generic limitations, as well as scholarly preconceptions in this volume has resulted in a collection that does justice to the complexity of the Robinsonade phenomenon and elucidates the dynamics of its ongoing transformations.

NOTES

1. Ian Kinane, *Theorising Literary Islands: The Island Trope in Contemporary Robinsonade Narratives* (London: Rowman & Littlefield, 2017), 12.
2. See Artur Blaim, *Robinson Crusoe and His Doubles: The English Robinsonade of the Eighteenth Century* (Frankfurt: Peter Lang, 2016). The blurb of the book reads, "The book is a study of the eighteenth-century English robinsonade, also known as desert island or castaway narrative." In a different context, Emily S. Davis asks, "What exactly are the key elements of the castaway story or Robinsonade?," a question that clearly implies an identification of the two concepts. Davis, "Teaching Coetzee's *Foe* in an Undergraduate Theory Classroom," in *Approaches to Teaching Coetzee's* Disgrace *and Other Works*, ed. Laura Wright, Jane Poyner, and Elleke Boehmer (New York: MLA, 2014), 182.
3. Maximillian E. Novak, for instance, defines the essence of the Robinsonade as "struggle against the forces of nature and ultimate success" and thus distinguishes *Robinson Crusoe* from the earlier tradition of castaway narratives, where the emphasis tended to be placed on isolation and survival. Novak, "Edenic Desires: *Robinson Crusoe*, the Robinsonade, and Utopian Forms," in *Transformations, Ideology, and the Real in Defoe's "Robinson Crusoe" and Other Narratives: Finding "The Thing Itself"* (Newark: University of Delaware Press, 2015), 112.
4. Peter Longueville, *The Hermit: or, The Unparalleled Sufferings and Surprising Adventures of Mr. Philip Quarll, an Englishman Who Was Lately Discovered by Mr. Dorrington a Bristol Merchant, upon an Uninhabited Island in the South-Sea; Where He Has Lived above Fifty Years, without Any Human Assistance, Still Continues to Reside, and Will Not Come Away* (London: Printed by J. Cluer and A. Campbell for T. Warner in Pater-Noster-Row, and B. Creake at the Bible in Jermyn-Street, St. James's, 1727), vi.
5. See Carl Fisher, "Innovation and Imitation in the Eighteenth-Century Robinsonade," in *The Cambridge Companion to "Robinson Crusoe,"* ed. John Richetti (Cambridge: Cambridge University Press, 2018), 101–102.
6. See Blaim, *Robinson Crusoe and His Doubles*, and Fisher, "Innovation and Imitation in the Eighteenth-Century Robinsonade."
7. See Ann Marie Fallon, "Anti-Crusoes, Alternative Crusoes: Revisions of the Island Story in the Twentieth Century," in Richetti, *Cambridge Companion*, 207–220.
8. See, for example, Celia Torke, *Die Robinsonin: Repräsentationen von Weiblichkeit in deutsch- und englischsprachigen Robinsonaden des 20. Jahrhunderts* (Göttingen: V&R unipress, 2011), and Ann Marie Fallon, *Global Crusoe: Comparative Literature, Postcolonial Theory and Transnational Aesthetics* (Farnham: Ashgate, 2011).
9. Kinane, *Theorising Literary Islands*, 11–12.

Part One
EXPLORING AND TRANSCENDING THE GENRE

1

"MUSHROOMS, CAPERS, AND OTHER SORTS OF PICKLES"

Remaking Genre in Peter Longueville's *The Hermit* (1727)

RIVKA SWENSON

NOTWITHSTANDING SOME FINE WORK ON Robinsonades, much remains to be said about the novelistic Robinsonade microgenre.[1] Individual examples old and new should be scrutinized, and the varieties of the microgenre (and their special relationships to both the rise of the Robinsonade and the larger rise of the novel) should be theorized. In fact, early Robinsonades' modern heirs (themselves more various than readers might assume) are inheritors of a tradition that is more complicated and more various than might be guessed at first blush, for the simple fact that some of the most interesting (and popular) specimens have been written off, prematurely, by modern critics. For example, today's readers have entirely forgotten the sensational jewel tones, the suggestions of dimensional tactility, and the robust description of smells and tastes and sounds that eighteenth-century readers savored at length in the different editions of Peter Longueville's very popular 1727 novel *The Hermit: Or, the Unparalleled Sufferings and Surprising Adventures of Mr. Philip Quarll, an Englishman*.[2] Amplifying the thrust of other recent recuperative work on early Robinsonades,[3] adding to the robust discussion that has recently sprung up around the senses in eighteenth-century Britain,[4] and intersecting with the burgeoning field of food and literature studies,[5] my essay is the first to treat Longueville's indeed *Surprising* (and surprisingly neglected) hermit Philip Quarll at any length. Illuminating in *The Hermit* an early untraced contributor to the Robinsonade microgenre's metafictional nature as well as a stunningly sensualized early chapter in the history of early Robinsonades and early novels alike, I show how Longueville's hermit meaningfully revises all that the hermit finds on his version of Crusoe's island and how the hermit processes all of these extant materials most lusciously and deliciously—with the help of the narrator-faux-editor-explorer Dorrington, who discovers Quarll living on an island off the coast of Mexico and who further processes the hermit's parchment documents—for a hungry reading audience. As we shall see by poring over Quarll's copious pickles, his rainbow fountain, and his innovative taxidermy, Longueville's descriptive sensory palate builds on Defoe's ingenuity by frankly and consistently defying what we usually expect to find in early prose fictions. That is to say, we expect to find a dearth of highly particularized, visualized, sensualized description, concomitant with our usual experience of premodern prose fictions,[6] but the hermit's work on the island and on the genre, at once both preservative and transformative, yields a rich bounty.[7] The protagonist's ability to transform everything that comes his way into something that can be smelled, heard, felt, and, above all, seen, tasted, or otherwise devoured and the narrator's commitment to describing the edible world for readers give flesh to the desires of the Crusoean microgenre that Longueville helps further imagine into being.

The Hermit offers something we are not much accustomed to finding in eighteenth-century novelistic fictions, including (famously) Daniel Defoe's *Robinson Crusoe* itself.[8] This is not to say that Defoe's *Crusoe* lacks all such description;[9] to the contrary, it is to say that Longueville capitalizes and expands upon such moments in *Crusoe* and writes them large: here is the sensually described world, the tasty world of colors, smells, textures, sounds, and, especially appropriate for the Robinsonade, tastes. Even that which is not literally consumable by Philip Quarll is rendered consumable for a readerly eye: the monkeys have "backs of a lively green," the "Face and Belly of a lively yellow," and "Coat[s] all over shining like burnish'd Gold" (19); the birds have a "fine Cin[n]amon Colour" on their backs, breasts of "Mazarine blue," bellies of "deep Orange," green necks, purple heads, and "Eyes, Bill[s] and Feet Red" (207). The other senses are no less neglected. For example, the hermit's bed is "a hard dry Hearth, very smooth and clean" with "a Mat about three Inches thick, made of a sort of Grass, which, tho' as dry as the oldest Hay, was as green as a Leek, felt as soft as Cotton, and was as warm as Wool" (7). Legendarily, we do not always find such a world in *Crusoe* itself. There are a lot of "things" in *Crusoe*, but we "see" hardly any of them (nor, to be sure, do we know what most of them taste like, despite the book's preponderance of words like "devour"). In *Crusoe*, we know there are earthenware vases, and we know some of them are misshapen. We know there is a parrot. We know there are cats and cheese and broad contours, but, with a few exceptions like the richly descriptive, synthetic (and queer-in-more-than-one-sense) scene in which Friday slumbers in the nude,[10] Defoe does not consistently dedicate himself to stimulating an interplay of senses nor even to instantiating a sensually consumable world. I would be loath to perpetuate the outdated notion, rightfully complained about by J. Paul Hunter in *Before Novels*, that "there was no 'literature' in the eighteenth century," and I do not mean to suggest any failing on Defoe's part;[11] Defoe particularizes and visualizes at carefully chosen key junctures, particularly when it comes to describing hybridity (Crusoe's own hybridized attire and appearance while on the island, or, obviously, the manly yet beautiful Friday). Longueville, however, takes the meat of those rare moments in Defoe—the texture of Friday's sharp eyes, soft smile, and hair not like wool, the almost-taste of his sweet lips and olive skin, and Crusoe's keen sense of all the colors Friday is and is not (from very tawny to not quite black to not-nauseous yellow to bright dun olive)—and makes of it his bread and butter as he indulges in the full color of gustatory delight.

Simply put, Quarll's world is highly edible, and usually literally so, as well. Longueville might not present us with the synthesized worlds that have been said to mark the modern novel, but we can see in reading him how insufficient some of the received wisdom on the novel (and its putative rise) actually is for assessing the world-building methodologies that inform early prose fictions such as this one.[12] Even Longueville's grass is a consumable marvel, whether described as being like "a Leek" (207) or as "a curious Grass, something like C[h]amomile, but of no Smell, and of an agreeable Taste" (3). Moreover, much of the book simply describes the things that the Hermit gives Dorrington to eat: from the "pickl'd Anchovies . . . , Mushrooms, Capers, and other sorts of Pickles" quoted in my title, to "diverse sorts of dry'd Fishes," to the endless retinue of dishes Dorrington so lengthily describes (10). For instance, "Butter, . . . Cream and Milk, several small Cheeses, . . . a Parcels of Roots like *Jerusalem* Artichoaks, which look'd to have been roasted" (7). Or, in another vein, "boil'd meat and Oyster-Sauce" and "Soop" (27), followed by "House-Lamb" and "several sorts of delicate Pickles I never eat of before, and Mushrooms, but of curious Colour, Flavour and Taste" (28). Dorrington also enjoys, for example, "Cabbage . . . season'd with the Fruit of the Piamento Tree" (50), and diverse roots, "some sweetish, others sharp and hot like Horse-Raddish . . . , some eating like Parsnips, others almost like a Carrot, but rather more agreeable, some like Beets and Turnips, . . . some being Bluish, others Black, some Red, and some Yellow" (202). To name just a few! Suffice it to say, the eating, and our explicit witnessing of said eating, goes on and on, making *The Hermit* a worthy heir to Crusoe's/*Crusoe*'s devouring ways and making us reconsider seriously, if we dare, the world-building practices of premodern authors.

Ultimately, Longueville's fiction gives proof to Cynthia Wall's recent assertion that our "expectations" about early imaginative prose require some further complication.[13] The *preparation* of the food is no less integral to what *The Hermit* does and to what Longueville imagined *The Hermit* could do (generically) to heighten and slake an already-sharpened (by Defoe) readerly appetite; *The Hermit*, like most (and arguably all) Robinsonades, is typically metafictional, marked by its obsession with being heir to, but also reviser of, the microgenre. Indeed, the hermit's transmutations of the world around him, as he prepares it for consumption, exemplify Longueville's own work in *The Hermit*. Quarll, unlike his successor Unca Eliza Winkfield in *The Female American*, does not feel limited to simply taking anything as it comes. To the contrary, as Quarll promises, "Roasted roots . . . eat much pleasanter than the fresh" (19). It is not an exaggeration to say that, in *The Hermit*, the singular, gemlike sweetmeat of Friday's raw sugar body in Crusoe's cave of fantasy is writ large onto a wildly colorful landscape that Quarll explicitly describes, refashions (usually by *pickling*), and consumes. Nor is it an exaggeration to say that the hermit pickles well-nigh everything, from fish to meat to mushrooms: "His good Success in making that sort of Pickle, encourages him to try another" (250). Not much escapes his picking, pickling grasp, from "a Plant in the Wood, that bears a final green Flower, which before it is blown looks like a Caper," and "*French* Beans," and "Cucumber," and indeed "every kind of Buds, Blossoms, and Seeds," and "wild Parsnip . . . , green and crisp" (250). And more. Pickling—the act of preserving and transforming—is Quarll's passion as much as it is (generically) Longueville's, and its appearance in *The Hermit* as a methodology for processing the stuff of the word is as bracing as it is unexpected.

Even the medium Quarll uses for his pickles (a piquant vinegar, like the medium of *The Hermit* itself) is a revision: when he comes upon wild pomegranates that have "outward Beauty" but no corresponding "goodness of the inside" because the "dull luctitiousness [is] too flat for eating," he sets the juice in the hot sun after combining it with "an Herb" like "Creasses," and makes vinegar (249). Thus the "flat," "dull" dreck, inside "a five gallon vessel" (249), now reborn as a transformative elixir, is able to do what Quarll does: remake everything that the powerful acid infuses. "These Pickles, sir," exclaims Dorrington, are "far exceeding any I ever did eat in *Europe*" (28). Similarly, Quarll's "Soop," with its fragrant aroma of "Artichoaks, Asparagus and Sallery" is "so excellent" that Dorrington vows he has "never eat[en] any comparable to it at *Pontack*'s, nor any where before" (26). So much for the roast beef of old England (punning aside, I return to this matter in concluding this essay). Quarll does not quarrel with Crusoean convention, but he does enliven it. Each time Dorrington grows full of one dish and complains that he "can find no room in [his] Stomach," Quarll serves up another collation of dishes, and Dorrington, "at his pressing Request tasted of 'em, and my Appetite renew'd at their inexpressible Deliciousness, so I fell to eating afresh" (28). Readers who, like Dorrington, have sometimes suffered the figurative "Disappointment of [not] having something more comfortable than Water to drink" can find themselves refreshed by the Hermit's "Cider," the better "to revive and keep up his Spirits, as well as to please his Palate and sute his Appetite" (251). Presented with a rainbow surfeit of pickles and other refashioned enchantments, readers may well become enchanted by Quarll Island, may become entranced, Persephone-like, Dorrington-like, by Quarll's shining, pomegranate-vinegar-infused world.

If pickling is part of *The Hermit*'s reflexively meta-generic self-engagement with the dual act of preservation and conversion, so is the packaging of the pickles, and so we hear almost as much about Quarll's containment vessels and his plating methods as we do about the pickles and other productions that those vessels hold. The very first paragraph of the novel anticipates what is to come when Dorrington, using "yellow maggots" to catch some fish that are of "divers beautiful Colours," observes indirectly that the effect of the content is dependent upon the form and context through which content is expressed: the fishes are either "more or less beautiful, according to the Serenity of the Weather" (2). Everything is consumable in *The Hermit*, but that which contains and contextualizes the novel's consumable imagery—the way the food is dressed, like the way language is dressed or the way the fishes are made vibrant due to tricks of the light and the workings of the environment—is a necessary factor in Dorrington's aesthetic gustatory bliss. Dorrington marvels at length, upon entering the hut, at the "Shells of different Sizes, some being callow'd at the Outside, as having been on the Fire, but extreme clean within, the rest were, both Inside and Outside, as fine as Nakes of Pearl" (9). Pleased, he finds that throughout the hut are "divers broad and deep Shells, as beautiful as those in the Kitchen" (11). Peeping at what these nacreous vessels encase, he finds, of course, the treasure of pickle upon pickle. Gratified by these workings of form and content together, and the effects of nature simultaneously preserved and altered, Dorrington exclaims the place "no hermitage, but rather what's needed to gratify the Appetite, as well as to support Nature" (11). When the Hermit tells Dorrington "if you can eat off of Shells, ye are welcome, I have no better Plates to give you," Dorrington replies that "these are preferable to Silver ones in my Opinion, and I very much question whether any Prince in *Europe* can produce so curious a Service" (26). So much for the dull, flat silver of old Europe. Who would not savor the fresh colors, the opulent dimensional layers, of *The Hermit*'s nacreous (or, as Longueville says, "nakes") mother-of-pearl shells?

Simply put, *The Hermit* is a major, unacknowledged participant in what Denise Gigante calls the "literary history of taste in all its full-bodied flavor."[14] Like other "writers in this history," Longueville seizes upon "the creative power of taste as a trope for aesthetic judgment and its essential role in generating our very sense of self."[15] If, as Gigante asserts, "modern aesthetics as evolved from the concept of taste involves pleasure, and pleasure is its own way of knowing," then *The Hermit* is a stunning link in that evolutionary process.[16] Moreover, consumption (by the hermit, by Dorrington, by us) is illuminated by Longueville as "an overdetermined, multivalenced concept, . . . grounded in the power of metaphor, and it is time for literary history to examine rigorously its related subsets of taste and appetite"; we can see the hermit as an example of a Lockean man whose identity is energized not by innate ideas but by what Gigante calls "a more complex . . . construct of selfhood dependent on how human beings process experience through the senses."[17]

But taste per se in Longueville is connected to the other senses, in a way that makes the hermit not only an eighteenth-century man but a modern one, too. Smell, for instance, is very important on the hermit's island, connected as it is to pickle making. Thus, the hermit's pickling practices, like Longueville's literary one, should be part of the necessary process that Emily C. Friedman calls the work of "olfactory recovery" within "sense studies."[18] As Friedman observes, "Olfactory experiences, not unlike . . . past reading practices, are tied to unique conditions of production and reception that have been altered and lost.[19] Why are pickles important to an early modern mind? Because of the vinegar, of course. Friedman notes that "in moments of distress, either physical or emotional, eighteenth-century genteel-class men and women, and their fictional counterparts, could turn to handheld devices filled with a variety of pungent materials to revive them."[20] These smelling bottles, what Friedman calls "personal scenting devices," included the "popular" vinaigrettes (as they were called), "small containers of vinegar-soaked sponges." Like the ammonia-based smelling bottle Friedman describes, aromatic vinegar-based ones could help to "prevent fainting or . . . revive those who have lost consciousness" by "irritating the nasal membranes, causing faster breathing."[21] In fine, the hermit's pickle-ridden island *wakes us up*. And, holistically speaking, we can easily sense while reading how, as Gigante explains, "taste is etymologically related to touch," and how smell is a kind of haptic touch, during an "era of sensibility" in which "the skin became an expanded organ of assimilation, the subjective interface by which human beings touch and taste the world of sensory reality."[22] The tasting and smelling and hearing and touching and seeing human being takes in pleasure "through every pore," a digesting process "that includes the entire organism in aesthetic experience."[23]

The freshness of *The Hermit* lies in its own nacreous layers and dimensions of description from whence we gain Longueville's invigorating experience of sights, smells, textures, sounds, and flavors. For instance, Quarll's spring from which he derives his drinking water, viewed from three different angles, is a kind of synesthetic masterpiece that resembles either a human breast with a "fountain of water sweet as milk," or an antique piece of architecture, or a seahorse, and Dorrington, ever Longueville's model reader, is delighted to find "three so very different, and yet rightly compar'd likenesses, being offer'd by one and the same unalter'd Object" (176). As the fountain expresses, multiple readers may be moved by such multivariate objects, as depth and interest are created by incorporating multiple layers of images that "conspire to make the fountain useful, convenient and agreeable" (37). The fountain, then, is an apt metaphor for the kind of work *The Hermit* does. Spotting the "fine rainbow, issuing as it were out of the mouth of a giant, lying on the rock, reaching quite over the lake," Dorrington, in the role of Longueville's ideal reader, is so enraptured by the reflection "at the bottom of" the pool that he "could not but stop to admire the various Colours it was of, which far exceeded in Beauty and Liveliness any [he] ever saw in the Skie" (35–36). The fountain's pool, reflecting the rainbow, creates a fiction even Sir Philip Sidney's poet maker would be proud of: a "world" more "golden" than nature's own "brazen" sky.[24] Dorrington's helper Alvarado thus responds when Dorrington "imagin[es]" that the rainbow "proceded from the Rays of the Sun upon some Pond or standing Water, whose Reflexions did rise and meet the Top, so caus'd that beautiful Circle": "*Alvarado*, . . . by what he had seen before, concluded that the Island was enchanted, said it was another Illusion, of which the place was full" (36). The fountain, like the larger fiction of *The Hermit*, is neither the equivalent of Crusoe's carefully plain earthenware jars nor a mere mimetic reflecting device. Instead, the fountain combines the already-beautiful rainbow with other elements, "adorned," as it is, "with various small Flowers and Herbs of divers beautiful Colours and most fragrant Smells" (37), and filled as it is not only with clear water but with gem-like fishes like "large Rubies, Emeralds, Jacinths and other colour'd Stones" that "look'd like Stars launching from Place to Place in the Sky" (40). In the fanciful sky of Quarll Island's quasi–reflecting pool, the fishes are shooting "stars" (40), ranging freely within, it seems, the "zodiac" (to borrow Sidney's phrasing) of Longueville's "own wit."[25]

But Longueville's most striking emblem for what he does with the Robinsonade microgenre—always pursuing, as he says in the novel's prefatory poem, a "fresh Scene" (ix)—is the magnificent bird his protagonist transforms through the fetishistic but also revisionary act of taxidermy. The bird is described at length: "of a changeable Colour, from Red to Aurora and Green; the Ribs of a delightful Blue, and the Feathers Pearl colour, speckl'd with a bright Yellow, the Breast and Belly (if it might be said to be of any particular Colour) was that of a Dove's Feathers, rim'd like the Back, divers[e]ly changing; the Head, which was like that of a Swan for make, was Purple also, changing according as mov'd; the Bill like burnish'd Gold; Eyes like a Ruby, with a Rim of Gold round it; the Feet the same as the Bill; the Bigness of the Bird, was between a middling Goose and a Duck, and the Make of a Swan" (199–200). This stunning description notwithstanding, it is what Longueville does with the bird that surprises the reader: "He carefully takes out its Flesh, which corrupting would spoil the Outside, then fills the Skin with sweet Herbs, which he dry'd for that Use, then having sow'd up the Place he had cut open to take the Flesh out, he set it up in his Lodge" (200). If most (arguably all) Robinsonades contain at least one self-reflexive emblem of the microgenre, this marvelous bird, renovated like the pomegranate juice and the pickles, stuffed and sewn (and sown, with the perfuming contents of "sweet herbs"), is arguably *The Hermit*'s own most salient emblem. Appropriately, the bird is "set . . . up in [Quarll's] Lodge" like the genius of the place (200).

While my focus here is on the novel's transformative descriptions, there are other good reasons, besides the nacreous shells, the rainbow fountain, and the stuffed bird, why modern readers should turn to *The Hermit*. The story of Quarll's life before he comes to the island, while excised completely from the late eighteenth-century and early nineteenth-century chapbook versions, is hardly dull, encompassing a childhood of orphaned hardship, earthy depictions of hardscrabble London life, multiple marriages, jailing for polygamy, transatlantic voyages chockablock with diverse adventures (for instance, Quarll acts as midwife for an African woman, Juno, who gives birth aboard the ship).

The novel's arrangement, no less than its plot, is fascinating, too, as a framed narrative that is energized by acts of preservation as well as transformation. Indeed, *The Hermit* formally resembles the Hermit's own nested shells of layered nacre. First, readers get Dorrington's sense of the island (Book 1), followed by the Hermit's tale of coming to the island as drawn by Dorrington from Quarll's parchment journal (Book 2), followed by, in the final volume (Book 3), the contents of Quarll's island journal (again recast through the eyes of Dorrington himself). The preface to the second of the two 1727 editions explains, "The *first* Book herein was wholly written by [Dorrington], and the *second* and *third* Books were faithfully transcribed from Mr. *Quarll*'s Parchment Roll, which was a Continuation of what my Friend had begun" (vii).[26] Complicated issues of narrativity and colonial appropriation thus arise at the formal structural level. Michael Seidel is right (as are many others) that *Robinson Crusoe* is not only "a primer on how to live on a remote island, but on how to write the experience up," and clearly Longueville's novel is, too.[27] Indeed, Coby Dowdell, though he does not elaborate, is right to say that "Longueville's *The English Hermit*" betrays its own "self-awareness of . . . narrative textuality."[28]

Ultimately, as a Robinsonade and as an early novel, *The Hermit* has more to recommend it than I can describe here. As in *Crusoe*, numerous small episodes surprise the modern reader and beg for a closer look, from: the arrival of rogues who steal Quarll's things (livestock, pets, an entire building, even his wonderful stuffed bird), and even attempt to steal Quarll himself so that they might display him along with his things in a raree-show; to Quarll's adoption of monkeys as servants; to the novel's resonance with contemporary travel narratives and its nods to other modes, genres, and forms; to the presence of national allegory in the hermit's dreams; to specific revisions of Crusoean imagery and plot points; to the changes in editions as the novel was converted into (children's) chapbooks. Issues of gender, untraced with respect to this novel and untheorized with respect to the Robinsonade tradition at large, also demand attention: Quarll has plenty to say about the perfidy of women, and he literally explains that he is happy to be an "Adam" alone in paradise with "no . . . Women to tempt a man" (207, 16), as if the island space is the antidote to some imagined dull English domesticity either on or off the page—even if in Quarll's weaker moments he carefully checks chests that wash ashore and hopes he might find "a Woman" inside (233). Notably, the later chapbook versions increase the level of consumable descriptive imagery (and the descriptive imagery of literally consumable things), even while omitting the entire section of the narrative concerned with Quarll's polygamous pre-island time—a dual revision that calls out to be pressed upon critically for what it tells us about the contextualized development of the Robinsonade microgenre's different trajectories.

At the same time, exciting new directions in food studies also make the hermit's edible world ripe for a closer look. What novel better "illuminate[s] and, at times obfuscate[s]" the "histories of colonialism and communalism, labor and leisure, scientific research and creative production, ethical consideration and environmental degradation" that Amy L. Tigner and Allison Carruth point to?[29] If the approach to food and literature "entails a complex terrain of social and biophysical systems," Longueville offers a special opportunity for historical scholars.[30] And, certainly, Longueville should be meaningful for scholars of literature and culture; Tigner and Carruth are right to consider how literature works to "whet" readers' "appetites," not merely for actual food but for description itself.[31] Thus, *The Hermit* ideally demands "an approach to literature and food that integrates the methods of cultural history, close reading, and archival research with concepts drawn from literary studies—such as narrative, rhetoric, form, audience, authorship, and taste—and food studies—such as foodways, food justice, gastronomy, and agrarianism."[32] If scholars want to "tease out relationships between cultures of food and major literary forms," in this case the utopian and dystopian concerns of the Robinsonade, the edible *Hermit* has to be part of the picture. To be sure, this novel can help us suss out what Jennifer Fleissner calls the connections between "aesthetic and gustatory taste."[33]

To return briefly to the matter of the roast beef of old England, which I jokingly referred to above, the hermit is not simply adapting English foodways to his edible island or vice versa. Rather, in his desire to stay on the island (he refuses to leave with Dorrington and Alvarado), he is also eager to assert one kind of fiction against another: the island is the space of fictional possibility and sensual flowering, as opposed to the gray realities the hermit sees being produced by that other island—England—he has left behind. As the hermit tells it, the dull reality of England and its history stands to interrupt the reveries of fiction; likewise, the marvelous fiction of Quarll's life is an antidote to the dreams of England that invade his sleep and threaten to upend his peace. Indeed, at the end of *The Hermit*, Quarll conveys how he was busy making pickles when the sky suddenly grew dark. Stepping outside, he finds a "vast number of dead birds" (252). Concluding that these deaths are "a prognostication of dreadful wars in *Europe*, from which he begs Heavens to protect his native country," he identifies these details as fatal to his space: "lest the dead birds that lay in great numbers should (with laying) infect the island, he and his monkey carried them to the other side of the rock, so threw them into the sea" (252). Picking and choosing what his island will encompass, Quarll nevertheless cannot resist reusing and transforming some part of the animals: "as many of them as had soft feathers on their breasts and bellies he plucked away to stuff a pillow" (252). He makes a pillow for his monkey, too. The pillow, however, proves injurious to Quarll's peace, inspiring nightmares of dead horses, of sons snatched from sobbing parents into press gangs, of men without arms or legs, of men with their smoking "Guts hanging out" (253). "The year, being 1707," he dreams of St. James's Park, he dreams of war in England, he dreams of thistles and oaks and roses growing together and "produc[ing] a plant which bore both roses and thistles" (256). The monkey is similarly disturbed, Quarll believes, as both he and the monkey start from sleep in great fright. Quarll "concludes the cause must proceed from the pillow" (257). The feather-stuffed pillows are the source, he decides, of the commotion that overtakes his dreams: "his eyes are took up with frightful objects, and his ears filled with a terrible noise, at which the rest of his senses have left their offices, and are become useless" (257). Where pickles stimulate, the stuff of his nightmares is a bloody bludgeon to the senses. Thus "inclined to believe that the pillow had really some influence on the imagination," he finds that without the pillow he has the kinds of lovely and sustaining dreams he had "before he used the pillow," and, now, without the pillow, both he and "his monkey slept very quiet" (257). The realities of England can only interrupt: "evil effluvias issued out of those feathers the pillow was stuffed with" (257): he dreams of "fierce and bloody battles," of "men and horses lying as thick upon the ground as grass in a meadow, and streams of blood running like so many brooks" (258). When the monkey refuses his own new-feathered bed, Quarll concludes "that there was a malignant quality into those feathers" and he "throws them into the sea, and fills the case with a sort of soft moss, which grew at the bottom of a particular tree, on which the creature lay very quiet ever after" (259). The world the hermit leaves behind is as bloody, chaotic, and dull as the hermit's pickles are sustaining, piquant, and colorful. Not all pillows, not all stories, dreams, or methodologies, are the same. Longueville's space of the imagination is a departure, a respite from the tainted feathers of stark history. No wonder the hermit does not want to leave his island.

There is more to say about *The Hermit*'s metafictionality, and Longueville's depictions of colonial gift giving, and many more things than what I can encompass here. But, if my essay lacks the space to describe those matters, much less pertinent connections with modern Robinsonades, I have made at least a partial assay to compensate for the long neglect of Longueville's seriously popular novel.[34] If Defoe's *Crusoe* is the deeply metafictional, self-reflexively sophisticated novel that its most sensitive critics take it to be, *The Hermit* is, too, in its own way, and we can do better than the mid-twentieth-century critic who "found nothing pertinent in the book except descriptions of a sea red as blood, a corposant, and fishes flashing like jewels, the use of the word clift, and a dream of a flaming ocean."[35] Glossing over such descriptions as if they are anything *but* pertinent, such a critique misses the point, and the mark, that Longueville was eager to make and that he *did* in fact make, for many readers, over many years. A slightly earlier twentieth-century reader (Henry Hutchins, a venerable Defoe scholar) came closer to the heart of things: "*The Hermit* is interesting reading, for those who are not devotionally enough inclined to appreciate Quarll's prayerful soliloquizings may marvel at the lake with its subterranean outlet to the sea, the perpetual rainbow, and the grotto with its impressive echo which sounds like choral music."[36] Longueville himself, noting in the first version of the 1727 preface how "*Robinson Crusoe, Moll Flanders*, and Collonel *Jack* have had their admirers" (v), asserts strongly in the second, alternate version of the 1727 preface that a new scene is frankly necessary, due to the "*the Book-Sellers Shops being already crowded with* Robinson Crusoe, Moll Flanders, *Colln*. Jacks" (vi). *The Hermit*, with all its pickling, nacreous shells, fish-filled rainbow fountains, and taxidermied delights, surely does offer the new scene its author aims at. And if *The Hermit* is, as Dorrington's traveling companion Alvarado says it is, an "enchanted" space, "all illusion, (36), it is also arguably Longueville's vision of "Nature" as "nature intended it," a paradise where one may happily decide against "punish[ing] himself by denying his Appetite, and only eat[ing] to support Nature, and not to please his Palate" (241). To be sure, Quarll's island is both an ingenious inheritor and progenitor. The way to this kind of eating and this kind of writing, implies Longueville, is accessible to all who pursue it. Indeed, in the opening paragraph of the book, it is as simple as "spying a Clift in the Rock, thro' which" we see "a Light," and having "a mind to see what was at the other side" (3).

NOTES

For help in developing this essay, thanks to postcolonialist Winnie Chan, the VCU Humanities Research Center, the students in my Robinsonade seminars, and the two anonymous readers at Bucknell whose advice was invaluable.

1. For recent work on Robinsonades, see, for instance, the three closing essays in John Richetti, ed., *The Cambridge Companion to "Robinson Crusoe"* (Cambridge: Cambridge University Press, 2018): Jill Campbell, "Robinsonades for Young People," 191–206; Ann Marie Fallon, "Anti-Crusoes, Alternative Crusoes: Revisions of the Island Story in the Twentieth Century," 207–220; and Robert Mayer, "Robinson Crusoe in the Screen Age," 221–233.

2. Peter Longueville, *The Hermit: or, The Unparalleled Sufferings and Surprising Adventures of Mr. Philip Quarll, an Englishman Who Was Lately Discovered by Mr. Dorrington a Bristol Merchant, upon an Uninhabited Island in the South-Sea; Where He Has Lived above Fifty Years, without Any Human Assistance, Still Continues to Reside, and Will Not Come Away* (London, 1727). Further references are to this edition and are given parenthetically. Coleman O. Parsons reports that "between 1727 and 1800, this pleasant little fiction went through thirteen editions. Coleridge remembered having read it at the age of six." See Coleman O. Parsons, "The Mariner and the Albatross," *Virginia Quarterly Review* 26.1 (1950): 102–123, 115. Michelle Burnham, in an appendix headnote, calls *The Hermit* "one of the most popular castaway imitations to follow in the wake of *Crusoe*." Michelle Burnham, ed., *The Female American*, by Unca Eliza Winkfield (Peterborough: Broadview Press, 2001), 157. Andrew O'Malley goes further: "the most popular early [Robinsonade] example was Longueville's *The Hermit* (1727), which enjoyed a popularity that, for a time, almost rivaled that of Defoe's work." O'Malley, *Children's Literature, Popular Culture, and "Robinson Crusoe"* (Houndmills: Palgrave Macmillan, 2012), 36. Despite this popularity, most critics merely mention (at best) *The Hermit*: for instance, Michelle Levy, in "Discovery and the Domestic Affections in Coleridge and Shelley," *Studies in English Literature, 1500–1900* 44.4 (2004): 693–713, remarks that Coleridge read *The Hermit* in some form; in another vein, Margaret Kinnell, in "Sceptreless, Free, Uncircumscribed? Radicalism, Dissent and Early Children's Books," *British Journal of Educational Studies* 36.1 (1988): 55, remarks on the "autonomy" of hermits such as Longueville's; Jerry Beasley, in "Portraits of a Monster: Robert Walpole and Early English Prose Fiction," *Eighteenth-Century Studies* 14.4 (1981): 406–431, is pithy but equally brief.

3. Most recently, Jason H. Pearl has brought attention to another neglected gem of an early Robinsonade, in "*Peter Wilkins* and the Eighteenth-Century Novel," *SEL Studies in English Literature 1500–1900* 57.3 (2017): 541–559.

4. See, for instance, recent books and articles: on taste in eighteenth-century British literature, Denise Gigante, *Taste: A Literary History* (New Haven, CT: Yale University Press, 2005); on smell in eighteenth-century British literature, Emily C. Friedman, *Reading Smell in Eighteenth-Century Fiction* (Lewisburg, PA: Bucknell University Press, 2016); on tactility in eighteenth-century British literature, Kristin Girten, "Mingling with Matter: Tactile Microscopy and the Philosophic Mind in Brobdingnag and Beyond," *Eighteenth-Century Studies* 54.4 (2013): 497–520; on sound in eighteenth-century British literature, Paula McDowell, *The Invention of the Oral: Print Commerce and Fugitive Voices in Eighteenth-Century Britain* (Chicago: University of Chicago Press, 2017); and, on vision in eighteenth-century British literature, my "Optics, Gender, and the Eighteenth-Century Gaze: Looking at Eliza Haywood's *Anti-Pamela*," *Eighteenth Century: Theory and Interpretation* 51.1–2 (2010): 27–43, and "The Poet as Man of Feeling," in *Oxford Handbook of British Poetry, 1660–1800*, ed. Jack Lynch (Oxford: Oxford University Press, 2016), 195–209.

5. See, for instance, the essays in Amy L. Tigner and Allison Carruth, eds., *Literature and Food Studies* (Oxford: Routledge, 2017). See also numerous discrete examples from the world

at large, for instance Jennifer Fleissner, "Henry James's Art of Eating," *English Literary History* 75.1 (2008): 27–62.

6. Of course there were some rare exceptions to the paucity of easily visualized description in premodern prose fictions; see my "'It Is to Pleasure You': Seeing Things in Mackenzie's *Aretina* (1660), or, Whither Scottish Prose Fiction Before the Novel?," *Studies in Scottish Literature* 43.1 (2017): 22–30.
7. See Cynthia S. Wall on the early eighteenth-century novelistic proliferation of things and the rise of description (if not the fully fleshed or sensualized variety we associate with modern novels) in *The Prose of Things: Transformations of Description in the Eighteenth Century* (Chicago: University of Chicago Press, 2006).
8. On the legendary plainness of Defoe's typical descriptive methods, see Samuel Taylor Coleridge, "Lecture XI," in *The Complete Works of Samuel Taylor Coleridge*, ed. W. G. T. Shedd (New York: Harper, 1853), 309–319. See also Virginia Woolf on Crusoe's plain pots, "*Robinson Crusoe*," in *The Second Common Reader*, ed. Andrew McNeillie (1932; New York: Harcourt Brace, 1986), 51–59.
9. Indeed, Maximillian E. Novak makes clear just how ingenious Defoe's occasional fully fleshed descriptions are. See Novak, *Transformations, Ideology, and the Real in Defoe's "Robinson Crusoe" and Other Narratives: Finding "The Thing Itself"* (Newark: University of Delaware Press, 2015).
10. See my "*Robinson Crusoe* and the Form of the New Novel," in Richetti, *Cambridge Companion*, 16–31.
11. See J. Paul Hunter, *Before Novels: The Cultural Contexts of Eighteenth-Century English Fiction* (New York, W. W. Norton, 1990), xiii.
12. Here I refer to some of the important classic studies that nevertheless do not make much room for taking seriously (in an aesthetic sense) prose fictions that do not adhere to modern standards for novelistic world building: e.g., Dorothy Van Ghent, *The English Novel: Form and Function* (1953; repr., New York: Harper & Row, 1961); Ian P. Watt, *The Rise of the Novel: Studies in Defoe, Richardson, and Fielding* (1957; repr., Berkeley: University of California Press, 2000); Ralph Rader, "The Concept of Genre and Eighteenth-Century Studies" (1973), in *Fact, Fiction, and Form: Selected Essays*, ed. James Phelan and David H. Richter (Columbus: Ohio State University Press, 2011), 58–81.
13. Wall, *Prose of Things*, 110.
14. Gigante, *Taste*, 2.
15. Ibid., 2.
16. Ibid., 3.
17. Ibid., 3.
18. Friedman, *Reading Smell*, 2, 3.
19. Ibid., 3.
20. Ibid., 51.
21. Ibid., 58.
22. Gigante, *Taste*, 2.
23. Ibid., 12.
24. Philip Sidney, "The Defence of Poesy," in *Sir Philip Sidney: The Major Works*, ed. Katherine Duncan-Jones (Oxford: Oxford University Press, 1989), 212–251.
25. Ibid., 216.
26. The alternate 1727 edition replaces Dorrington, as author-editor, with Longueville himself. About the two editions, see Arundell Esdaile, "Author and Publisher in 1727: 'The English Hermit,'" *The Library (The Transactions of the Bibliographic Society)* 4.2(3) (1921): 185–192. See also Eve Tavor Bannet, *Transatlantic Stories and the History of Reading, 1720–1810: Migrant Fictions* (Cambridge: Cambridge University Press, 2011), 240n1.

27. Michael Seidel, *Robinson Crusoe: Island Myths and the Novel* (Boston: Twayne, 1991), 79.
28. Coby Dowdell, "The American Hermit and the British Castaway: Voluntary Retreat and Deliberative Democracy in Early American Culture," *Early American Literature* 46.1 (2011): 149.
29. Tigner and Carruth, "Introduction: Genealogies and Genres of Food Studies," in *Literature and Food Studies*, 1.
30. Ibid., 2.
31. Ibid., 2.
32. Ibid., 4.
33. Fleissner, "Henry James's Art of Eating," 28.
34. Connections with modern Robinsonades are as various as Marianne Wiggins' portrayal of the edible colonial world as nightmare. Marianne Wiggins, *John Dollar* (New York: Harper & Row, 1988).
35. Parsons, "Mariner and the Albatross," 115.
36. Henry Hutchins, "Some Imitations of Robinson Crusoe—Called Robinsonades," *Yale University Library Gazette* 11.2 (1936): 33.

2

"IF I HAD..."

Counterfactuals, Imaginary Realities, and the Poetics of the Postmodern Robinsonade

PATRICK GILL

THERE IS A RECOGNIZABLE SET of key factors with which modern rewritings of Daniel Defoe's classic novel can set out their stall as regards their relation to their parent text, and they usually proceed from the respective author's decision as to the nature of their setting. Once it has been determined what the modern equivalent of Robinson's island should be, most other things follow more or less automatically: if, as in Rex Gordon's 1956 science fiction novel *No Man Friday*, our castaway finds himself on a distant planet, the roles of both the cannibals and of Friday are likely to be taken up by alien creatures, and his ingenuity will be required not to rear goats but to procure water and oxygen. However, this essay argues that a no less telling aspect of Robinsonades (and of understanding the tremendous changes the Robinson story has undergone) is to be found in counterfactuals or, in more general terms, realities intradiegetically marked as imaginary. Hilary Dannenberg defines the counterfactual as "an alternate version of events that is created by a thought experiment that takes the conditions of the actual world and then constructs an altered model which diverges from this reality because of a strategic change in the past of that world."[1] While the emphasis on imagining alterations *in the past* makes perfect sense in many contexts such as in alternate histories, when used for the purposes of a narratological enquiry, discussion of the counterfactual in this strict sense ought to be flanked by consideration of other phenomena: characters imagining what might be going on at the same time in a different place, for instance, or even characters hypothesizing about future events. After all, while a separation of these phenomena is technically useful, even necessary, when discussing the strict logical proposition that is counterfactual history or alternate-world fiction, when the projection of an imagined reality takes place at a certain point in a character's mind rather than as a global fantasy constituting the premise of the entire narrative itself, the distinction is not only harder to make but much less useful. The present discussion needs to introduce a third notion besides the counterfactual and the somewhat vaguer concept of imagined realities: that of authorship or textual authority. Since imagined realities are a mental phenomenon, their nature and function depend on the fictional characters to whom they are ascribed, and the way the reader is told about these imagined realities is reflective of the respective character's interests and ethos, but also of the control they have over the telling of the story as a whole.

Taken together, these three factors of counterfactuals, imagined realities, and notions of textual authority and authorship form the incontrovertible basis of what the present essay terms the postmodern Robinsonade's poetics. As the discussion of the following examples serves to illustrate, the questions of how reality is imagined and who gets to express their version of reality based on what authority have undergone a persistent development away from certainty, univocality, and narrative control toward not only a destabilization of individual versions of events but also a questioning of the very nature of storytelling itself. In order to demonstrate the nature of this development in the postmodern Robinsonade's poetics, three novels from different decades of the past sixty years are here contrasted in terms of their use of counterfactuals, imagined realities, and textual authority, with Daniel Defoe's original text.

ROBINSON CRUSOE (1719)

Given its island setting, *Robinson Crusoe* offers the perfect sandbox scenario in which only a limited number of phenomena can occur, making suppositions regarding possible outcomes and alternate timelines more plausible. To some extent, these alternative scenarios envisioned by the castaway Robinson (or retrospectively imagined by a more mature Robinson sitting down to write his memoir) serve the simple purpose of foregrounding the sheer interiority the reader encounters in the novel. When, after years on the island, Robinson contemplates his outer appearance in a lighthearted episode and says that "had any one in *England* been to meet such a Man as I was, it must either have frightened them, or rais'd a great deal of Laughter" (108), the reader witnesses Robinson imagining himself in another place and then speculating on the reaction he might provoke in others. Employed in this manner, such counterfactuals can be understood as invitations to the reader to participate in the novel's empathetic structures. Furthermore, being let in on the lonely Robinson's absurd fantasy provides the story with a strong identification with the narrator through whose eyes all of this is presented and adds to Defoe's realism, which, as Richetti argues, results from "his vivid evocation of individuals as they examine the conditions of their existence and explore what it means to be a person in particularized social and historical circumstances."[2]

Sometimes counterfactuals and imagined realities are invoked to engender a sense of jeopardy, as is the case when Robinson considers what his fate would have been had he not managed to salvage anything at all from the ship (95). At other times, though, this immediate sense of jeopardy is alleviated by the distance to events created in the narrative. When the older Robinson, remembering his erstwhile plans for sailing from the island, concedes that he "made no Allowance for the Dangers of such a Condition, and how [he] might fall into the Hands of Savages," and then goes on to assess that "if [he] once came in their power, [he] should run a hazard of a thousand to one of being killed" (91), the hypothetical consideration of those dangers in the text is not aimed at making them feel immediately present. It is instead a case of the older Robinson having a lesson to impart.

If the reader parses these discourses—the capturing of firsthand emotions on the island, on the one hand, and the careful reflection on events in retrospect, on the other—the counterfactuals and imagined realities in *Robinson Crusoe* also speak to one of the core conflicts in Defoe's novel, and that is the question of the balance between free will and providence. The latter not only was important specifically to Defoe or his time but is a staple of didactic storytelling: story arcs bend toward poetic justice where the good will be rewarded and the bad punished. That said, free will is an equally important narrative ingredient as stories of complete preordination lack in suspense. Robinson's counterfactuals help to enact that balance between free will and predestination by providing us with versions of the world in which Crusoe's behavior is controlled first by the one and then by the other. This is the case with his plan of slaughtering the cannibals periodically visiting the island: "After I had thus laid the Scheme of my Design, and in my Imagination put it in Practice" (123), Robinson explains that doubts befall him. But these doubts appear only after an extended description of his imagined reality, which, as Seidel argues, "is almost indistinguishable from the scenes that he describes as real. . . . It is only when a reader actually begins paying close attention to Crusoe's language that he or she realizes how much of what happens on the island exists in the supplemental or projected realm."[3] Later on, a calmer Robinson less bent on slaughter can reflect on what would have ensued had he executed his plan: he would have been as sinful and inhumane as the evil Spanish in committing "a meer Butchery, a bloody and unnatural Piece of Cruelty, unjustifiable either to God or Man" (125).[4]

The double layer of projections, one in Robinson's time on the island, the other one retrospectively activated during the writing of his memoirs, offers readers the chance to vicariously live through decisions based on free will at the time and make sense of them taking the long view. Together they form a powerful matrix of psychological insight, practical instruction, and religious didacticism. As Johnson argues, "Even the apologists for Providentialism recognize that God figures along a dual time scheme, in which the older, narrating Crusoe contrasts the day-to-day flow of events in diegesis with a plotting of those events according to a divine conversion narrative."[5]

Just as importantly, they also help readers understand that as narrator Robinson gains dominion over his narrative as he does over the island. Just as he "asserts his authority—his ordering capacity—over more and more important and wider and wider areas" of the island,[6] he also continuously expands his authority over his narrative, turning his earlier self's doubts into the certainty of the convert: "Not only does Crusoe frequently keep accounts as a way of imposing a sense of orderliness on his life, but he gives an account of his life that makes it add up to something."[7] And in this design of turning firsthand experience into both psychological realism and Christian didacticism, Robinson avails himself fully of counterfactuals and other forms of imagined reality. How this aspect of the Robinsonade is taken up and developed in the second half of the twentieth century, from the tentative beginnings of postmodernism in the 1950s via its application in a critique of colonialism in the 1980s to its culmination at the end of the age of irony, is the subject of the following discussions of individual texts.

ROBINSON (1958)

Unusually for a Robinsonade, in Muriel Spark's "proto-postmodernist" novel,[8] the survivors of a plane crash stranded on an island are given the promise of salvation at the very start of the story when they are told that a boat will arrive for its annual visit in three months' time. They find themselves in the well-provisioned dwelling of a hermit-like man under whose guidance they will simply have to sit out the time until the arrival of their rescuers in comfortable surroundings. The occasional gesture toward a relative dearth of provisions aside, then, it is clear from the start that abject loneliness and bare survival are not the primary concerns of this text.

The three survivors, narrator January Marlow among them, are looked after by Robinson, who informs them that they have come to an island called Robinson. It is not just in their names that there seems to be a coincidence between man Robinson and Robinson island—the book features a map of the island emphasizing the fact that its basic shape is that of a human being with individual peninsulas given anatomical names such as the North Knee and the Headlands. Right from the beginning, then, it seems that the survivors' host is in complete control over the island, over his life as well as theirs. Far from being a hapless victim herself, the narrator January also brings with her some experience in writing, as she imagines she might turn her account of survival on the island into a novel (2).[9] She is even encouraged by Robinson to write her journal, although he admonishes her to "stick to facts" (13) throughout the novel. January's first-person account is for the most part narrated retrospectively, although the reader is occasionally given a glimpse of the contemporaneously written journal, often to receive information on characters' backstories as January discovers them.

As far as any authority over the narrative is concerned, then, the reader is firmly in the hands of January Marlow, but she in turn is dependent on Robinson not just for her initial rescue but for guidance and information regarding the island and its current inhabitants. As the story progresses, Robinson appears ever more capricious and unreliable, at one point even going so far as to feign his own murder and disappearing for several weeks, turning the second half of the novel into a whodunit, a search for meaning and clear-cut explanations. Finally questioned about his motivation in staging this elaborate fiction, Robinson seems to think himself not just beyond reproach but beyond mere human comprehension: "Yours is, of course, the obvious view. Well, my actions are beyond the obvious range. It surely needs only that you should realise this, not that you should understand my actions" (170).

But it is not just the characters themselves that prove unreliable by choice or incompetence in Spark's Robinsonade. Much of their failure to grasp reality is based on the fact that reality is difficult to grasp. Beginning with confusions about their names (as January's is that of a month and Robinson's is shared with the island itself [5–6]) and extending to their speculation on their fellow castaways' motivation, stable meaning can rarely be attributed to anything on the island of Robinson. As Spark's biographer puts it, "[*Robinson*] is a sequence of apparently unrelated vignettes spliced with excerpts from the heroine's journal. Although it looks like a realist novel, it plainly is not. January scrutinises the 'facts' but the facts will not explain the reality. She constantly changes her interpretation of data, laying out lists of events and possible motivations for the protagonists' actions and reactions, but the link between intention and action, cause and effect, collapses."[10] It is in the novel's counterfactuals and imaginary realities that this collapse in the relationship between cause and effect is played out most tellingly. When, for instance, January sees one of her companions disappear on the horizon where, unbeknownst to her, there is an entrance to a secret cave, she briefly imagines a reality where none of her companions had ever actually existed and where life on the island was merely "a dead woman's dream" (34). At another point, reminiscing about a time when her brother-in-law, a religious and moralistic zealot, stalked her to discover whether she was conducting an affair, January tells the reader, "He was always . . . trying to catch me in an illicit love affair, but he never succeeded; and whether this was because I never, in fact, had a lover, or whether I had, but effectively concealed the fact, you may be sure [he] is still guessing" (84). In this instance, then, by leaving us suspended between two possible versions of the truth, January stays in control of the narrative, disclosing only as much as she wants to. But the episode also foregrounds the notion that what is truly important is not what empirically happened in actual life but only the impression her brother-in-law has: perception trumps objective truth.

These counterfactuals serve to undermine rather than support faith in a stable reality. Where Defoe's Crusoe can retrospectively construct a providentialist narrative making sense of his fate, and where he can use counterfactuals to imagine how without his intelligence or without a providential God to look after him, something much worse might have befallen him, January seems to be less certain the more facts she learns. Her destabilizing use of counterfactuals gains traction when she considers the early death of her significantly older husband: wondering "how it would have been had he lived" (20). Rather than mourning his early death, her verdict seems to imply that she is better off without him. This use of counterfactuals against common expectations is perhaps best exemplified by a passage in which the survivors of the plane crash chat fairly innocuously about the catastrophe:

> "I wish," said Jimmie, "I stay at home. I commence to think I want my head examined for making this dangerous journey."
>
> "Same here," I said, without really meaning it. I did wish to go home, but not that I had never come away. If I had stayed at home, there might have been a fire in the house, or I might have been run over, or murdered, or have committed a mortal sin. There is no absolute method of judging whether one course of action is less dangerous than another. (37)

In expressing an uncertainty regarding the turns her life might have taken had she stayed home, January directly counters the certainty with which Defoe's Robinson can look back on his life and discern the exact workings of providence. The pinnacle of the undermining of substantive truths in favor of fleeting impressions is achieved at the end of the novel, when, having been rescued from her castaway existence, January reads in a newspaper article that the island is slowly sinking and expected to have fully disappeared "within three years" (185). This literal impermanence of Robinson island takes the reader back to the novel's very first sentence: "If you ask me how I remember the island . . . I would answer that it was a time and landscape of the mind if I did not have the visible signs to summon its materiality" (1).

Critics have commented on "the strange doubleness that plays itself out over the course of the novel, where nothing that happens seems to be without significance, but where only some of the meanings of events are conveyed."[11] Equally, it has been attested that, in her work in general, Spark's "presentation of life suggests an essential fragmentation, an essential incoherence."[12] This phenomenon frequently has critics reaching for the one approach, the one key that will help integrate all the loose ends of Spark's *Robinson* into a coherent story with a clearly defined intention behind it, which is why allegorical readings of the novel abound.[13] What the present discussion has shown, however, is that read alongside Defoe's *Robinson Crusoe*, particularly as imagined realities and textual authority are concerned, Muriel Spark's *Robinson* foregrounds questions of epistemology that do not have to be seen as stepping stones on the way to a univocal understanding of the novel, be it religious or political. Instead, these epistemological questions and the fact that they remain unanswered is what is at the very core of Spark's project, a novel that appears in the guise of realist fiction but then resists the integration of the many strands and items of information it provides into a coherent whole. What happens when a novel completely relinquishes the appearance of realism in problematizing questions of counterfactuality and textual authority can be seen in our next example.

FOE (1986)

J. M. Coetzee's 1986 novel is another instance in which a female narrator functions as a witness to the goings-on on the fabled desert island, although it has to be pointed out that *Foe* takes the reader back to the eighteenth century. In doing so, it goes against Defoe's novel in situating the action in the adult Defoe's lifetime rather than in the mid- to late seventeenth century. Coetzee's novel is divided into four parts: the first of these gives Susan Barton's testimony on her sojourn on Robinson's island and the time spent there with a distinctly gruff Cruso, as he is called here, and a Friday muted by having his tongue cut out at an earlier stage. At the end of this, we discover that the first-person account has an addressee who in this section's final paragraph is revealed to be called Mr. Foe. The second part consists of a series of letters penned by Susan Barton and addressed to Mr. Foe, a professional writer (and obvious stand-in for the historical figure of Daniel Defoe). Having left the island, buried Robinson at sea and taken Friday to London, Susan Barton exhorts Foe to help her turn her adventure into a story fit for publication.

Unfortunately, Foe has had to go into hiding from his creditors and so is difficult to get hold of. In part 3 Susan and Friday finally meet up with Foe and join him in hiding, where Susan conducts a series of discussions on the nature of writing and reality with him. They are joined by two other women (one of whom has already put in an appearance in the second part) whose ontological status is never quite clear: they may be mere apparitions conjured up by Foe or some other author, or they may be flesh-and-blood people. The reader may be interested in having this question answered for its own sake, but to Susan the answer has more far-reaching implications: "But if these women are creatures of yours [i.e., Foe's], . . . then who am I and who indeed are you?" (133).[14] As Susan is confronted with these spectral beings dissolving the boundaries between story and reality, she begins to lose confidence not only in her storytelling ability but also in herself on a much more fundamental level: "Nothing is left of me but doubt. I am doubt itself. Who is speaking me? Am I a phantom too?" (133). The brief fourth section introduces an unnamed twentieth-century narrator whose sole function is descriptive, and what they describe is a dreamlike sequence revisiting some of the scenes of the book from a centuries-long distance and gradually focusing on the character of Friday who closes the novel.

Whereas Spark's *Robinson* presents an epistemological quandary, enquiring into how we know what we know and how sensible it is to act on our presumed knowledge, Coetzee's *Foe* can be read as an ontological enquiry, a foray into questions of our state of being, or rather into questions of the relationship between stories and reality. And as such its use of ideas of the counterfactual varies as the story progresses and uncertainty seeps in. The first section in the novel is the one most immediately recognizable as a Robinsonade, and at first the narrator's use of imagined realities follows predictable lines. When, for instance, she first sees Friday, Susan imagines having "come to an island of cannibals" (6) in a classic ploy to raise the stakes for a castaway character. On the very next page, however, Susan lists a number of desert-island clichés to serve as a foil for her widely divergent experiences on Robinson's island. The idea that things will not be quite as the reader might expect is further introduced by Susan's judgment on the stories Cruso tells her: "I would gladly now recount to you the history of this singular Cruso, as I heard it from his own lips. But the stories he told me were so various, and so hard to reconcile with one another, that I was more and more driven to conclude age and isolation had taken their toll on his memory, and he no longer knew for sure what was truth, what fancy" (11–12). Not only does this serve to withhold information from the reader, it questions Cruso's entire authority over his own story. Trust in his authority is further undermined by a series of facts that appear in stark contrast to Defoe's novel and thus serve as alternative realities when the earlier work is taken into consideration. Cruso has no will to leave the island (13), keeps no journal (16), and has not salvaged any firearms from the wreck (15), and while he is continuously engaged in constructing terraces, presumably for agricultural purposes, he has no seed and no intention of ever planting anything on those terraces (33).

With his authority over the island as well as over the story waning, all of Cruso's actions are suddenly up for debate, and so Susan can bring up a series of counterfactual scenarios appearing in the innocent guise of practical considerations but really designed to undermine trust in Cruso's good faith and basic competence. "It seemed a great pity that from the wreck Cruso should have brought away no more than a knife," Susan tells the reader. After all, "had he rescued even the simplest carpenter's tools . . . , he might have fashioned better tools" (16). But while this "great pity" can be put down to bad luck or adverse circumstances, there is an attribution of blame to be found in the way Susan judges Cruso's refusal to teach Friday English beyond comprehension of a few orders barked at him: "Yet would it not have lightened your solitude had Friday been master of English? You and he might have experienced, all these years, the pleasures of conversation. . . . What benefit is there in a life of silence?" (22).

So while the first section of Coetzee's *Foe* does contain the occasional echo of Defoe's use of counterfactuals—as in Susan's realization that life on Cruso's island is not that bad since she "might as easily have been cast away on an island infested with lions and snakes" (25)—their real purpose is to gradually erode faith in Defoe's master narrative and to undermine the authority Cruso has over his island and over his story. That said, the end of that section also demonstrates the constructive power of imagined realities when Susan consoles a dying Cruso with stories of how they "will buy a sack of corn" and return to the island to finally plant it (44).

The second section of *Foe* initially continues with the counterfactual speculation on what life on the island would have been like had one particular condition been different. Susan quibbles with the contention that Cruso could have built a boat had he rescued more tools (55) and imagines how life on the island would have been improved, had Cruso taught Friday to speak (56). Soon, though, her thoughts turn to her present situation, and her loss of certainty and authority becomes palpable. A pivotal moment in this development can be found when Susan questions her own motivation in educating Friday: "I tell myself I talk to Friday to educate him out of darkness and silence. But is that the truth? There are times when benevolence deserts me and I use words only as the shortest way to subject him to my will. At such times I understand why Cruso preferred not to disturb his muteness. I understand, that is to say, why a man will choose to be a slaveowner"

(60–61). This encapsulation of much of the hypocrisy behind the project of colonialism confers a new question onto the narrative. Where Susan was concerned with survival during her time on the island, her perambulations around London afford her time to consider how her story ought to be told. With this reflection also comes doubt: doubt in her own status, doubt in her ability to make the right decisions, and—gradually but increasingly—doubt regarding her treatment of Friday. Not surprisingly, the letters she writes to Foe in the second section of the book are increasingly characterized by an abundance of question marks, and the alternative realities she imagines come in the form not of assertions but of questions. This part of the novel thus is primarily not concerned with hard facts that can be contrasted with imagined realities. Instead, the second section of *Foe* concerns itself with the potential of the story Susan wants Foe to write. As the focus shifts from physical objects (islands, apeskin shoes, terraces) to ideational factors, Susan's stance becomes ever more precarious, open to negotiation.

The feeling that what is negotiated in *Foe* is the intangible continues in the third section and will entirely dominate the fourth. As Susan remarks, the story "doggedly holds its silence" on account of "the loss of Friday's tongue" (117). Revolving around a perpetual absence, that of Friday's voice, this section of the novel no longer deals in counterfactuals that can serve as foils to the real and substantive facts. Instead, all boundaries between the real and the imagined are dissolved and everything has the potential of being true: fictional characters are perhaps real and Susan may perhaps be a fiction (133). Finally, the characters reassure themselves that they are real: "We are all alive, we are all substantial" (152). The only one left out of these avowals is Friday, who, given his missing tongue, cannot participate in the conversation. However, the third section ends with Friday's tentative steps toward learning to write, before the fourth section has our disembodied modern narrator focus mostly on Friday and his underwater roar, intimating that the time for Friday's story may have come at last.

The change in the use of counterfactuals and imagined realities in the different sections of *Foe* shows the passing of textual authority from the Robinson figure to Susan: "The masculinist, imperialist world has produced Cruso, with his arid spirituality, and Foe with his immoral exploitation. . . . Coetzee, by inserting Susan Barton between them, deconstructs that patriarchy, but through Susan also deconstructs white liberalism."[15] This deconstruction of the "putatively feminine"[16] liberal project is mirrored by the preponderance of questions in the second section and the blurring of ontological boundaries in the third, as the newly acquired power of shaping the story is shown gradually slipping through Susan's fingers. And while the baton cannot be passed on immediately, as no pretender to the narrative throne seems to be waiting, the closing pages of section 3 as well as all of section 4 strongly suggest that the hitherto silent Friday—paradoxically foregrounded throughout the novel through his silence—will be the next to shape our perception of the archetypal castaway story. That our understanding of stories is contingent, that meaning is not monolithic and permanent is also an idea reflected in the final Robinsonade to be discussed in the present essay.

LIFE OF PI (2001)

The absence most keenly felt in Yann Martel's *Life of Pi* when it is considered as a Robinsonade is that of an island. To be fair, an island features prominently in chapter 92, but overall *Life of Pi* tells of the "magical, realistic, surrealistic and allegorical journey"[17] that Piscine "Pi" Patel is forced to undertake in his lifeboat following a shipwreck in which everyone else is killed. Despite the obvious difference of barely featuring a desert island, *Life of Pi* clearly harkens back to Defoe's *Robinson Crusoe* in terms of the foregrounding of religion as well as in its continuous interest in questions of otherness.[18] It also ties in with the other postmodern Robinsonades in not merely revisiting the action of its precursor but in problematizing the very notion of discourse and storytelling.

To this end, the story employs a frame narrative in which the implied author travels to India and is told to look up a certain survivor of a shipwreck in Canada as he will "*have a story that will make you believe in God*" (xiii).[19] Having found that person, Pi Patel, the author figure is then told how young Pi survived 227 days in the Pacific alone in a lifeboat with a Bengal tiger. The story, which is told in a storytelling situation typical of much older texts but also supported by documents such as Pi's diary, some newspaper cuttings, and a recorded interview, contains increasingly unlikely elements that test the reader's credulity, and to some extent the reader is given a surrogate within the text at the end of the novel, when two Japanese officials are sent to interview the shipwreck survivor and are told his extraordinary story of survival alongside a Bengal tiger. Incredulous, they ask Pi to tell them "what really happened" (405), and Pi, after a short pause, proceeds to tell them a story that is more realistic and does not involve animals but that also happens to be even more traumatic than that which he has already told them: "So tell me," Pi asks them, "since it makes no factual difference to you and you can't prove the question either way, which story do you prefer? Which is the better story, the story with the animals or the story without animals?" (424). In the end, like the Japanese officials, the author surrogate and the reader need to entertain both versions of the story.

While Yann Martel's novel does contain a number of interesting (oftentimes amusing) cases of imagined realities, what follows focuses on the narratological structure of the book as a whole. To be sure, there are different types of imagined reality to be found in the novel and they serve different purposes. Many of the conditionals employed throughout the book are prospective in nature, thus letting us into Pi's plans and giving an explanation on whatever strange experiment he might be conducting next. This is in line with traditional castaway stories, providing some insight into the narrator's psyche as well as familiarizing readers with the practicalities of improvised island living.

Stylistically, the most characteristic use of imagined realities in *Life of Pi* is to instill an absurdist kind of humor into a desperate situation, as when the shipwrecked Pi reads his lifeboat's survival manual, a document written with clearly a different than the prevailing reality in mind, when it recommends "community singing" as a "sure-fire way to lift the spirits" to the lone (human) survivor of a shipwreck (222). Other uses of the counterfactual are more akin to the standard fare in castaway stories, lending weight to the idea of imminent jeopardy in short sentences such as "If there hadn't been the lifebuoy I wouldn't have lasted a minute" (139). What really sets this novel apart and turns it from a "tall tale with a magical realist feel"[20] to "a postmodern meditation on the very nature of story"[21] is the fact that the reader is left with two competing stories neither of which they are fully prepared to believe: "Martel's narrative is ultimately inconclusive; the question of whether the first telling of the tale or the second, abbreviated and horrific telling is the factual one is ultimately a narrative crux."[22]

In confronting the reader with the impossible choice between two versions of its tale, *Life of Pi* brings "the metadiscursive tradition of the Robinsonade genre as a whole"[23] to its current point of evolution: Defoe's Robinson holds uncontested sway over his narrative, the only difference in perception being that between his younger self living through the adventure on the island and his older self retrospectively seeing Providence at work in his life. Muriel Spark's Robinson only labors under the illusion of being in control, when in fact given the limitations of human knowledge and the obvious multiplicity of meaning in any social interaction, he can neither remain in command of the island nor regulate communication about and among the castaways for long. Coetzee's Cruso does not even attempt to preserve his own story and is frequently shown to deviate from Defoe's hero in some telling aspects. However, when Susan Barton tries to take control of the narrative, she soon finds herself in hock to the professional storyteller Foe—until they both belatedly realize that they have wrongfully wrested the story from someone who was there all along and who should be the one to tell it, even though—in his tongueless state—he may lack the means. Martel's novel, finally, turns the struggle for control over the narrative from an intradiegetic quandary into an extradiegetic one. In *Life of Pi*, it is no longer fictional characters having to determine the meaning of a story: that burden is placed squarely on the shoulders of the reader.

In pursuing this project of questioning intradiegetic authorship and textual authority in the Robinsonade, of offering "a self-reflexive, critical meta-commentary on the remediation at work in the genre more generally,"[24] these novels from different decades employ a multitude of means, but as the present discussion has shown, the use of counterfactuals and imagined realities is often to be found at the heart of such endeavors. Their function in Spark's novel may appear the most noticeable as they simply do the opposite of what they are supposed to do in Defoe's book: they make the world a less certain place, outcomes more difficult to anticipate, and empathy less likely to take hold. In Coetzee's *Foe*, counterfactuals are still present in the first section, where they also partly undermine Cruso's authority over the island, but then they gradually disappear as all of the characters' existence is shrouded in doubt and there are no certainties left to serve as foils for any counterfactual speculation. And in *Life of Pi* the character Pi presumably knows what his journey really entailed but decides to offer up two stories for the reader to choose between—two parallel universes rather than a univocal division of the world into what is and what is not, into real and imagined.

NOTES

1. Hilary P. Dannenberg, "Divergent Plot Patterns in Narrative Fiction from Sir Philip Sidney to Peter Ackroyd," in *Proceedings of the Conference of the German Association of University Teachers in English*, vol. 21, ed. Bernhard Reitz and Sigrid Rieuwerts (Trier: WVT, 2000), 415.
2. John Richetti, "Defoe as Narrative Innovator," in *The Cambridge Companion to Daniel Defoe*, ed. John Richetti (Cambridge: Cambridge University Press, 2008), 121.
3. Michael Seidel, "*Robinson Crusoe*: Varieties of Fictional Experience," in Richetti, *Cambridge Companion*, 184–185.
4. It is worth noting that this resistance to slaughtering the savages (along with condemnation of Spanish colonial attitudes) gradually recedes in the course of *The Farther Adventures*, a book that also features a much lower incidence of first-person introspection and far fewer counterfactual constructions of the "If I had" type than the original *Robinson Crusoe*.
5. Daniel J. Johnson, "*Robinson Crusoe* and the Apparitional Eighteenth-Century Novel," *Eighteenth-Century Fiction* 28.2 (Winter 2015–2016): 244.
6. Virginia Ogden Birdsall, *Defoe's Perpetual Seekers: A Study of the Major Fiction* (Lewisburg, PA: Bucknell University Press, 1985), 30.
7. Ibid., 37.
8. Eluned Summers-Bremner, "'Another World Than This': Muriel Spark's Postwar Investigations," *Yearbook in English Studies* 42 (2012): 152.
9. Muriel Spark, *Robinson* (London: Macmillan, 1958). Further references are to this edition and are given parenthetically.
10. Martin Stannard, *Muriel Spark: The Biography* (London: Weidenfeld and Nicolson, 2009), 188.
11. Summers-Bremner, "'Another World Than This,'" 161.

12. Judy Sproxton, "The Women of Muriel Spark: Narrative and Faith," *New Blackfriars* 73.863 (September 1992): 439.
13. The two critics cited here fall into this category, though offering vastly different keys: in the eyes of Sproxton, *Robinson* has to be understood in religious terms, while Summer-Bremner, in "'Another World Than This,'" maintains that only consideration of "the Cold War Zeitgeist" (155) can fully elucidate the text's hidden meanings.
14. J. M. Coetzee, *Foe* (London: Penguin, 1987). Further references are to this edition and are given parenthetically.
15. Paula Burnett, "The Ulyssean Crusoe and the Quest for Redemption in J.M. Coetzee's *Foe* and Derek Walcott's *Omeros*," in *Robinson Crusoe: Myths and Metamorphoses*, ed. Lieve Spaas and Brian Stimpson (Houndmills: Macmillan, 1996), 245.
16. Ibid., 245.
17. Bhagabat Nayak, "Magic Realism in Yann Martel's *Life of Pi*," in *Studies in English Literature*, vol. 11, ed. Mohit K. Ray (New Delhi: Atlantic, 2005), 169.
18. Chapters 54 to 56 of *Life of Pi* outline Pi's plans for killing Richard Parker, the Bengal tiger, thus providing a similar quandary to Robinson's plans for the slaughter of the cannibals. The very theme of cannibalism is intricately woven into the fabric of *Life of Pi* as well.
19. Yann Martel, *Life of Pi* (Edinburgh: Canongate, 2002). Further references are to this edition and are given parenthetically.
20. Louise Squire, "Circles Unrounded: Sustainability, Subject and Necessity in Yann Martel's *Life of Pi*," in *Literature and Sustainability: Concept, Text and Culture*, ed. John Parham, Adeline Johns-Putra, and Louise Squire (Manchester: Manchester University Press, 2017), 228.
21. Daniela Janes, "The Limits of the Story: Reading the Castaway Narrative in *A Strange Manuscript Found in a Copper Cylinder* and *Life of Pi*," *Mosaic: An Interdisciplinary Critical Journal* 46.4 (December 2013): 110.
22. Ibid., 122.
23. Ian Kinane, *Theorising Literary Islands: The Island Trope in Contemporary Robinsonade Narratives* (London: Rowman & Littlefield, 2017), 218.
24. Ibid., 217.

Part Two
NATIONAL CONTEXTS

3

CASTAWAYS AND COLONIALISM

Dislocating Cultural Encounter in *The Female American* (1767)

Przemysław Uściński

> Miranda: How came we ashore?
> Prospero: By Providence divine.
> —William Shakespeare, *The Tempest*

> The world was all before them, where to choose
> Their place of rest, and Providence their guide.
> —John Milton, *Paradise Lost*

IN HIS ESSAY "FROM PILGRIM to Tourist" Zygmunt Bauman proposes to see modernity in terms of a gradual transition, generally speaking, from pilgrimage to tourism. "The figure of the pilgrim was not a modern invention; it is as old as Christianity. But modernity gave it a new prominence and a seminally novel twist," Bauman observes.[1] The idea of life as a pilgrimage that prevailed in the early modern period later gave birth to the "mutations" of that idea, which Bauman distinguishes as four types of modern traveler: the stroller (flaneur), the vagabond, the tourist, and the player. Those modern types contrast with the pilgrim inasmuch as the idea of pilgrimage means that one "can *reflect* on the road past and see it as *a progress towards*, an advance, a coming *closer* to; one can make a distinction between 'behind' and 'ahead' and plot the 'road ahead' as a succession of footprints yet to pockmark the land without features. Destination, the set purpose of life's pilgrimage, gives form to the formless, makes a whole out of the fragmentary, lends continuity to the episodic."[2] Unlike pilgrims, tourists do not rely on the idea of final destination, or on the secure guidance of providence; they rather move here and now, episodically, in the everlasting present of the immediate (aesthetic) enjoyment: "What the tourist buys, what he pays for, what he demands to

[39]

be delivered (or goes to court if delivery is delayed) is precisely the right not to be bothered, freedom from any but aesthetic spacing."[3] What seems to be lacking in Bauman's typology, however, is the figure of a castaway, one which, admittedly, may simultaneously prove to be a pilgrim of sorts, especially if the shipwreck is read as a sign of a providential plan rather than as a mere accident. Before being a pilgrim, however, the castaway stranded on a desert island, such as Robinson Crusoe, is, as Ian Kinane observes, above all an individual: "There is a disjunction—and certainly a tension—between the desires of the castaway existing in isolation on the island and the pull exerted upon him by the social consciousness of civilisation from whence, presumably, the castaway came."[4] Located, at least temporarily, outside the reach of civilization, the castaway remains nonetheless its embodiment, an ambassador of civilization, the achievements of which may, however, come under scrutiny within the now distanced, isolated mind of the castaway. Commenting on the trope of isolation in Nietzsche's writing, Kinane also notes that

> it is the voice of the "herd" within the text that tells Zarathustra that "all isolation is wrong," and that "he who seeketh may easily get lost himself." Like Zarathustra in his cave, the individual castaway, *separé comme une île*, is able to examine the foundations of his/her own societal model from without that system. Though Zarathustra acknowledges that the "voice of the herd will still echo long in thee," he asserts that he still finds a great appeal in the man "who seeketh to create beyond himself"—one who transcends his/her given societal role and who seeks self-reflection beyond the "herd" of society.[5]

A castaway is lost, but potentially to be found (or to find himself/herself), through self-reflection, as a pilgrim on an independent, inner journey of self-becoming, a journey that Bauman, after Max Weber, refers to as that of "vocation," but one presumably guided by a call from beyond the Nietzschean "herd" of civilization, one proscribing an individual, sanctified mission to be accomplished. In Daniel Defoe's *Robinson Crusoe* (1719) such self-reflection comes, for instance, at the moment that Crusoe refers to as his "first Prayer" in years (67). It is at that point that Crusoe realizes that by taking the "foolish Step" of embarking upon a dangerous voyage he "rejected the Voice of Providence" that secured for him a comfortable, safe existence at home, "wherein I might have been happy and easy," as he admits (67). By abandoning the security of his home not out of economic necessity but in search of excitement and adventure, Crusoe committed a sin against providence, disregarding or misreading its signs—a mistake he realizes only when alone, with "no Help, no Comfort, no Advice" (67).

In what follows I read a later, anonymous castaway narrative, *The Female American* (1767), in the context of, among others, the postcolonial critique of the rhetoric of providence and destiny prominent in the imperialist discourses that accompanied and often guided the process of colonization. Through such a reading I discuss how the generic and narratorial strategies that the novel elaborates correspond with its treatment of the vital ethical and political questions related to the problem of cultural encounter. As Michelle Burnham and James Freitas observe, "[Although] the heroine's central experience of living on a remote island somewhere in the Atlantic ocean may be analogous to Crusoe's, *The Female American* revises the narratives of capitalist accumulation, colonial conquest, and political imperialism that have been associated with Defoe's book. Winkfield's story engages instead in fantasies of a feminist utopianism and cross-racial community, both of which are enabled, however, by a specifically religious form of imperialism."[6] While paying due attention to both the analogies and contrasts between the anonymous text and Defoe's earlier novel, I focus in particular on Unca Eliza Winkfield—the protagonist of the story and its narrator—as a figure of a castaway who, unlike Crusoe, devotes herself to widescale missionary endeavors. Her imagined (dis)location, geographical but also—with regard to other castaway narratives—intertextual, can be read in a number of ways pertaining to, among others, what Homi K. Bhabha, in his study *The Location of Culture*, terms the "third space." Relatively isolated, the islands on which the castaways are typically stranded provide a space other than one assigned to a given term within the dichotomy colonizing/colonized. The notion of "third space" aims at troubling the fixity of any cultural identity, for instance by foregrounding the fact that any culture—even when it attempts to posit itself as a coherent whole—is always an effect of numerous influences, encounters, translations, and disparities: "It is that Third Space, though unrepresentable in itself, which constitutes the discursive conditions of enunciation that ensure that the meaning and symbols of culture have no primordial unity or fixity, that even the same signs can be appropriated, translated, rehistoricized and read anew. . . . We should remember that it is the 'inter'—the cutting edge of translation and negotiation, the in*between* space—that carries the burden of the meaning of culture."[7] It is the "inscription and articulation of culture's hybridity" that deconstructs the myth of fixity, purity and cohesion of culture, revealing it as an entangled web of reinscriptions, disparities, appropriations, and ongoing negotiations; it may hence allow for "envisaging the national anti-nationalist histories of the 'people.'"[8] In the case of a castaway narrative, the possibility of a protagonist experiencing a relative isolation and/or encountering "alien" cultures gives the possibility of experimenting with and reflecting upon the relation between the individual and society, also by testing the coherence of the protagonist's acculturation amid the novelty of unexpected encounters, or through the protagonist's prolonged isolation. This dimension seems to give castaway narratives much of their enduring appeal, but it also provides a platform—indeed a space—for reconsidering various culturally shaped norms and ideas, for instance by imagining how they work "outside" civilization, or at least outside their usual context.

Unca Eliza Winkfield, the eponymous heroine of *The Female American*, is a daughter of a Native American princess Unca, who saved from death and subsequently married, in a Pocahontas-like manner, an English sailor, a son of Edward Maria Winkfield, whose name clearly echoes that of Edward Maria Wingfield, the first president of the Virginia colony. As Cathy Rex observes, "Each portion of the name, *Unca Eliza Winkfield*, also signifies upon a distinct aspect of the heroine's complex identity: she is Indian, she is a woman, she is a direct descendant of the founding fathers of America. In this continuation of the Pocahontas narrative, the heroine is not simply 'Rebecca' or 'Matoaka,' but both simultaneously."[9] What is more, the name *Unca*, as Betty Joseph notes, "stands as a feminized version of an important player in American history. 'Uncas' was chief of the Mohicans when the tribe joined the Puritan settlers in a war against a fellow tribe (the Pequots) in the 1630s. . . . Uncas, a traitor to native struggles, remained a hero for the British, whom he aided in all their struggles till his death in 1683."[10] Unca Eliza's biracial identity is further complicated by the fact that she spends her childhood among the Indian (probably Algonquian) tribe in Virginia (Wingandacoa), but later is educated in England, where she arrives at the age of seven and where, as she reports,

> My tawny complexion, and the oddity of my dress, attracted every one's attention, for my mother used to dress me in a kind of mixed habit, neither perfectly in the Indian, nor yet in the European taste, either of fine white linen, or a rich silk. I never wore a cap; but my lank black hair was adorned with diamonds and flowers. . . . My uncommon complexion, singular dress, and the grand manner in which I appeared, always attended by two female and two male slaves, could not fail of making me much taken notice of. I was accordingly invited by all the neighboring gentry, who treated me in a degree little inferior to that of a princess. (58)[11]

In England she makes "a great progress in the Greek and Latin languages, and other polite literature," but she also receives what she calls "pious instructions," that is, a very "methodical" and "exact" religious training, conducted in "a warm and affecting manner" (59–60). Unca Eliza's hybrid, equivocal identity thus combines culturally significant lineages within and across two cultures. This identity fosters and corresponds to the confounded identity of the text—purportedly autobiographical, it remains anonymous, and though first published in London in 1767, its subsequent editions in America, around 1790 and in 1814, further mystify the matters as regards the novel's possible authorship, its geographical or national origins, as well as its intended audience.[12]

Upon her trip back from America to England, after she visited her ill father, Unca Eliza falls prey to the tricks of a greedy captain, who takes her captive on his boat, demanding all her possessions and killing her slaves after she refuses to comply with his demands.[13] Unca Eliza herself is cast on the island with nothing but, as she recollects, "a box of clothes" and "my bow and quiver of arrows" (64). Isolated on the island, she sinks in religious meditations, in a manner not much different from Robinson Crusoe, and she places herself in the hands of the Almighty:

> I ought therefore to thank God for this escape, and to commit myself to his providence. indeed, in the hour of affliction we are ready enough to pray to God for help; but are so taken up with a sense of our miseries, that we forget that we have any mercy to be thankful for. We should always sing a *Te Deum* before we sigh a litany; for our sighs will sink before they reach heaven, unless raised thither by the wind of praise. Filled with these ideas I fell on my knees, and thanked God, who had delivered me out of the hand of the wicked, and that now I was in his only. (65)

Unca Eliza's religious premonitions about her destiny are further advanced by her reading of the Bible, a copy of which she finds in a hermit's cave on the island. The diseased hermit, Crusoe-like, also left in his "cell" a manuscript containing instructions on how to survive on the island and avoid the Natives, who visit it regularly once a year. That these and other provisions should be found on the seemingly desert and distant island for Unca Eliza was a matter of "great improbability," and she takes it as "an earnest of a future deliverance" (73).

It is in the vicinity of the cave that she also discovers a giant "idol," a hollow stone structure, a colossal figure resembling partly a man and partly a woman, called by the Natives "the Oracle of the Sun," with a subterranean passage leading to its interior. Unca Eliza is fascinated particularly by one technological feature of the giant structure—its ability to modulate and fortify the volume of any sound uttered inside it: "This image, particularly the head of it, it seems, was so wonderfully constructed as to increase the sound of even a low voice to such a degree as to exceed that of the loudest speaker," she observes, adding that "[it was] natural for me to conclude than that this image was anciently used to give out oracles: I tried to sing an hymn in my usual pitch of voice; but the sound was too much for my ears to bear, and I was obliged to lower my key" (88). It is there that Unca Eliza decides to hide at the moment of the Natives' yearly visit, and it quickly occurs to her that the statue of the idol will fittingly serve that purpose she has undertaken—to peacefully convert "Indians" to Christianity: "if I might become an instrument to promote the knowledge and glory of God, and the salvation and happiness of any of his creations, I might have his blessing on my endeavours" (92). Much like Robinson Crusoe, Unca Eliza frequently sees herself as an object on which the mysterious workings of divine providence operate, especially in the face of assault, violent storm, earthquake, and other traumatic, near-death experiences. Yet she also takes, arguably, a much more active, missionary approach when it comes to her interaction with the Natives: the novel cogently "emphasizes Unca Eliza's social instincts at the expense of solipsism of Defoe's protagonist."[14] Her decision "to convert [the Natives] from their idolatry" is made effective though a peaceful but cunning manipulation of the Natives' indigenous religious structures and practices: articulated from within the mighty statue, her thunderous voice interrupts their nocturnal rituals, and instructs them to discard the worship of the Sun (which "was made by God, to give you light and heat, and has no understanding"), replacing it with the worship of "God, who hath all power only, and who is good and gracious" (103). It is thus the hollow idol's "panoptic capabilities" and its exceptional acoustic features that provide Unca Eliza with possibilities for nonviolent conversion, granting her "an 'opening' that is consistent with the narrative's putting aside of the priorities of male conquering force for female civilizing."[15]

    As in the case of many events in the narrative, the convenient existence of a fittingly shaped stone idol is read as a sign of divine providence: during the earthquake that takes place right before the yearly visit of the Natives to the island, Unca Eliza once again recommends herself "into the hands of God" (95), and while the earthquake completely destroys her former habitation, it conveniently leaves the idol intact, prompting Unca Eliza to take her hiding there and put to the test her plan of converting the "Indians." Mathew Reilly sees Unca Eliza's autobiographical narrative as portraying a movement of "self-formation outside the constraints of society," a narrative in which the island "serves as a metaphor for her escape from religious and political orthodoxy."[16] Arguably, however, Unca Eliza's isolation from the constraints of society is mitigated by her recurrent adherence to the notion of divine providence, and while the narrative is a "physical and philosophical bildungsroman" of sorts,[17] it also tells a story of colonial and cultural encounter beyond individual quest for maturation. This broader focus of the narrative suggests what Laura Brown calls in her study a "cultural fable" of "imperial fate," which appears as the set of persistent discursive tropes that combine British imperialism and colonialism with the notions of fate and divine providence. Among others, this cultural fable fosters "a world mapped out by the historical force of mercantile capitalist expansion, a world whose fate is framed within the moral system generated by that force."[18] Colonialism thus produces its own maps and narratives, and accommodates the notions of fate, destiny, and divine providence to its own logic of expansion and domination. As a castaway on an unknown, as yet unmapped island, Unca Eliza is less concerned with practicalities of survival (mostly due to the fact that the hermit's manuscript provides her early on with plentiful instructions) and more with her civilizing mission, which she frames, initially at least, within the larger context of her own, often "miraculous," biographical fate, or destiny, as well as her hybrid identity, which involves the "exact" religious education she received in England, her knowledge of the Bible, and, conveniently, her fluent use of the Indian language.

Unca Eliza's use of the stone idol to effectuate her conversion tactics is a pivotal moment in the narrative with regard to her interactions with the Natives. As she decides to join the Natives in person, she also uses the idol to announce the arrival of the female teacher: "A person shall come to you, like yourselves, and that you may be the less fearful or suspicious, that person shall be a woman, who shall live among you as you do. She shall bring with her the holy writings I have been speaking of, and shall teach all of you, especially your priests, who shall instruct you after her departure, the knowledge of the true God" (119). Thus, Unca Eliza provides for herself a respectable place among the Natives, which allows her to continue her teachings, mingle with the tribe, and even translate the Bible, the Catechism, and "most of the prayers in the Common Prayer-Book" into the Indian tongue (127). Reflecting on her missionary efforts, she provides the following comment:

> I remembered when I was in England, that I used to look into some of the deistical writers in my uncle's study. These writers laboured to prove, that Christianity was repugnant to plain uncorrupted reason. Yet I found this assertion intirely [sic] false; for, here a people, who had no other guide but their reason, no sooner heard Christianity plainly and firmly expounded to them, but they soon embraced it. And I am fully persuaded that whenever any unprejudiced person tries the religion of Christ by his reason, though he may find it in some measure above his reason, he yet will not find it contrary to it, and that it is worthy of his assenting to it. (128)

Characteristically, the comment about the relatively easy absorption of Christianity among rational humans comes after the narrator has already implemented the somewhat manipulative conversion techniques through her use of the stone idol—a manipulation that preceded her later interactions with the Natives in person, on a presumably more equal footing. What is more, if "Indians" have "no other guide but their reason," this would suggest the reasonableness of their native religion—the worship of the sun. In short, if the rhetorical trajectory of the whole narrative seems directed toward the possibility of successful, peacefully conducted missionary endeavors (in contrast with the rhetoric of conquest and forceful submission), such endeavors need to be already framed within the larger putative narrative of destiny and divine providence, which provide much needed supplements to the otherwise purely "rational" conversion. This seems to be the case with a number of fortuitous circumstances related in the novel, including the presence of an imposing stone idol, which allows Unca Eliza to sleekly, and indeed peacefully, infiltrate the cultural/religious space of the Natives before meeting them face-to-face.

By substituting the colonial (male) force with the more "feminine" tactics (masquerade, charm, polite persuasion) of civilizing mission, the texts seems to accomplish a symbolic displacement, whose reading needs to be at least twofold. On the one hand, it can be read as proposing a nearly utopian alternative to the brutal colonialism of conquest, forceful conversion, murder, and slavery, an alternative that builds its cultural legitimacy by evoking, among others, the telling precedent of Pocahontas, a female agent of compassion, "a figure whose historical memory is not adequate to the unilinear narratives of nationalist mythmaking."[19] Like Pocahontas, Unca does not belong to one nation, or one nationalist history (either British, American, or even Indian), and her final decision not to leave the island and not to return to England (a point I will discuss later) might suggest that the hybridity of her identity resists the narratives of infiltration, colonization, or submission. Her subjectivity, in such a reading, both plays out and testifies to a peaceful and potentially enriching flow of interactions and encounters between cultures/ethnicities, in a "third space" beyond the power relations of dominance or violence. In such a reading, Unca Eliza, herself a product of numerous cultural encounters, and receptive of different influences, would stand in sharp contrast with Defoe's protagonist. As Matthew Reilly puts it, "Whereas Crusoe models the private, assertive self whose productive activity is bound up in a characteristically rationalist separation between wilful subject and external objects, Winkfield demonstrates how individual consciousness might be endangered and altered through embodied relations within a contingent environment."[20] On the other hand, however, the symbolic displacement in question may suggest a series of mere substitutions (female instead of male, openness instead of destruction, peaceful conversion instead of violent conquest) within the otherwise fixed dominant structure of the narrative of "imperial fate" that I have briefly discussed. As a benign, half-Indian female missionary, Unca Eliza would, under a logic of such interpretation, herself become a token of good faith, a ventriloquist substitute voice, but one residing inside a giant idol representing colonialism with all its disdain for native practices and customs condemned as "idolatry." Her gentle ways of (self-)conversion thus not only sustain the narrative of "imperial fate" but also persuasively conceal the gruesome reality of actual brutal colonialism, including missionary colonialism: "both English and Indian, [she] appears unthreatening to both populations because she is female," and hence a "perfect embodiment of colonial relations, especially in her expansion of a benign Christian and English empire."[21] Though it has been argued that the protagonist of *The Female American* "becomes the locus for the critique of the colonial and patriarchal discourses governing not only race and identity, but also intermarriage, cultural assimilation, [and] religious conversion,"[22] it is worth noting that, despite her status as a castaway, Unca Eliza does not stand for the contingent, unpredictable character of cultural encounter, since her role is scripted, and her future foreshowed early on, for instance in her musings about her "exact" religious training, which was to prove "of the highest use" (60).[23] In other words, there is within Unca Eliza's ostensibly hybrid identity a discernible asymmetry: her Indianness, from the very outset of the narrative, is prescribed as merely subordinate in relation to the teleological importance of her later education/training (*Bildung*) as a Christian (Anglo-)American.

The insistence on the driving force of divine providence, recurrent throughout the text, structures the text by providing coherence to the seemingly random "adventures" narrated and enframes the entire story within a religious metanarrative. Another pivotal moment in the novel when it comes to Unca Eliza's relations with the Natives occurs upon the arrival of the "European ship" with Mr. Winkfield, Unca Eliza's pious cousin, on board. Spotting two Englishmen on the island, the heroine considers the safety of the Natives:

> Whatever might be the cause of their landing, I had much to fear. Indeed I was safe where I was; but how was I to get home? and to stay long in such a place I could not. My next fear was for the poor Indians, who would come in the evening, and not finding me by the shore, as usual, would no doubt come upon the island, in search of me, and be taken for slaves. Nor might the evil stop thus; their country might be discovered, and probably invaded, and numbers of the people be carried away into slavery, and other injuries committed. (129)

Though longing to reveal her identity to her cousin, Unca Eliza again hides in the stone idol, wary of the possible threats to herself and the Natives that she identifies with the colonizing practices of the Europeans. Though unintentionally, her words uttered from within the idol and her later appearance alarm her cousin's companion and, in effect, horrify the entire crew, which decides to depart and leave

Mr. Winkfield on shore. This chain of events is interpreted, this time by Mr. Winkfield, as very fortuitous: "It seems . . . as if providence, though by a somewhat adverse stroke, designs that I shall carry my resolution to teach the Indians into practice, and spend my days with my dear Unca" (145). Resolving to continue the missionary work together, Unca Eliza and Mr. Winkfield further accentuate their separateness from the colonial endeavors toward the end of the novel when they cautiously forbid "the sailors to come any farther upon the island, than just to land the goods, that no discovery of our habitation might be made," and when they declare, in the final sentence of the novel, that they never intend "to have any more to do with Europe" (162).

These gestures of separation, Betty Joseph argues, "enact a secession from Europe (as the Declaration of Independence will do soon), but this secession does not simultaneously consolidate a national space as much as it proposes a retreat from all such exercises."[24] The novel thus fosters an image of community and cross-cultural exchange and encounter that remain different from, and possibly critical of, the dominant colonial perspective governed by the logic of conquest and nationalist consolidation in terms of territory, identity, and property. Still, however, a "retreat" suggests also a form of a pastoralist escape from the constraints and pitfalls of colonial trade, conquest, travel, and labor, an escape that *The Female American* tries to propose, somewhat ambiguously, as a relatively plausible alternative that cannot help appearing, however, as utopian. Not only the accumulation of fortuitous circumstances (including Unca Eliza's mixed-race identity) but also the framing of the narrative within the generic caption of "the Adventures" in the novel's title largely predetermine the limits of the text's potential critical capabilities. On the one hand, the novel aims at reclaiming the picaresque tradition for a female agent, partaking, in effect, in a "counter-tradition of anti-domestic female adventure that unfolded across a global landscape of oceans and islands."[25] On the other hand, however, as the novel employs the rhetoric of divine providence to render respectability to its account of often marvelous occurrences, its "defining terms are exuberantly fantastic rather than realist,"[26] which hardly makes *The Female American* an epitome of a serious anticolonial or antislavery discursive engagement.[27]

The novel needs a distant island and a quasi-religious account of providentially guided story to envision "a third space" that salvages the more fluid and peaceful cultural encounter from the violence of colonialist exploitation—a violence that seems otherwise inescapable. Consequently, "as it ends, the novel imagines *a complete release* from history" as "Unca believes the island can escape colonialism, piracy, the transatlantic slave trade, bonded labour, and all those events that actually stand in the way of a successful proselyte."[28] This protective and protectionist "complete release from history," though it proceeds from the "original" fluidity and complexity of cultural identity personified by Unca Eliza Winkfield and her family history, needs a final resolution in the form of a full separation to preserve that fluidity and openness, however mitigated they remain by the novel's insistence on missionary activity, which itself is somewhat uncritically juxtaposed with direct violence against the Other.[29] Unca Eliza becomes a successful missionary devoted to her newly established Indian community of Christian proselytes, in a marked contrast with Robinson Crusoe's individualist pursuit of self-reliance. Yet she also figures as an emblem of state-sponsored conversion efforts that might thrive undisturbed only within the remote, topographically isolated—and hence fully controllable—space that, paradoxically, excludes any exteriority connected with the possibility of contingent foreign influences. Unca Eliza's tactics of mimicry and infiltration that ultimately aim at conversion would prove futile in a milieu where plentiful voices and perspectives are available. As a self-fashioned solitary evangelist, she is able to perform effectively because her massage remains undisturbed by conflicting accounts or theological disputes that are, arguably, part and parcel of the history of Christianity. In short, if *The Female American* celebrates a peaceful cultural encounter, it also suggests that such peacefulness is possible only elsewhere, outside history, in the confined space provided by a remote island.

Castaway narratives often serve as allegories of the relation between the individual and society that imaginatively probe into matters of the border(s) between self-definition and social determinism (or between chance and decision), yet in the case of *The Female American* such probing seems to come to a halt whenever Unca interprets the events and her own actions as instrumental to the operations of divine providence. In comparison with Defoe's novel, these interpretative gestures seem less problematized within the narrative, since Unca Eliza becomes simply composed and self-assured about her prospects whenever she evokes the concept—it is this assurance, however, that means she never questions her own accountability, using the rhetoric of providential design as sufficient justification for her actions.[30] Likewise, in a gesture parallel to the logic of "cultural fable" of "imperial fate," and perhaps in complicity with it, the novel reinscribes missionary activity as an acceptable, even commendable, motivation for cultural expansionism governed by divine providence, within what Brown identifies as the second phase of colonial expansion, coming "after midcentury, when the first flash of the *pax britannica* and first era of English imperial expansion is complicated by the social, political and cultural adjustments that emerge in the growing movements opposing the slave trade and advocating social and political reform."[31]

If *The Female American* belongs, however tentatively, to that historical moment of cultural self-reflection, this is visible in the ways it foregrounds the

[49]

contradictions of colonialism, particularly in relation to the very import and future of Christian missionary endeavors. The novel uses the frame of castaway narrative, however, to dislocate its account of cultural encounter and provides the figure of biracial female missionary as a proxy for colonialist power, thereby avoiding to address (rather than resolving) the historically urgent questions about justice, agency, and accountability in the colonial context. This avoidance is encoded in the novel's plot and its escapist conclusion, but is traceable also in its narratorial reliance on the notion of divine providence.

NOTES

1. Zygmunt Bauman, "From Pilgrim to Tourist—or a short History of Identity," in *Questions of Cultural Identity*, ed. Stuart Hall and Paul du Gay (London: Sage, 2003), 19.
2. Ibid., 21–22. Bauman's remarks could fit well as a description of John Bunyan's *The Pilgrim's Progress* (1678), a narrative that elaborates on the idea of life as pilgrimage, that is, as a journey in which all episodic and seemingly accidental occurrences are linked together and form a single coherent itinerary.
3. Ibid., 30.
4. Ian Kinane, *Theorising Literary Islands: The Island Trope in Contemporary Robinsonade Narratives* (London: Rowman & Littlefield, 2017), 141.
5. Ibid., 109.
6. Michelle Burnham and James Freitas, "Introduction," in *The Female American; or the Adventures of Unca Eliza Winkfield. Compiled by Herself*, ed. Burnham and Freitas (Peterborough: Broadview, 2014), 12.
7. Homi K. Bhabha, *The Location of Culture* (London: Routledge, 2004), 55–56.
8. Ibid., 56.
9. Cathy Rex, *Anglo-American Women Writers and Representations of Indianness, 1629–1824* (London: Routledge, 2015), 116. Rex refers here to both the "original" name of Pocahontas and the name (Rebecca) she adopted after her marriage with John Rolf.
10. Betty Joseph, "Re(playing) Crusoe/Pocahontas: Circum-Atlantic Stagings in 'The Female American,'" *Criticism* 42.3 (Summer 2007): 321.
11. Burnham and Freitas, *Female American*. Further references are to this edition and are given parenthetically.
12. Apart from Defoe's novel, the text clearly draws on travel accounts such as Thomas Hariot's *Brief and True Report of the New Found Land of Virginia* (1590), George Percy's "Discourse of Virginia" (1624), and John Smith's *Generall History of Virginia* (1624). See Elizabeth Bohls, "Age of Peregrination: Travel Writing and the Eighteenth-Century Novel," in *A Companion to the Eighteenth-Century English Novel and Culture*, ed. Paula R. Backscheider and Catherine Ingrassia (Oxford: Blackwell, 2005), 103.
13. This particular situation resembles one in Aphra Behn's *Oroonoko, or the Royal Slave* (1688), when a duplicitous, nameless captain invites the prince Oroonoko to embark upon his ship. The seemingly friendly captain, with whom Oroonoko traded in slaves in the past, now takes the prince and his entourage captive to sell them as slaves for the plantation is Surinam.
14. April London, *The Cambridge Introduction to the Eighteenth-Century Novel* (Cambridge: Cambridge University Press, 2012), 124.
15. Joseph, "Re(playing) Crusoe/Pocahontas," 322.

16. Mathew Reilly, "'No Eye Has Seen, or Ear Heard': Arabic Sources for Quaker Subjectivity in Unca Eliza Winkfield's *The Female American*," *Eighteenth-Century Studies* 44.2 (Winter 2011): 262–263.
17. Ibid., 263.
18. Laura Brown, *Fables of Modernity: Literature and Culture in the English Eighteenth Century* (Ithaca, NY: Cornell University Press, 2003), 88.
19. Joseph, "Re(playing) Crusoe/Pocahontas," 331.
20. Reilly, "'No Eye Has Seen, or Ear Heard,'" 273.
21. Roxann Wheeler, "The Complexion of Desire: Racial Ideology and Mid-Eighteenth-Century British Novels," *Eighteenth-Century Studies* 32.3 (Spring 1999): 326–327.
22. Rex, *Anglo-American Women Writers*, 116.
23. Although that particular comment is made by the narrator as she recollects the events post-factum, it adds to the general narratorial scheme whereby the supposedly accidental but felicitous circumstances are typically revealed as contributing to Unca Eliza's coherent pilgrimage—though a castaway, she is never entirely lost.
24. Joseph, "Re(playing) Crusoe/Pocahontas," 323.
25. Burnham and Freitas, "Introduction," 32.
26. London, *Cambridge Introduction*, 123.
27. This is to say not that utopian thought or imagery cannot be potentially critical or transformative but rather that the novel underscores the utopian (idealized, unrealistic) character of its vision of cultural encounter through its own generic identification and narratorial enframing.
28. Joseph, "Re(playing) Crusoe/Pocahontas," 323, emphasis added.
29. Unca Eliza's account of her religious practices emphatically fashions them as peaceful and consensual: "Though I had no right to administer the sacrament of the Lord's supper, yet I was well satisfied, that under the circumstances we were in, I might baptize. But I never did so, till I was well satisfied that the party had a tolerable notion of the christian religion, and earnestly desired to be baptized" (127). Yet her manipulation through the stone idol and her use of threats and gifts reflect the questionable character of even the relatively lenient missionary activities.
30. Crusoe's psychological portrait in Defoe's novel seems more complex than that of Unca Eliza, though ultimately in both cases the notion of providence gives much-needed comfort to the protagonists. As John Richetti puts it in his classic study, "Just as Crusoe survives physically by watching for favourable forces in the chaotic appearances of nature, he survives on a psycho-spiritual level by learning to see God's presence in the minutest disposition of his circumstances." John Richetti, *Defoe's Narratives: Situations and Structures* (Oxford: Clarendon, 1975), 43.
31. Brown, *Fables of Modernity*, 89.

4

SETTING THE SCENE FOR THE POLISH ROBINSONADE

The Adventures of Mr. Nicholas Wisdom (1776) by Ignacy Krasicki and the Early Reception of *Robinson Crusoe* in Poland, 1769–1775

JAKUB LIPSKI

*T*HE ADVENTURES OF MR. NICHOLAS WISDOM by Ignacy Krasicki (1776) is a typical starting point for historical investigations into the development of the modern novel in Polish literature.[1] For one thing, it is difficult not to admit the novelty of the narrative in the context of the romance tradition dominating the realm of prose narrative in the preceding decades: Krasicki's book has been labeled "anti-romance" to highlight the difference on the grounds of its openly parodic undertones.[2] For another thing, the figure of the author, which in Polish literature is comparable to that of Alexander Pope,[3] legitimates attempts to put him in the role of originator or trend setter. Indeed, the critics of the Enlightenment in Poland, especially the Stanislavian Age—the reign of King Stanislaus (1764–1795), who ushered in far-reaching cultural reforms—have been basically unanimous in labeling the narrative "the first Polish novel."[4]

Derivative as it was, *Nicholas Wisdom* transposed onto Polish soil a number of narrative conventions that had already been flourishing in French and English literature (the two main points of reference for Krasicki and the other Stanislavian *literati*). A first-person narrative, the novel opens in a manner typical of fictional memoirs. Nicholas is a member of Polish nobility and is about to learn what the world is like. The first section recounts his childhood, education, and Grand Tour, recycling elements known from didactic rake's progresses in the Hogarthian style, such as gambling and amorous misfortunes. It closes with the Robinsonade moment, when Nicholas is marooned on an unknown island. This is followed by the utopian section featuring the happy Nipuans living in a state of nature. In this part, Nicholas receives his "natural" education from Master Xaoo and changes his worldview. In the third section, Nicholas returns to Europe and Poland and has a chance to understand the superiority of the Nipuan ideas over the civilized customs and political relations on the Continent and in his own motherland.

SETTING THE SCENE FOR THE POLISH ROBINSONADE

Toward the end of the utopian section (chapter 15, book 2), shortly before Nicholas is able to leave the island on a boat he has himself mended and prepared for departure, the protagonist enters the wreck of the ship that marooned him. Like Robinson, Nicholas retrieves a number of goods, which he then stores in a cave. He then presents a meticulous list of items retrieved, in a manner imitating Crusoe's systematic discourse. This is perhaps the closest Krasicki gets to the Defoevian idiom, but such moments do not dominate the narrative. In total, the motifs that Krasicki would have taken from *Robinson Crusoe* include storm and shipwreck, initial despair on the beach and fear of wilderness, reentering the wreck, using a cave as a store, rescue from a Spanish ship, and imprisonment by a slave trader sailing to Brazil. In addition, the narrative occasionally echoes Robinson's reflective passages, concerned with the role of the Providence and self-analysis, such as the following: "Walking alone along the coast line, exactly where I had been cast away, I started reflecting upon my present condition and, in general, upon all of my life's adventures."[5] As indicated above, *Nicholas Wisdom* can be considered not a fully-fledged Robinsonade but a quasi-Robinsonade at best, not least because of the fact that the crucial shipwreck and island motif is promptly transformed into a utopian narrative,[6] which, in turn, does not take more than a third of the whole novel. Admittedly, the reader of *Nicholas Wisdom* is bound to recognize that Krasicki would have been equally indebted to Jonathan Swift and his *Gulliver's Travels* (1726), and perhaps more to Jean-Jacques Rousseau's *Emile* (1762) and Voltaire's *Candide* (1759).[7] Nevertheless, the diffused elements of Wisdom's Robinsonade, even if indirectly, begin a relatively rich tradition of Polish reworkings of the pattern.[8] In fact, it was immediately readopted by Krasicki too in his *History* (1779)—a novel inspired by the tradition of imaginary voyages and dialogues with the dead. In *History*, the time-traveling narrator is at one point tired of the world and decides to retire into the wild. He finds a pleasant mountainous spot somewhere in China and is bent on spending his days "in peace" and "far from human company."[9] Like Robinson, Krasicki's time traveler reenacts the story of agricultural and civilizational change:

> When I had enough wood at my disposal, I built myself a hut—a dwelling not magnificent but comfortable. I started to work the land: I planted seeds of vegetables and herbs that appeared edible and ended up being very well provided.... Then I caught a few deer-like animals, still rather little. I tamed them so well that they would not leave me for a second. I did the same with various species of bird. They would sing songs to me and I fed them as the land was fertile.
>
> Necessity is the mother of invention, so I learnt to be proficient in all the crafts.[10]

[53]

Although he published *History* three years after *Nicholas Wisdom*, Krasicki was in fact working on the two texts almost at the same time,[11] which may lead to the conclusion that despite the brevity of the two Robinsonade sections, the novelist was elaborating on a convention and an idea that were thought topical and relevant at the time of writing. The specificity of the historical moment is all the more significant as the Robinsonade proper, as a fully-fledged genre, did not start to develop in Polish literature before the mid-nineteenth century. My aim in this chapter is to locate Krasicki's interest in the Robinsonade in the literary and intellectual context of the author's time, in particular in the several years preceding the writing and publication of *Nicholas Wisdom*, beginning with the 1760s—a decade of changes in the literary tastes ushered in by the Anglophile king Stanislaus August Poniatowski.

This chapter re-creates the literary milieu that became the scene for the emergence of the Robinsonade in Polish. The first Polish translation of *Robinson Crusoe* in 1769 will be seen as a response to the heightened interest in Defoe's novel in the 1760s, while the subsequent editions in the 1770s and finally the publication of *Nicholas Wisdom* in 1776 will be taken as testimony to the enduring presence of *Crusoe* in the literary life of the Stanislavian Age, in a decade characterized by a growing demand for prose fiction.

Tellingly enough, the 1769 translation was the first translation of an English novel into Polish, with the others not coming before the late 1770s. In the same year, the flourishing demand for narratives of adventures and sentimental affairs was satiated by Polish translations of Alain-René Le Sage's *Gil Blas* (1715–1735) and Antoine Prévost's *Manon Lescaut* (1731). As Jan van der Meer points out, in 1769 the number of modern novels published in Poland for the first time exceeded ten.[12] Van der Meer later indicates that the real change in the novel production was brought in 1776, when *Nicholas Wisdom* was published.[13] The period studied here, then, framed by these two publishing events, appears to have been the formative time for the development of the modern novel in Polish. In reconstructing this historical moment, I show how the publication of the first Polish translation of Defoe's novel testified to some of the strategies characterizing the literary life of Warsaw at the beginning of King Stanislaus's reign. The appearance of *Robinson Crusoe* and the Robinsonade in Poland was a multifaceted literary event, which involved the king's close circle of literary associates and some of the most influential figures in the literary sphere.

The early reception of *Robinson Crusoe* on Polish soil exemplifies the general tendencies in the afterlife of English fiction in Enlightenment Poland. First of all, the translations came out relatively late, just as the market for modern prose narrative started to develop several decades later than in England and France, basically with King Stanislaus's succession to the throne and the proper beginning of the Polish Enlightenment (the preceding reign of August III is usually considered as the final stage of the Baroque). Second, a number of English novels were translated not from the original but from the French versions, often rather loose and abbreviated. Finally, *Robinson Crusoe*'s early reception in Poland, just like the reception of the other highlights of modern fiction (for example, Le Sage, Henry Fielding, and Laurence Sterne) is to be credited to the circle of King Stanislaus—a trendsetter in modern Enlightenment culture and the early stages of Polish Anglophilia.[14]

Richard Butterwick suggests that translations of English novels were conducted independently of the king and that the king's Anglophilia "remained largely a private matter."[15] This might have been the case when one searches for explicit commissions and archival remnants of influence. However, I argue that literary phenomena should not be analyzed in this manner only. The Royal Library in Warsaw was far from being a private sphere and exerted an impact on the women and men of letters, including Ignacy Krasicki,[16] who gathered their own collections and modeled them on the one owned by the monarch. The king's circle of friends were affected by his tastes, as revealed in the rich literary life of the Czartoryski circle, first in Warsaw and then in Puławy.[17] I do not claim that the king alone was instrumental in the early reception of *Robinson Crusoe* in Poland; rather, the literary life of the Royal Castle was an important, if not the most important, element in the intellectual network of the 1760s and 1770s, which was the scene for the appearance of Defoe's novel in Poland.

Though fiction did not dominate the collection, the king and his librarians were responsive to the modern trends in narrative prose. *Robinson Crusoe* was one of the first novels to be ordered for the library. An early receipt for books obtained in the period between 1767 and 1775, the first extensive list of books for the royal library, features a three-volume French edition ("*La vie et avantures de Robinson Crusoe*, t. 1–3, Paris 1761") and a two-volume English edition. The list includes 278 titles, so no hasty conclusions should be drawn from the presence of Defoe's novel. However, bearing in mind the fact that the market for prose narrative was to start developing at the turn of the 1760s and 1770s, the few novels included should be taken seriously. The canonical examples of modern prose fiction first ordered by the king and his librarians included only the following: Le Sage's *Gil Blas* in the first Polish translation from 1769; Marie Jeanne Riccoboni's *Lettres de Milady Juliette Catesby* (1760) in the original, which was promoted by Voltaire himself; and Sterne's *A Sentimental Journey* (1768) in the French translation by Frenais; the rest was dominated by travels, histories, and philosophical treatises. It should be noted that only *Robinson Crusoe* was ordered in two different editions, including an English edition.[18] The novel was also collected in the other significant libraries of the nobility in the Stanislavian period (including Ignacy Krasicki's library): Zofia Sinko located eleven copies throughout the country, which is one of the highest numbers for novels translated into Polish in the 1760s and 1770s.[19] Needless to say, library collections should not be treated as decisive evidence for anything other than themselves, but it is worth bearing them in mind when reconstructing the literary scene.

The receipt also provides insight into the prospective ways modern fiction in Polish was to start developing, the dominant points of reference being the picaresque and the sentimental. Admittedly, *Robinson Crusoe* in the 1760s was read as belonging and contributing to both variants, given the adventurous element, on the one hand, and the commentary on a state of nature, on the other. Generically heterogeneous as it was, Krasicki's *Nicholas Wisdom* encapsulated these conventions, beginning like a rake's progress tinged with sentimental affairs (Nicholas repeatedly refers to his "sentimental education") only to become a Rousseauvian utopia in book II.

One does not risk much interpreting the early reception of *Robinson Crusoe* in Poland in the context of Jean-Jacques Rousseau's thought. The interest in Defoe's novel among the Polish intellectual elite was most likely due to the famous recommendation put forward by Rousseau in his *Emile, or On Education* (1762). *Emile* was known and read in Poland, though not uncritically, already in the 1760s,[20] and the periodical *Monitor*, modeled on the *Spectator*, published excerpts from the treatise in 1765 (nos. 31–32). The utopian section of Krasicki's *Nicholas Wisdom* promotes a system of education very much in line with the ideas of the French philosopher: the teacher first learns about the pupil and then tries to eliminate the wrong habits so as to be certain that the seeds of moral truths he proceeds to plant will fall upon clean and fertile soil; finally, he ensures that the theory will be successfully put in practice.[21] Having been taught the Nipuan way of life and gradually coming to realize the artificiality of "civilized" societies, Nicholas has no alternative but to accept the superiority of the Nipuans. He now understands why he himself is being called a "savage," thus self-reflexively implying that in Krasicki's Robinsonade the role of Friday is reserved for the marooned protagonist.

Rousseau's thought fueled the French reception of Defoe's novel, with a visible increase in a number of editions published.[22] In 1766 there appeared a new translation/adaptation by Joseph Feutry (1720–1789),[23] which would serve as the model for the translator into Polish. As for the recommendation itself, *Crusoe* is promoted as "the most felicitous treatise on natural education": "This book will be the first that my Emile will read. For a long time it will alone compose his whole library, and it will always hold a distinguished place there. It will be the text for which all our discussions on the natural sciences will serve only as commentary. It will serve as a test of the condition of our judgment during our progress, and so long as our taste is not spoiled, its reading will always please us."[24] The remark is then followed by Rousseau's interpretation of the model including a clearer formulation of its educational merits:

> Robinson Crusoe on his island, alone, deprived of the assistance of his kind and the instruments of all the arts, providing nevertheless for his subsistence, for his preservation, and even procuring for himself a kind of well-being—this is an object interesting for every age and one which can be made agreeable to children in countless ways. . . . The surest means of raising oneself above prejudices and ordering one's judgments about the true relations of things is to put oneself in the place of an isolated man and to judge everything as this man himself ought to judge with respect to his own utility. . . .
>
> This novel, disencumbered of all its rigmarole, beginning with Robinson's shipwreck near the island and ending with the arrival of the ship which comes to take him from it, will be both Emile's entertainment and instruction throughout the period which is dealt with here.[25]

Rousseau's interpretation, in a way, gave way to some dominant reception trends in the later decades of the eighteenth century, irrespective of what the novel was really like. These, at least to some extent, were based on misconceptions. First, Crusoe was not deprived of "instruments of all the arts," and rather than establishing himself on the island from scratch, he depends on the remnants of civilization that he has managed to retrieve from the ship. Second, Rousseau's remark that the book can be "made agreeable to children in countless ways" implied the potential of the story to become children's literature—a quality that would not have been projected by Defoe.[26] Finally, the French thinker appears to have appreciated only the island section of the narrative, which in Defoe's novel is only part of a larger, much more complex whole. The rest is dubbed "rigmarole" and considered redundant. These three observations formed a model of reception that, arguably, survived in the popular imagination well into the twenty-first century. More immediately, in turn, it provided a formula for what might be termed the Rousseauvian Robinsonade, "beginning with Robinson's shipwreck near the island and ending with the arrival of the ship which comes to take him from it," suited particularly for adolescent readers. The first of this kind was Joachim Heinrich Campe's *Robinson der Jüngere* from 1779, which immediately became very popular reading throughout Europe. The Polish translation (1793) appeared beyond the time frame for this chapter, but it is worth highlighting the still prevalent Rousseauvian understanding of *Crusoe* as implied in the publishing announcement of the new version: "This work . . . is

JAKUB LIPSKI

one of the best to shape a child's heart and mind. It teaches in an entertaining manner and does not cause the young reader's interest to wane."[27]

The reception of *Crusoe* in Rousseau's manner transcended the confines of literature and entered garden design. When the Rousseauvian appreciation of natural sceneries, based on the writer's descriptions in *La nouvelle Heloise* (1761) and *Emile*, contributed to the reform of the French garden and establishment of the tradition of the picturesque garden on the Continent (much indebted to the tradition of the English garden, too), "Robinson Crusoe hut" was among the many recommended "garden follies, or . . . *fabriques*,"[28] though Rousseau in *La nouvelle Heloise* was rather critical of such additions as artificial ruins or temples. In 1774, King Stanislaus's architect and advisor August Fryderyk Moszyński presented the monarch with his *Essay sur le jardinage Anglois*, where among the several dozen recommended embellishments "Robinson Crusoe's habitation" is described as a fashionable addition to the Royal Gardens in Łazienki, Warsaw:

> The remnants of what used to be a path and the few fallen trees make one curious to delve into the forest. Having taken some turns through trees and bushes, the visitor reaches Robinson's habitation, just as it was described in the novel. The hut can be entered by an underground passage, and the interior corresponds to what it was like for Robinson. His tools are hung on the walls and serve as embellishments. A wooden palisade, masked by the brush from the outside, encloses and conceals the hut when one views it from the meadow located in this part of the forest. . . . One can walk back taking the same path or turn right and go further into the forest to reach Trophonius' cave.[29]

There is no evidence that the proposed plan materialized, but the context helps better understand the idea. The neighboring Trophonius' cave suggests that Robinson's hut as an element of garden design should be viewed in the context of other "caves," "grottos," "huts," or "hermitages." As such, it appears to have been testimony to the sentimentally Rousseauvian reading of Defoe's novel, with the reader's focus centered on the relationship between the solitary individual and Nature—an ideal form of contact encouraged by these elements of the picturesque garden.[30]

Having sketched the background for the appearance of *Robinson Crusoe* in Poland, it is now time to introduce the two main agents of this literary event— the translator and the publisher. Jan Chrzciciel (Giovanni Battista) Albertrandi, the first translator of *Robinson Crusoe*, was closely affiliated with the king: first as his reader, then librarian, and finally principal archivist. Like the king himself, Albertrandi cooperated with Michał Gröll—a German printer who moved to

Warsaw from Dresden and established a printing house that would dominate the literary scene of the late 1760s and 1770s. Following the modus operandi adopted in Western Europe, Gröll published not only popular works of fiction but also literary periodicals that set the ground for the books by way of reviews, publishing announcements and essays aimed at shaping the literary taste. The best-known fruit of Albertrandi and Gröll's cooperation was the literary weekly *Zabawy przyjemne i pożyteczne* (Pleasant and Useful Diversions, 1770–1777), which energized the literary life of Warsaw in accord with the ideas of the king (duly supported in the weekly). It was published by Gröll and edited by Albertrandi.

As for the 1769 translation itself,[31] the paratext of the edition consists of several aspects that should be noted here. The book opens with a dedication to Lady Jadwiga Lubieńska, who is credited with having provided the translator with the time and space needed for the carrying out of the translation: the work began in 1767 and took Albertrandi six weeks. Then comes the translator's preface, which is an important contribution to the developing novelistic discourse in Poland. The periodical *Monitor* was known for its criticism of romance writing, thus setting the scene for the emergence of realist fiction. Albertrandi in his preface anticipates the possible criticism for presenting the Polish readers with "another Romance" and recycles the common remarks used to denigrate the genre: irrationality, no applicability to real life, and waste of readers' time (vii–viii). Then, the translator proceeds to argue for *Robinson Crusoe*'s distinctiveness from the romance tradition, referring to the examples of Fénelon and Ramsey (the translator of Fénelon and author of the popular *Travels of Cyrus* from 1727, Polish translation in 1770): "In contrast to their works, what we learn from the adventures of Robinson is applicable in everyday life" (ix). Robinson is understood to exemplify the instability of the human mind, the workings of Providence, courage, hard work, and prudence. All these, the translator has it, are to be taught to people, and the attractive form of history makes it easier and more delightful (x). The conclusion accords with the *utile et dulce* principle—it is not a waste of time if entertainment becomes a form of education.

The apologetic passage is then complemented by the so-called *uwiadomienie*—a short note about the book, its author, and publication context. It contains a factual error, which, however, may tell us more about the Polish context for the appearance of *Robinson Crusoe*. The writer credited with authoring *Robinson Crusoe* is Richard Steele, who is praised as the principal contributor to the *Spectator*, a periodical published to "correct the habits and customs" of people and repeatedly referred to and translated in "our Monitor" (xi). Intentionally or not, by linking the release of his translation of *Robinson Crusoe* with the intellectual policy of the *Monitor*, Albertrandi not only highlights its difference from the romance tradition but also argues for its applicability to the intellectual program of the Warsaw literary and political elite. Apparently, the Polish translator is repeating the error made by Feutry, who misattributed the novel to Steele in his own preface to the 1766 French translation. The possible reason for the confusion was Steele's role in popularizing the history of Alexander Selkirk, which, however, used the platform of another journal—the *Englishman* (3 December 1713). It cannot be determined if Steele's authorship of *Robinson Crusoe* was assumed by the other members of the *Monitor* circle. The French edition owned by both the king and Ignacy Krasicki did not feature the name of Defoe as the author, while the publishing details of "*Robinson Crusoe* en anglois" (the entry for the English edition) are unknown. This is yet another piece of evidence that for the most of the eighteenth century the fame of Robinson did not add to the fame of its actual author.[32]

Then, concluding the preface, Albertrandi refers to the French afterlife of the novel, writing that notwithstanding the praise it received, it was criticized for the lengthy and "useless" remarks irritating the impatient readers (xii). This held especially for the third volume, which was full of "unrelated, random remarks," with no merits at all, spoiling the general impression. The critical remark is not linked with any names, but the obvious point of reference seems to have been Rousseau. There appeared a "general demand," Albertrandi writes, that someone "polishes the imperfections," a task that was eventually performed by Mr. Feutry, who abbreviated the novel into two decent volumes, preserving "everything worth reading" (xiii).[33] As such the novel merited a translation into Polish, which, the translator hopes, will be well received just as the other "more serious" (xiv) educational pieces he authored.

The publication of the first Polish translation of *Robinson Crusoe* was accompanied by related reviews published in some of the most important periodicals. The French-language *Journal Polonais* was focused on the books published by Michał Gröll, and accordingly, in volume 3 there is a review of Feutry's edition, most probably copied from a relevant French journal.[34] *Wiadomości Warszawskie* (Warsaw News, 1769, 73/13 IX) features an advertisement written by Gröll himself: "The Adventures of Robinson Crusoe merit a Polish edition. Apart from the dominant romance element, which keeps the reader interested throughout, the book makes for a wonderful treatise on natural education."[35] The advertisement thus relates to two important aspects of the critical discourse of the 1760s in Poland—the antiromance tendencies, still dependent on taxonomical inconsistencies ("romance" is seen as tantamount to adventures), and the possible, indirect benefits to reading fiction, here clearly by alluding to Rousseau. As such, the advertisement joins Albertrandi's preface in the attempt to distinguish *Robinson Crusoe* from the romance by virtue of its educational potential.

The second and third editions of Albertrandi's translation in 1774 and 1775, respectively, indicate a relatively lively publishing life—by Polish eighteenth-century standards, that is. The editions were printed by Łukasz Szlichtyn from Lwów (today Lviv), whose publishing house operated under a special privilege granted by King Stanislaus.[36] The information about the privilege is introduced in the title page, which apart from legitimizing the publisher's ventures, indirectly exudes an aura of royal consent given for the further establishment of *Robinson Crusoe* in Stanislavian literary culture.

In 1775 Szlichtyn also published a relatively prompt Polish translation (anonymous) of *Naufrage et aventures de M. Pierre Viaud* (The Shipwreck and Adventures of Mr. Pierre Viaud, 1768)—a very popular Robinsonade in 1770s Europe, today attributed to Jean Gaspard Dubois-Fontanelle. It would have been known by Krasicki too, though the author of *Nicholas Wisdom* is unlikely to have been inspired by such scenes as Viaud devouring the "Friday" figure and preparing smoked chops as provisions. On the other hand, the transformation of the Robinson figure into a "savage," a structural move already implied in book IV of Swift's *Gulliver's Travels* as a form of indirect criticism of *Crusoe*'s positivism,[37] testified to the anxieties of the age, which would have been recognized by Krasicki too: his Robinson/Nicholas, when confronted with the Nipuan utopia, also finds himself in the position of Friday.

By 1776, when *Nicholas Wisdom* was published, *Robinson Crusoe* had already established itself in the Stanislavian literary life. It is not surprising, in light of the international afterlife of Defoe's novel, that its reception in Poland, on the one hand, was "authorless"—with no awareness of the actual author figure—and, on the other, had many agents: the king and his cultural reforms; the publishers and the translator coming from the royal circle; the French translator, who provided the source text; Rousseau, who determined its content and the manner of reading that transcended the confines of literature; Richard Steele, the alleged author, who metaphorically brought the novel closer to the aesthetic norms promoted in literary periodicals; and finally the fictitious Pierre Viaud, who exposed the generative potential of the Robinsonade pattern. When Krasicki worked on *Nicholas Wisdom* and *History*, this pattern was not part of a literary history told through names of authors and their output. Rather, it had already become part of what Gérard Genette calls the architext—a transcendent textual network out of which any new literary work emerges.[38] It had become an orphaned paradigm, deprived of the fatherlike author, and thus welcoming new ways of adoption and appropriation; a potential vehicle for new meanings, particularly suited to a reading culture that appreciated fictional travels, adventures, and sentimentalized uses of nature. The several years framed by the appearance of *Robinson Crusoe* in Poland and Krasicki's employment of the Robinsonade pattern illustrate the emergence of a new literary culture in the Stanislavian Age: a dynamic network of connections, involving politics, book market, and periodical production. In this modern literary sphere, in a manner similar to what had been happening in England from the beginning of the eighteenth century, texts often lived lives of their own, disconnected from their authors. The *Robinson Crusoe* received in 1760s and 1770s Poland may not have been exactly what Daniel Defoe had written, but indeed the distance between Defoe's novel and its adaptations has been what has catalyzed the development of the Robinsonade as a genre in the past three hundred years.

NOTES

Research for this chapter was funded by Narodowe Centrum Nauki, grant Miniatura II (2018/02/X/HS2/03216).

1. The novel has been translated into English, and I am using the English title proposed by the translator, though a more accurate translation would be "Nicholas Experience." See Ignacy Krasicki, *The Adventures of Mr. Nicholas Wisdom*, trans. Thomas H. Hoisington (Evanston, IL: Northwestern University Press, 1992).
2. See Mieczysław Klimowicz, "Wstęp," in Ignacy Krasicki, *Mikołaja Doświadczyńskiego przypadki*, ed. Klimowicz (Wrocław: Zakład Narodowy im. Ossolińskich, 1975), xxiv–xxxi. All quotations from the novel as well as other Polish sources are given in my translation.
3. See Czesław Miłosz, *The History of Polish Literature* (Berkeley: University of California Press, 1983), 177.
4. The romance novel dialectic, as elaborated upon by Ian P. Watt in *The Rise of the Novel* (1957; repr., Berkeley: University of California Press, 2000), has been for at least three decades taken with a pinch of salt in English studies. See Margaret Anne Doody, *The True History of the Novel* (New Brunswick, NJ: Rutgers University Press, 1996). Admittedly, it appears to have enjoyed a longer life in Polish literary criticism. See Paweł Bohuszewicz, *Od "romansu" do powieści: Studia o polskiej literaturze narracyjnej (druga połowa XVII wieku—pierwsza połowa XIX wieku)* (Toruń: Wydawnictwo Naukowe Uniwersytetu Mikołaja Kopernika, 2016).
5. Krasicki, *Mikołaja Doświadczyńskiego przypadki*, 132.
6. Not that there is a clear-cut boundary between these two genres. See Artur Blaim, *Robinson Crusoe and His Doubles: The English Robinsonade of the Eighteenth Century* (Frankfurt: Peter Lang, 2016).
7. A useful evaluation of Krasicki's reliance on *Robinson Crusoe* and *Gulliver's Travels* is offered in Zofia Sinko, *Powieść angielska osiemnastego wieku a powieść polska lat, 1764–1830* (Warszawa: Państwowy Instytut Wydawniczy, 1961), 62–65.
8. Jadwiga Ruszała published two monographs on the Robinsonade in Poland: *Robinson w literaturze polskiej* (Robinson in Polish literature) (Słupsk: Wydawnictwo Wyższej Szkoły Pedagogicznej w Słupsku, 1998) and *Robinsonada w literaturze polskiej* (The Robinsonade in Polish literature) (Słupsk: Wydawnictwo Akademii Pomorskiej w Słupsku, 2000). Her work offers a useful overview of the phenomenon, especially in the nineteenth century and the first half of the twentieth. She includes *Nicholas Wisdom* in her list of quasi-Robinsonades but does not comment on the novel beyond briefly noting that it is an example of a utopia with a Robinsonade element. The best-known and most successful Robinsonades in Polish include works by Władysław Ludwik Anczyc (1823–1883), who also abbreviated *Robinson*

Crusoe in 1867, Adolf Dygasiński (1839–1902), and Arkady Fiedler (1894–1985), the author of the Robinson trilogy including *Wyspa Robinsona* (Robinson Crusoe Island, 1954), *Orinoko* (Orinoco, 1957), and *Biały Jaguar* (White Jaguar, 1980).

9. Ignacy Krasicki, *Historia* (Kraków: Universitas, 2002), 119.
10. Ibid., 119.
11. See Klimowicz, "Wstęp," xxvii.
12. Jan IJ. van der Meer, *Literary Activities and Attitudes in the Stanislavian Age in Poland (1764–1795): A Social System?* (Amsterdam: Rodopi, 2002), 60. This number shows that studies of Enlightenment "print culture" in Poland should recognize the difference between Poland's fledgling literary market and what was happening in England at the same time.
13. Van der Meer, *Literary Activities and Attitudes*, 61.
14. The Stanislavian period was the time when the love for things French in Poland was gradually accompanied by the love for things English (often through French mediation). There have appeared studies of the phenomenon in Polish criticism, but the emphasis has been placed on such "isms" as sternism and ossianism, and the reception of *Robinson Crusoe* at the time has not yet been properly examined.
15. Richard Butterwick, *Poland's Last King and English Culture: Stanisław August Poniatowski, 1732–1798* (Oxford: Clarendon, 1998), 182.
16. Krasicki's library, including several thousand items, was one of the biggest collections among the Polish nobility. For the inventory, see Sante Graciotti and Jadwiga Rudnicka, eds., *Inwentarz biblioteki Ignacego Krasickiego z 1810 r* (Wrocław: Zakład Narodowy im. Ossolińskich, 1973).
17. The Czartoryskis were great lovers of things English, from Wedgwood porcelain to economic ideas and literature. Once they separated from the king's immediate circle, they moved to Puławy in southeastern Poland and established a cultural center that would energize the Polish reception of Shakespeare, Ossian, and Laurence Sterne, to give three significant names. See Zofia Gołębiowska, "British Models and Inspirations in Czartoryskis' Country Residence in Puławy at the Turn of the Eighteenth Century," in *Culture at Global/Local Levels: British and Commonwealth Contribution to World Civilisation*, ed. Krystyna Kujawińska-Courtney (Łódź: Wydawnictwo Biblioteka, 2002), 139–150.
18. Jadwiga Rudnicka, ed., *Biblioteka Stanisława Augusta na Zamku Warszawskim: Dokumenty, Archiwum Literackie* 26 (1988): 67–83. By the 1760s, King Stanislaus had acquired the necessary command of the English language, as testified by his correspondence with the English diplomat Sir Charles H. Williams, who was instrumental in the evolution of Stanislaus's taste for England and English culture. See chapter 4 of Butterwick, *Poland's Last King* ("The Influence of Sir Charles Hanbury Williams"), 86–101.
19. Zofia Sinko, "Powieść zachodnioeuropejska w Polsce stanisławowskiej na podstawie inwentarzy bibliotecznych i katalogów," *Pamiętnik Literacki* 57.4 (1966): 581–624.
20. Dorota Żołądź-Strzelczyk, "Kilka uwag o znajomości dzieła Jana Jakuba Rousseau *Emil, czyli o wychowaniu* w Polsce przełomu XVIII i XIX wieku," *Problemy wczesnej edukacji* 2.29 (2015): 7–14.
21. Klimowicz, "Wstęp," xlii–xliii.
22. "Editions in French and Some Other Translations," in *Robinson Crusoe at Yale. Yale University Library Gazette* 11.2 (1936): 28–32.
23. As Sinko points out, Feutry's version was in fact an adaptation/abbreviation of the already existent 1721 translation by Saint-Hyacinthe. Sinko, *Powieść angielska*, 19.
24. Jean-Jacques Rousseau, *Emile, or On Education*, ed. and trans. Christopher Kelly and Allan Bloom (Hanover, NH: University Press of New England, 2010), 332.
25. Ibid., 332.

26. "It is *Rousseau* who begins Crusoe's life as a hero of specifically childhood reading." Teresa Michals, *Books for Children, Books for Adults: Age and the Novel from Defoe to James* (Cambridge: Cambridge University Press, 2014), 38.
27. Quoted after Ruszała, *Robinson w literaturze polskiej*, 30.
28. John Dixon Hunt, *A World of Gardens* (London: Reaktion Books, 2012), 221. Robinson's hut as a "garden folly" was an equivalent to Emile's hut, also a typical embellishment in a French picturesque garden. See Agnieszka Morawińska, "Osiemnastowieczna wizja ogrodu," in August Fryderyk Moszyński, *Rozprawa o ogrodnictwie angielskim, 1774*, ed. Morawińska (Wrocław: Zakład Narodowy im. Ossolińskich, 1977), 30.
29. Moszyński, *Rozprawa o ogrodnictwie angielskim*, 110.
30. Jakub Lipski, "Picturing Crusoe's Island: Defoe, Rousseau, Stothard," *Porównania* 25 (2019), 85–99.
31. [Daniel Defoe], *Przypadki Robinsona Krusoe*, trans. Jan Chrzciciel Albertrandi (Warszawa: Nakładem Michała Grela, 1769). Further references are to this edition and are given parenthetically.
32. Throughout the eighteenth century Defoe was not considered to be part of the new novelistic tradition. For a study of this phenomenon and the change ushered in by Walter Scott's appreciation of Defoe, see Homer Obed Brown, "The Institution of the English Novel: Defoe's Contribution," *Novel: A Forum on Fiction* 29.3 (1996): 299–318.
33. Apart from the *Serious Reflections* volume, the notable cuts included Crusoe's diary, merchant-like summaries, and most of Friday's religious education and the christening of his people. These could be explained by the intellectual trends promoted by the French Enlightenment philosophers.
34. *Journal Polonais* 3 (1769): 81–85. See Ruszała, *Robinson w literaturze polskiej*, 29.
35. Quoted after Ruszała, *Robinson w literaturze polskiej*, 29.
36. Maria Juda, "Uprzywilejowane drukarnie we Lwowie doby staropolskiej," *Folia Bibliologica* 55/56 (2013/2014): 16–17. For the third edition, Szlichtyn preserved the details of the first edition, including Michał Gröll's name as publisher, in the preliminary pages.
37. This tension is nevertheless present in *Robinson Crusoe* too. Robinson repeatedly expresses his anxiety over becoming a "beast," while in *The Farther Adventures* "the young Woman" whom Robinson saves thus recounts the hunger she experienced when on board the ship: "had my Mistress been dead, as much as I lov'd her, I am certain, I should have eaten a Piece of her Flesh." Daniel Defoe, *The Farther Adventures of Robinson Crusoe*, ed. W. R. Owens (London: Routledge, 2017), 117.
38. Gérard Genette, *The Architext: An Introduction* (Berkeley: University of California Press, 1992).

5
THE RISE AND FALL OF ROBINSON CRUSOE ON THE LONDON STAGE

FREDERICK BURWICK

THIS ESSAY TRACES RADICAL SHIFTS in representation in the London staging of the Robinson story. In spite of the enthusiastic reception and numerous editions and imitations during the course of the eighteenth century, over sixty years passed before Daniel Defoe's castaway tale was first adapted to the stage. In *Robinson Crusoe, or Harlequin Friday* (Drury Lane, 29 January 1781),[1] Richard Brinsley Sheridan used the structure of the harlequinade as satire to oppose the slave trade. Performance through the 1790s similarly adapted the plot to denounce the French Revolution and then the Napoleonic Wars until 1815, and in the 1820s Sheridan's satire was again modified to support the reform movement. In describing this trajectory, I acknowledge a pivotal redirection in René-Charles Guilbert de Pixérécourt's heroic melodrama *Robinson Crusoe* (Paris, 2 October 1805) and its influence on Isaac Pocock's politically charged *Robinson Crusoe; or, The Bold Bucaniers* (Covent Garden, 7 April 1817). Even in the course of promoting self-sufficient individualism, these plays exposed Crusoe's authoritarian impulse to exploit and enslave. Performed as comic satire, the Crusoe plays avoided the racism and colonialism of Daniel Defoe's novel of 1719, by ridiculing enslavement of peoples and usurpation of properties, as in Mark Lemon's burletta *Robinson Crusoe* (Olympic, 21 March 1842), *Puck's Pantomime; or, Harlequin and Robinson Crusoe* (Drury Lane, 24 December 1844), Edward L. Blanchard's burlesque *Robinson Crusoe* (Strand, 12 May 1845).

It would be misleading to imply that these plays of the 1840s reveal a trajectory guided by a pervasive impulse, a spirit of the age. For one thing, playwrights were strongly influenced by the successes of the novelists and Continental theater. For another, entertaining the audience was more crucial than the political polemics. Further, what was performed in the provinces did not always echo what was performed in the metropolis. Even in London, the playbills of the illegitimate theaters exhibit rivalry rather than conformity to the preferences of licensed theaters. Fueled by class differences that occasionally grew riotous, the rivalry was made institutional with the passing of the Licensing Act (1737), intended to prevent political agitation and to shield church and state from scurrilous satire. All plays to be performed at any theater required the approval by the Examiner of Plays under the Lord Chamberlain. The Licensing Act privileged the legitimate theaters with the exclusive right to perform traditional comedy and tragedy. The licensed theaters were Covent Garden and Drury Lane. Haymarket secured a license for the summer season. The illegitimate theaters were originally directed to perform only musical entertainment and pantomime. In spite of these limitations, the illegitimate theaters proliferated in London, from three in 1780 to twenty-two in 1830.[2]

Following its publication in 1719, *Robinson Crusoe* went through dozens of editions and was appropriated in hundreds of adaptations. Predominantly works of prose fiction, the Robinsonades proliferated rapidly in the course of the eighteenth century. The staging of Crusoe's adventures was a relatively belated phenomenon, emerging in the appropriate theaters and theatrical genre. Plot and incident were altered to suit the canine drama, nautical drama, melodrama, pantomime, and harlequinades of the illegitimate theaters. The trivial media often served as the vehicle for effective social satire.

In spite of being cast in the form of a harlequinade, the first stage play based on Defoe's novel was performed at one of licensed theaters. *Robinson Crusoe, or Harlequin Friday* (Drury Lane, 29 January 1781) achieved remarkable inaugural promotion because it was the work of England's foremost playwright, Richard Brinsley Sheridan, who had acquired in 1776 David Garrick's share in the Drury Lane patent and in 1778 purchased the remaining share. All of Sheridan's later plays were produced at Drury Lane. *Robinson Crusoe, or Harlequin Friday* continued to be performed at Drury Lane through the 1790s and was soon being played in the provinces and in the minor theaters of London where frequent harlequinades delighted the crowds.

With the expansion of Continental trade at the beginning of the Restoration, street performances of Punch and Judy shows were introduced in London. Stage performances of harlequinades followed at the beginning the eighteenth century. Both were popular entertainment adapted from *commedia dell'arte*. Punch, derived from the stock character of Pulcinella, was featured in puppet theater as a slapstick trickster. Harlequin, derived from Arlecheno, was brought to stage along with other characters of *commedia dell'arte*, including his beloved Columbine, her miserly father Pantaloon, the servant Pierrot or Pedroline, and the mischievous Clown. The typical plot involved the eloping lovers pursued by the angry father and servant. The audiences of Venice or Naples would call for a favorite story to be improvised by the masked stock characters, who would then adapt the roles to suit the characters. Although the pantomime players of the English stage were untrained in improvisation, the Harlequinades were structured to reveal the stock characters performing in their "story" roles and then dropping those roles to complete the plot in their *commedia* identity. This two-part structure engendered the illusion of a play about a play. Utilizing spectacular stage effects, the great amusements in the harlequinades were the magical changes in character, costumes, and props in the transformation scene.

Following his dramatic synopsis of Crusoe's adventures, the transformation gave Sheridan the leverage to critique the systems of political economy represented by Crusoe and Friday. The composition and performance of this harlequinade coincided with Sheridan's election to Parliament as an ally of Charles James Fox, furthering the Whig support of American independence while also denouncing the dependency on slave labor. In rallying the abolitionist movement, William Wilberforce was opposed by Lord John Russell and Colonel Banastre Tarleton, the MP for Liverpool, but gained the support of Sheridan and Fox as well as William Pitt, William Smith, William Grenville, and Henry Brougham. Defoe's characters are reconceptualized to suit the issues of the age. Sheridan's Friday evaded every attempt of his "Master" to render him less than human.[3] As David Worrall has revealed, Sheridan infused the harlequinade with serious moral and ideological polemics.[4] Although he echoed arguments on the American Revolution and anticipated those of the French Revolution, Sheridan's *Robinson Crusoe, or Harlequin Friday* did not endorse the bloodshed as a means to liberation. He did, of course, acknowledge the cruelty, as depicted in the prison scene that stage artist Philip James de Loutherbourg prepared for the performance of 1781. The scene painting has been lost, but de Loutherbourg's watercolor maquette survives.[5] Imprisonment, mutiny, and shipwreck were also deployed in subsequent plays as tropes for the revolution.

Not just the playwright, actors too might contribute to the abolitionist polemics in their performance of *Robinson Crusoe*. This was especially notable in the comic routines of Joseph Grimaldi, who from 1781 to 1822 performed as Friday and then, at the magical transformation, as Clown. To emphasize the revelatory power, Grimaldi always introduced the transformations with the catchphrase "Here we are again!" In this moment, four of the characters step out of their roles and become Harlequin, Pantaloon, Clown, and Columbine, and the second half becomes a critique or commentary on the first half.[6] Grimaldi's performance as Friday and Clown in *Robinson Crusoe* led to his acclaim as the foremost pantomime performer of the age. With Joseph Grimaldi as the star of the harlequinade,

Sheridan's *Robinson Crusoe* was revived at Drury Lane in 1796 and again in 1798, starring Grimaldi as Clown.

One might think that the abolitionist movement in Britain would come to an end when Parliament passed the Act for the Abolition of the Slave Trade in 1807, but that act addressed only the marketing, not the holding of slaves. The act of 1807 was ineffective in stopping the slave trade even to British colonies, for many rogue British ships continued transporting slaves for the high profits. The Slavery Abolition Act was not passed until 1833. Throughout his career Grimaldi continued his campaign against slavery, playing the role of Crusoe as the arrogant master or Friday as the exploited servant. In his engagement at Manchester, he commenced as Crusoe (29 March 1811), then played Friday on alternate nights, an alternation that he repeated in 1815.[7]

For Charles Farley's *Aladdin, or the Wonderful Lamp* (Covent Garden, 19 April 1813), Grimaldi played Kasrac, the suffering slave.[8] For Charles Dibdin's nautical *Kaloc; or, The Slave Pirate* (Sadler's Wells, 14 August 1815), Grimaldi played the title role when the melodrama was revived (Sadler's Wells, 28 July 1820). When Kaloc escapes the cruelty of the Bashaw of Tunis, he is joined by other runaways. They commandeer a Turkish galley and become formidable buccaneers. Obsessed by desire for revenge against his former master, Kaloc abducts the Bashow's daughter. The Bashow sets sail in relentless pursuit. Overwhelmed and fatally wounded, Kaloc perishes on the deck. A contemporary critic gave a full synopsis of the plot and praised Grimaldi's performance: "His delineation of the part was just, and his execution vigorous and impressive."[9]

During the summer of 1822, the final season of his career, Grimaldi accepted a six-week engagement at the Coburg. Two Robinsonades were featured on the playbills: a revival of *Philip Quarl*, Charles Dibdin's castaway melodrama of 1803, and *De la Perouse; or, The Desolate Island*, John Fawcett's shipwreck adventure of 1801. On Monday, 15 July (the third week of his engagement), Grimaldi prepared a new pantomime, *Disputes in China; or, Harlequin and the Hong Kong Merchants*, which called for him to transform from a boorish English traveler into Harlequin. The audience was especially impressed by scene of the Whampoa River, a stage design executed by William Clarkson Stanfield, drawn from the sketchbook of Far Eastern voyages as a merchant seaman, contributed greatly. Grimaldi was given the opportunity to show off a lively comic song, "Hot Codlings," with which he astonished John China-man.[10] Grimaldi's legs, injured by his acrobatic antics on stage, could scarcely hold him up, and he was required to interrupt his engagement by two weeks before he could complete the remaining three weeks.

When he returned to the Coburg on 29 July, *Philip Quarl* was again the main attraction and Grimaldi continued his role in *Disputes with China*. For the week of 12 August, he performed as Kanko, the island native in *De la Perouse; or, The Desolate Island*, a Robinsonade by John Fawcett that had premiered twenty-one years earlier (Covent Garden, 28 February 1801). Comte de Lapérouse, a French naval officer, embarked in 1785 on a lengthy voyage of exploration, after leaving Botany Bay in 1789, there was no further report of ship or crew. Fawcett presents an imaginary account of the captain and his crew. Fawcett correctly surmised the ship's destruction on an isolated island. Not until 1826 were the remains of the wreck discovered in the islands of Santa Cruz. For Grimaldi, the role of Kanko was virtually a reprisal of his role as Friday, a fitting farewell for a comic actor who had devoted much of his career to the abolitionist cause.

Performing at the Lyceum during the following year, Grimaldi's son, Joseph Samuel Grimaldi, assumed his father's style and many of his roles. In the comic pantomime, *Monkey Island; or, Harlequin and the Loadstone Rock*, J. S. Grimaldi played General Jackoo, Commander of Guard, who transforms into Clown. The peculiar geological properties of the island's huge loadstone rock enable the monkeys to fly. J. S. Grimaldi must have acquitted himself well in his monkey role, for in the following season he was cast in the title role of the nautical melodrama *Jacko! or, The Ape of Brazil* (Sadler's Wells, 6 June 1825).

An established role in many of the melodramatic productions, a monkey often served in place of a Friday as a companion to the shipwrecked castaway. Among the more raucous imitations to appear during the first decade after the initial publication of *Robinson Crusoe* was Peter Longueville's *The Hermit: or, The Unparalleled Sufferings and Surprising Adventures of Mr. Philip Quarll, an Englishman* (1727). Charles Dibdin's stage adaptation *Philip Quarll; or, The English Hermit* (Sadler's Wells, 9 May 1803) featured a monkey, whom Quarll named Beaufidelle. When William Barrymore revised the melodrama as *Philip Quarl! The English Hermit* (Coburg, 14 September 1819), he announced on the playbill that it was "founded on the story of a Robinson Crusoe character, who had a chimpanzee as his 'man' Friday." For the first season Quarll was played by O. Smith, who throughout his career was cast again and again as seaman, captain, pirate, or buccaneer.[11] His companion and his retinue of five additional boys were all costumed in monkey suits.

The Robinsonades also brought to the stage several performing dogs. Barrymore's monkeys in *Philip Quarl* were a modest follow-up to the sensational dog that performed in Barrymore's *The Dog of Montargis or the Forest of Bondy* (Covent Garden, 30 September 1814), rapidly adapted from Charles Guilbert de Pixerécourt's *Le chien de Montargis* (Théâtre de la Gaîté, 18 June 1814). This highly successful play prompted an epidemic of canine melodrama in the theaters of London: Sadler's Wells, Covent Garden, the Royal Pavilion in Marylebone, the

Italian Opera House, and the Alhambra Theatre in Leicester Square. Barkham Cony was the right man in the right time and place. With his trained dogs, Bruin and Hector, he was ready to make his fortune. He needed only a tale suited to the many tricks his dogs might perform. With the assistance of William Blanchard, he prepared a Robinsonade loosely based on the exploits of the Scottish castaway Alexander Selkirk. It was truly the case of the tale wagging the dog.

Selkirk's story had first been told in the *Voyages* (1712) of Edward Cooke. Marooned by his captain on Más a Tierra, an uninhabited island in the Juan Fernández archipelago, 420 miles off the coast of Chile, Selkirk survived four years and four months (1704–1709). Dangerous situations arose on the island when Spanish pirates would anchor in search of water and provisions. Cony and Blanchard were wildly inventive in adding skirmishes with "Indians," pirates, cannibals, a damsel in distress, or a child in peril. Either Cony or Blanchard would assume a minor role to be on stage to give a signal to Hector or Bruin.[12] An early version was *The Red Indian; or, Selkirk and His Dog* (Surrey, 26 August 1822). As performed the following year, *The Pirates; or, The Shipwreck'd Seamen and the Cannibals* (Royalty, 10 March 1823), Selkirk's name was dropped in favor of the more familiar Crusoe. Anderton played the part of Crusoe, and Mrs. Gallot played Innis, Crusoe's wife, just arrived on the ship sent to rescue the shipwrecked seaman. Cony was frequently on stage as Nipcheese, the ship's steward. There were five Indian girls in need of rescuing by the brave dogs, one rescue achieved when Bruin dove into a "pond" of water on stage to pull the drowning girl ashore. In act 2 the ship's captain and the Indian chief engaged in a dagger and tomahawk battle, until Bruin and Hector intervened and disarmed both antagonists.

Cony's *The Red Indian; or, The Shipwrecked Mariner and His Faithful Dogs* (Surrey, 9 March 1824) introduced a few minor changes to display the intelligence of his dog. Their most elaborate performance took place at Sadler's Wells. The gigantic tank—ninety feet long, twenty-four feet wide, and three feet high—installed in 1803 and removed in 1824, was replaced by a smaller set of upper and lower tanks that allowed for a pond and waterfall. The playbill announcing the performance of *Indian Perfidy; or, Hector & Bruin the Faithful Dogs* (Sadler's Wells, 1 June 1829) included a summary of the tricks performed by Cony's dogs:

> Incidental to the piece, the dog Hector conveys a signal from his master on shore to the ship. The faithful dog dashes the cup of poison from the treacherous Indian's hand at the very moment his master is on the point of drinking it. He then prevents the malignant and disappointed Indian from stabbing his Master. Bruin endeavours to break open the chest in which the ferocious Chief is concealed. Thus he preserves his master from destruction and then pursues the Savages in order to rescue the lost wife

and child of the distracted Master. Terrific combat... [interrupted dogs]. Bruin in his pursuit carries a lighted Torch to the Lady who burns the cord by which she is bound, and the faithful dog procures his Mistress's release. Grand Combat between Hector and the Ferocious Chief, to save the Infant from destruction, in which Hector proves victorious. The dog likewise preserves the child from an enormous Serpent, and is conveyed to his parents by the ever faithful dog. They fetch the boat's crew, who engage a general combat with the Savage, in which the sailors are completely triumphant, and the treacherous Indian Chief falls under the Fate of the irresistible and victorious dogs, Hector and Bruin.[13]

In *De la Perouse*, Grimaldi performed the Friday role as Kanko, the island native. In *Indian Perfidy* Martin played Kanko, William Walbourn played the castaway, and the perfidious Indian of the title was played by Wood. What had been the major roles were now reduced to the supporting cast, while Bruin and Hector were cheered as the heroes of the piece.

Melodrama had not utterly gone to the dogs. Tracing the performances of *Robinson Crusoe; or, Harlequin Friday* through the decades following the premiere in 1781, the evidence persists that the harlequinade was recognized for its social relevance. The abolitionist message of Sheridan and of Grimaldi could not be ignored. It could, however, be reinforced. When performed at Blackburn New Theatre (25 April 1787), the transformations of act 2 opened with a view of Liverpool docks, St George's Church, and Exchange buildings, a stark reminder that Liverpool was one of the busiest slave-trading ports on the Atlantic. Ships out of Liverpool transported 40 percent of the African captive to the slave plantations of the New World.

While it was abundantly evident that the wealth of Liverpool and Bristol was accumulated through the lucrative slave trade, it remained less obvious that the northeastern ports were involved. The active abolitionists in Tyneside offered support and a safe haven to those who managed to escape the bonds of slavery. Nevertheless, direct links have been traced between the plantations of the New World and some of the wealthiest estates of the North East.[14] Ten years after the first performance at Drury Lane, *Robinson Crusoe; or, Harlequin Friday* was the featured sensation of the season at the Theatre Royal at Newcastle upon Tyne. The manager from 1791 to 1806 was Stephen Kemble, brother of John Philip Kemble and Sarah Siddons. At the invitation of Kemble and his wife, Elizabeth Satchell, Sheridan himself traveled to Newcastle to take part in the revival.

In the revisions of 1791, Sheridan was concerned in making the abolitionist message even more prominent. Upon first meeting with Friday, Crusoe provides him with food and a gun to defend himself. They are rescued at the close of act 1 and the transformations of act 2 take place in inquisitional Spain. Friday, who is now treated as property, falls into deep despair over his fate. Cupid descends in a chariot of gold and gives Friday the gifts of a Magician.

> Here, take this purse, this sword, and cap of fame,
> Friday no more! Be Harlequin thy name.[15]

Sheridan himself played the role of Clown. Fanny Kemble, Stephen's niece and active abolitionist, played the liberty-granting Cupid. E. D. Davis played the double role of Friday transformed into Harlequin, and Mrs. Davis his wife performed Columbine, who marries Harlequin in the final scene.[16] The Kembles were committed in their contribution to the abolitionist movement.[17] Elizabeth Satchell's most famous role was Yarico from George Colman's antislavery play *Inkle and Yarico* (Haymarket, August 1787).

The role of Yarico raises a question of whether other encounters were defined by gender as well as racial difference. Shipwrecked in the West Indies, Inkle survives with the help of Yarico, a native of the island. They fall in love, but when Inkle returns to England, he wants an English wife and intends to sell Yarico as a slave. Alexander Selkirk and Philip Quarll as well as Robinson Crusoe exist in predominantly masculine worlds. Agnes Strickland's *The Rival Crusoes* (1826) and Barbara Hofland's *The Young Crusoe* (1828) present proper evidence that the Robinsonades were not the exclusive province of male novelists. Strickland, who wrote for young ladies an extensive series on the Queens of England, did not on this occasion give attention to the development of feminine character. Were castaway characters an exclusively a male role?

Ann Fraser Tytler's *Leila* (1833) makes the case that women too might be lost at sea. In Tytler's story, a father is shipwrecked with his daughter, Leila, and her nurse. The island is fraught not with dangers but with challenges that Leila must meet and overcome. Her encounters teach her patience and discipline. When she is rescued she exhibits a maturity and strength of character beyond that of other young women of her circle. Similar to other Robinsonades addressed to juvenile readers, Tytler's version stood apart as an *Erbauungsbuch* intended for young women. A majority of the Robinsonades were written primarily for children and were often less than subtle in stressing their moral and pedagogical intentions.[18]

In Charles Dibdin's *Hannah Hewitt, or the Female Crusoe* (Drury Lane, 7 May 1798), the audience might perceive two moral purposes, and the latter contradicted the former. Isolated on a desert isle, Hannah is a self-sufficient and enterprising woman, who successfully constructs a dwelling place, tends garden fruit and vegetables, and keeps herself fit in mind and body.[19] Until the final scenes, she is impressive for strength and independence. Rescued and returned to society, she realigns her character to conform to the docile and passive model expected of a young lady in Britain. In performing the role, Maria Theresa De Camp provided the audience with sufficient nods and winks to hint that she was not as demure and compliant as she pretended. Richard Suett played Buntline, the sailor who follows Hannah ashore and becomes co-conspirator in her "reformation."[20] De Camp acquired a stage reputation in performing strong-willed young women who resist male authority. She was Portia in *Merchant of Venice*. As Katherine, she let the audience know that she found it advantageous to let Petruchio consider her tamed. She was, as Maximillian Novak described her, a women of the revolutionary liberation.[21]

In its discrimination of a natural hierarchy of individual capabilities distinct from the hierarchy of a class system ordained by wealth and social convention, *Hannah Hewitt* can be seen as an anticipation of James M. Barrie's *The Admirable Crichton* (1902). Loam, his family and friends, with their servant Crichton are shipwrecked on a deserted tropical island. The resourceful Crichton is the only one of the party with any practical knowledge, and he assumes, initially with reluctance, the position of leader. Two years pass under Crichton's governance. When the rescuers greet the castaways, he resumes his status as butler. Too many embarrassing recollections remain for Crichton to continue in their service. In *Masterman Ready; or, The Wreck in the Pacific* (1841), Captain Frederick Marryat also examined the role reversals of master and servant and borrowed from Johann Wyss's *Swiss Family Robinson* (1812, English translation in 1814) in presenting the family cooperative as the proper survival economy.[22]

From 1781 to 1817, *Robinson Crusoe; or, Harlequin Friday* was performed with local variations as a favorite shipwreck adventure and harlequinade. Then in 1817 a competing melodrama was introduced. One year after Sheridan's death, Isaac Pocock's *Robinson Crusoe; or, The Bold Bucaniers* (Covent Garden, 7 April 1817) opened with success and subsequently sustained similar status as the most successful of the stage adaptations. Sheridan's version dominated for the thirty-five years, and for the next thirty-five years Pocock's melodrama was revived with equal frequency.

Pocock based his play on Pixérécourt's *Robinson Crusoe* (Porte-Saint-Martin, 2 October 1805), or rather on the revival of that play in the very different political climate of 1814. Pixérécourt launched his career amid the dangerous Reign of Terror in 1794. He survived by capturing the revolutionary spirit with plots of liberation and liberty. His first play was *Sélico ou les Nègres généreux* (Sélico, or The Magnanimous Slaves; Théâtre-Français, 1794). His first great success was *Cœlina ou l'Enfant du mystère* (Théâtre de l'Ambigu-Comique, 1800), which was also successful in Thomas Holcroft's translation, *A Tale of Mystery* (Covent Garden, 13 November 1802). Pixérécourt produced play after play that would run a year or more. One such play was *Robinson Crusoé*, which ran without interruption for a whole year. The play had been on the boards for less than three weeks when the news reached Paris that the French navy had been defeated at Trafalgar, but Admiral Lord Nelson was killed. Pixérécourt reinterpreted the significance of mutiny: what had been a revolution against authority in 1805 became in 1814 the betrayal of a greedy crew. When the play was revived in 1814, it was in the context of Napoleon's abdication (11 April 1814) and his exile to the island of Elbe (3 May 1814).[23] A satirical print was circulated of "Le Robinson de l'Ile d'Elbe" (The Robinson Crusoe of Elba), with Napoleon wearing a lion skin and holding an umbrella topped by golden imperial eagle on the top. Friday, on the lookout, follows behind him.[24]

In his theater review (*Examiner*, 13 April 1817), William Hazlitt revealed his preference for Sheridan's version over Pocock's. He warned theatergoers not to be fooled. This was "not the old favorite with the public." Recalling two of Sheridan's effective scenes, Hazlitt regretted the absence of anything comparable. Missing was "the striking incident of the notched post," which enabled Sheridan, Crusoe, and the audience to mark the passage of time. Missing too was Crusoe's discovery of "the print of the human footstep in the sand," which communicated Crusoe's loneliness, isolation, and both eagerness for a companion and fear of company. What did Pocock offer instead? Well, Hazlitt conceded, "there is a poodle dog in it." The main differences of the new melodrama were in the "innumerable savages, English and Caribbee," and the more complex skirmishes of the Spanish, British, and Pirates who impede the effort to escape the island.[25]

The audience was invited to compare Pocock's new melodrama with Sheridan's familiar harlequinade, because *Robinson Crusoe; or, The Bold Bucaniers* featured Grimaldi in his familiar role as Friday. Robinson Crusoe was played by Charles Farley, known to London audiences for his roles as the magician Abanazar in *Aladdin, or the Wonderful Lamp*, as the dumb Francisco in Holcroft's *Tale of Mystery*, and as Timour in M. G. Lewis's *Timour the Tartar*. As in his depiction of the smuggling trade in *The Miller and His Men*, Pocock's imagination was stimulated by the poverty, riots, and continuing conflicts in the years following the Napoleonic Wars. In August 1816 British ships sailed into the Bay of Algiers to bombard the city, ostensibly to halt the slave trade by the North African Barbary states. The year 1816 ended with the Spa Fields Riots. Working-class families were starving. Three months later, in March 1817, the Blanketeers left Manchester on a futile march to London to demand fair wages.[26]

Pocock departed from Sheridan in emphasizing the family. Friday's father, Iglou, is Carib chief with a horde of Carib followers. Diego, Crusoe's son, is captain of a ship in search of his father with Ines, his mother and wife to Crusoe aboard. When Diego's ship arrives at the island on which Crusoe was wrecked, Diego loses hope of rescuing his father because of a mutiny of his crew. Brought onto the island in chains, Diego and Ines are to be left marooned. Crusoe finds his wife and son, yet in his attempt to help them escape, Crusoe too is caught by the mutineers. Meeting with the few sailors loyal to Diego, Iglou gathers his tribe of Carib natives, takes the mutineers as his prisoners, and releases Crusoe and his family.[27]

Like Sheridan before him, Pocock wove abolitionist themes into his dramatization. Unlike Sheridan, he stressed the values of family and community. The attention to family as the unit of survival was shaped by the reform movement and found assertion in adventure novels for children, as in Mary Jane Godwin's translation of Johann David Wyss's *Swiss Family Robinson* (1816) or Barbara Hofland's *The Young Crusoe* (1828). The castaway narratives on stage, like many of those in contemporary novels, reflected cultural values. The Robinsonades of Sheridan and Pocock were performed most frequently, with Charles Dibdin's *Hannah Hewitt* and *Philip Quarll* also repeatedly on the stage during the Regency years. As performed in the provinces, the theatrical Robinsonades were subject to a variety of local changes.

Sheridan's harlequinade was transformed in series of dances in the adaptation at Stockport (16 December 1799). Act 1 introduces Crusoe as a Castaway, and moves rapidly to his meeting with Friday. The next scene shows the "Landing of the Savages," who perform by moonlight "the Original Savage Dance," as "a Ship in Full Sail" crosses the backdrop, a panorama of a tropical isle. Set back home in Stockport, the scene reveals "the Mail Coach and the Cobler's Stall." With his familiar cry, "Here we are again," Harlequin leaps through a window. Perhaps borrowing from a previous production, the characters act "the favourite Dying and Skeleton Scenes." Act 2 closes with "a General View of Stockport, taken from the New Road, and a Dance by the Characters."[28] As performed under H. H. Rowbotham's direction, *Bold Buccaneers; or the Caribs* (Coburg, 15 May 1826) still featured the characters of Robinson Crusoe and Friday, but the production was more of a stage spectacle, as the title indicates, with a battle between the cannibalistic Caribs and the ruthless Buccaneers.

When Brother Manderson brought his acting troupe, the Somerset Company, Wiveliscombe to perform *Robinson Crusoe, and His Man Friday* (14 October 1833), his playbills featured the Masonic symbols, and the play itself was sufficiently modified to emphasize the doctrine of mutual help (solidarity, but also banking, loans, health services, education) that the Freemasons promoted during the years when trade unions were rigorously prohibited by the Combination Acts. Although the plays continued to be staged in subsequent years, the adventures of

Crusoe and Friday, or the Buccaneers and the Caribs, were seldom informed by any ideological argument. Edward Blanchard's production of *Robinson Crusoe* (Strand, 12 May 1845) was a burlesque sustained by slapstick rather than by satire. That same year an anonymous Robinsonade, *Alexander Selkirk* (3 November 1845), was performed as adventure drama at the Victoria (formerly the Coburg, subsequently the Old Vic). No longer called into service as vehicle of political purpose, the theatrical Robinsonade still carried its story of adventure, survival, and Britishness. Nostalgia was the major attraction for the performance of *Robinson Crusoe!!; or, The Bold Bucaniers* at the Edinburgh Theatre Royal (1850). The production celebrated the visiting acting couple: Mr. and Mrs. Charles Kean. Charles Kean was the famous son of the even more famous Edmund Kean. Ellen Kean, the former Ellen Tree, appeared on the stage, since their marriage eight years earlier, exclusively in roles opposite her husband. On this occasion Charles Kean was Crusoe, Ellen Kean was Ines, wife to Crusoe.

The early adaptations of *Robinson Crusoe* for the London stage owed their continuing success to their satirical engagement with major political issues, and their effective use of the popular genre of melodrama and harlequinade. Most often repeated in the provinces as well as in the metropolis were Richard Brinsley Sheridan's *Robinson Crusoe, or Harlequin Friday* (1781) and Isaac Pocock's *Robinson Crusoe; or, The Bold Bucaniers* (1817). In his Robinsonades Charles Dibdin specifically supported the exploited and unfranchised members of society: women in *Hannah Hewitt* (1798); or *Philip Quarll* (1803), who preferred the independence as hermit to the demeaning status as itinerate laborer; or *Kaloc* (1813), the slave who rebelled against the cruelty of his master. The attraction of the theatrical Robinsonade did not wane during the latter half of the nineteenth century, rather it changed. Harlequinades fell out of fashion, melodrama became more simplistic, and the music halls became a venue for a new mode of satire. The targets turned from the global to the domestic. The Punch-and-Judy shows of the streets share many of its characters: the lewd rent collector, the overzealous bailiff, the haranguing mother-in-law, the drunken husband, the shrewish wife, the gambler. Patriotism remained important but on stage was scarcely distinguishable from chauvinism. The tropic isle of the shipwrecked sailor was quickly transformed into a recognizable domestic space.

NOTES

1. The dates of the plays are taken from the playbills in the vast collection of the British Library, British Library Mic. C 13137, Playbills, 166–377. Correspondence on the licensing is taken from the Larpent Collection at the Huntington Library, John Larpent, *Examiner of Plays (1778–1824)*, catalogue of the John Larpent Plays (San Marino, CA: Huntington Library).

2. To read more on the Licensing Act of 1737 and its impact on theatrical life, see three chapters in Julia Swindells and David Francis Taylor, eds., *The Oxford Handbook of the Georgian Theatre, 1737–1832* (Oxford: Oxford University Press, 2014): David Thomas, "The 1737 Licensing Act and Its Impact," 91–106; Julia Swindells, "The Political Context of the 1737 Licensing Act," 107–122; and Matthew J. Kinservik, "The Dialectics of Print and Performance after 1737," 123–139.
3. John McVeagh, "*Robinson Crusoe*'s Stage Début: The Sheridan Pantomime of 1781," *Journal of Popular Culture* 24.2 (Fall 1990): 137–152; Julia Swindells, "Abolitionist Theatre," in *Encyclopedia of Romanticism*, 3 vols., ed. Frederick Burwick, Nancy Goslee, and Diane Hoeveler (Oxford: Wiley-Blackwell, 2012), 1:7–14.
4. David Worrall, *Harlequin Empire: Race, Ethnicity and the Drama of the Popular Enlightenment* (London: Pickering & Chatto, 2007), 23–55.
5. Allardyce Nicoll, *The Garrick Stage: Theatres and Audience in the Eighteenth Century*, ed. Sybil Rosenfeld (Manchester: Manchester University Press, 1980), 138, 180.
6. Richard Findlater, *Grimaldi: King of Clowns* (London: Magibbon & Kee, 1955), 9.
7. Andrew McConnell Stott, *The Pantomime Life of Joseph Grimaldi* (Edinburgh: Canongate Books, 2009), 101.
8. Findlater, *Grimaldi*, 60, 76.
9. Anon., Review of *Kaloc* (Sadler's Wells, 3 April 1818), *European Magazine, and London Review* 73 (May 1818): 434; Charles Dickens, *Memoirs of Joseph Grimaldi* (London: Richard Bentley, 1846), 118.
10. Dickens, *Memoirs of Joseph Grimaldi*, 156–157.
11. Frederick Burwick and Manushag Powell, *British Pirates in Print and Performance* (Houndmills: Palgrave Macmillan, 2015), 38, 44, 50–52, 90.
12. Claudia Alonso Recarte, "Canine Actors and Melodramatic Effects: The Dog of Montargis Arrives on the English Stage," *Cahiers victoriens et édouardiens* 86 (Automne 2017), http://journals.openedition.org/cve/3345; Charles Day, *Joe Blackburn's A Clown's Log*, 2nd ed., ed. William Slout (Rockville, MD: Borgo Press, 2007), 11–12.
13. Playbills 284, British Library Mic. C 12137, Sadler's Wells, 1 June 1829.
14. John Charlton, *Hidden Chains: The Slavery Business and North East England* (Newcastle upon Tyne: Tyne Bridge, 2008), 27–31.
15. Richard Brinsley Sheridan, *Robinson Crusoe; or, Harlequin Friday. A Grand Pantomime, in Two Acts, as Performed at the Theatre-Royal, Newcastle upon Tyne, in 1791* (Newcastle upon Tyne: Printed by Hall and Elliot, 1791).
16. Ibid.
17. Worrall, *Harlequin Empire*, 23–55.
18. Andrew O'Malley, *Children's Literature, Popular Culture, and "Robinson Crusoe"* (Houndmills: Palgrave Macmillan, 2012), 130, passim.
19. Rebecca Weaver-Hightower, *Empire Islands: Castaways, Cannibals, and Fantasies of Conquest* (Minneapolis: University of Minnesota Press, 2007), 57.
20. John Genest, *Some Account of the London Stage, from the Restoration to 1830* (Bath: H. E. Carrington, 1832), 7:537.
21. Maximillian E. Novak, "Ideological Tendencies in Three Crusoe Narratives by British Novelists during the Period Following the French Revolution: Charles Dibdin's *Hannah Hewit, The Female Crusoe*, Maria Edgeworth's *Forester*, and Frances Burney's *The Wanderer*," *Eighteenth-Century Novel* 9 (2012): 261–280.
22. Daniel Schierenbeck, "The Adventure Novel," in *Encyclopedia of Romanticism*, 3 vols., ed. Frederick Burwick, Nancy Goslee, and Diane Hoeveler (Oxford: Wiley-Blackwell, 2012), 1:19–27.

23. For a study of Pixérécourt's *Robinson Crusoé*, see Christopher Smith, "Charles Guilbert de Pixérécourt's *Robinson Crusoé* (1805)," in *Robinson Crusoe: Myths and Metamorphoses*, ed. Lieve Spaas and Brian Stimpson (Houndmills: Macmillan, 1996), 127–140.
24. Katherine Astbury, "Le Robinson de l'Ile d'Elbe: The Robinson Crusoe of Elba," www.100days.eu/items/show/2.
25. William Hazlitt, *Complete Works of William Hazlitt*, ed. P. P. Howe after the edition of A. R. Waller and Arnold Glover (London: J. M. Dent and Sons, 1930–1934), 5:362.
26. Frederick Burwick, *British Drama of the Industrial Revolution* (Cambridge: Cambridge University Press, 2015), 159.
27. Genest, *Some Account of the London Stage*, 8:609.
28. Playbills 284, British Library Mic. C 12137, Stockport, 16 December 1799.

6

ISLANDS IN ROBERT LOUIS STEVENSON'S *KIDNAPPED* (1886)

A Counter-Robinsonade

Márta Pellérdi

David Balfour, the seventeen-year-old hero of Robert Louis Stevenson's *Kidnapped* "beg[ins] the most unhappy part of [his] adventures" as a miserable castaway on the island of Erraid in the Inner Hebrides of Scotland after suffering shipwreck "in a place so desert-like and lonesome" that it awakens in him "a kind of fear" (82).[1] It takes him four days to realize that at low tide he could have easily walked over to the other shore of the Isle of Mull. But before David discovers that the "desert-like" place is only a tidal island and his condition as a castaway has never been as hopeless as Robinson Crusoe's, he passes days of hardship suffering from rain, cold, and hunger. At one point he remembers the books that he read as a boy: "In all the books I have read of people cast away, they had either their pockets full of tools, or a chest of things would be thrown upon the beach along with them, as if on purpose. My case was different" (83). In this passage David wistfully remembers not only Defoe's *Robinson Crusoe* and the way Crusoe systematically salvaged useful items from the wreck of the ship in order to survive, but the Robinsonades that he used to read as a boy. Although David is aware that despite the similarity in their fates he is not at all as self-reliant and inventive as Crusoe, his memoir from 1751 resonates with echoes of the famous mariner's narrative.

Stevenson acknowledged his admiration for Defoe in several writings. In his essay "A Gossip on Romance," for instance, Defoe is listed as one of those remarkable writers who succeeded in what only great artists managed to achieve: "embody[ing] character, thought, or emotion in some act or attitude that shall be remarkably striking to the mind's eye."[2] The scene in which "Crusoe recoil[s] from the footprint"[3] discovered in the sand, he suggests, is one of the most memorable scenes in literature. Defoe's influence on Stevenson's writing was also noted by his early critics: for example, the success of his first adventure novel *Treasure Island*

[79]

(1883), published three years before *Kidnapped*, led one anonymous contemporary reviewer to call "Mr. Stevenson . . . the Defoe of our generation."[4]

Nevertheless, upon first reading Robert Louis Stevenson's *Kidnapped*, the reader has the impression that the author is more indebted to the historical Waverley novels of Sir Walter Scott than to Defoe. First published in 1886, *Kidnapped* was Stevenson's first attempt at merging two genres, the historical novel in the manner of Walter Scott with the novel of adventure, as codified by Defoe. *Kidnapped* was originally intended for the entertainment of young readers, "to steal some young gentleman's attention from his Ovid," as the author confesses in the dedication (3). Stevenson's readers were quick to observe Defoe's influence in the motifs, incidents, and style of the book. Arthur Conan Doyle, for instance, who admired both *Treasure Island* and *Kidnapped*, argued that both novels were "direct, eminently practical and Defoe-like narratives."[5] According to John Robert Moore, who has written the most detailed account of Defoe's influence on Stevenson so far, *Kidnapped* has "passages imitated from *Robinson Crusoe*."[6] J. R. Hammond points out that "Stevenson's affinity with Defoe is plain at numerous points in the story."[7] More recently, however, Rebecca Weaver-Hightower has included *Kidnapped* in the list of those "postcolonial texts" that dispute "the island fantasy" of traditional Robinsonades that developed from Defoe's famous novel.[8] It is along these lines that a century and a half after its publication, it is worth reinvestigating and reappraising Stevenson's classic novel.

When Stevenson was writing *Treasure Island* and *Kidnapped*, the novels of adventure that made him famous, it was not simply *Robinson Crusoe* that was at the back of his mind, but the Victorian Robinsonades written for boys, such as *The Coral Island* by R. M. Ballantyne (1858). Ever since James Joyce's seminal observation on Crusoe being "the true prototype of the British colonist," a great deal of critical attention has focused on the theme of colonialism in the source of all Robinsonades, *Robinson Crusoe*.[9] Richard Phillips, just like Joyce and numerous critics in his wake, argues that "through its narrative of colonisation and transformation on and of an island" Defoe's work "represents, promotes and legitimates a form of colonialism."[10] But Victorian Robinsonades, according to Phillips, also support the idea of colonialism, "mapp[ing] variations on the generic theme of British identity and imperial geography."[11] *Treasure Island*, Stevenson's first Robinsonade, however, can be regarded as a critique of such imperial narratives.[12] Diane Loxley, for instance, suggests that it is possible to see the fortune-hungry pirates as representatives of the declining British Empire in the second half of the nineteenth century, "desperadoes feeding off the system's decaying parts," presenting "an image of the fragmentation effected when the code and discipline of Empire falls apart."[13] Similarly, Stevenson's *Kidnapped*, a story about the adventures of a young Lowlander David Balfour and his Jacobite friend Alan Breck Stewart from the Highlands, shows not only a "tragically divided nation"[14] after the Union, but a "politics of resistance to dominant literary and imperialist constructions,"[15] as Nathalie Jaëck has argued, by "rewrit[ing] an alternative story of Scotland; ... celebrat[ing] Scottish solidarity against English rule."[16] It is in this light that it is worth regarding *Kidnapped* as a text subverting the traditional Victorian Robinsonade, or rather, as a counter-Robinsonade. For the purpose of demonstrating my point, I am adopting Janet Bertsch's wider definition of the Robinsonade, which not only is limited to "a story or an episode within a story where an individual or group of individuals with limited resources try to survive on a desert island," but can be used in a wider context as a "convenient way of identifying certain universal characteristics in novels that employ a common set of motifs in a similar way."[17] The island trope, which is so prominent in the first volume of *Robinson Crusoe*, is also significant in Stevenson's Scottish counter-Robinsonade; it is cleverly employed by Stevenson to suggest that the novel tackles delicate political issues that were controversial not only in the eighteenth century but also in the late Victorian period.

When Stevenson pays conscious literary homage to Defoe in his third novel, he transforms the traditional progressivist colonial narrative of the Victorian Robinsonade in order to produce an alternative, politically more complex historical novel of national survival set against an actual historical and geographical background. It is symbolic that David becomes a castaway on an island (Erraid) and begins his Highland adventures on the Isle of Mull. He then travels across the metaphorical isle of the Highlands in Alan's company. All of these geographical and metaphorical islands are situated in Scotland, a country within another country that is located on the greatest island of the British Isles. "The trope of the island," as Ian Kinane has recently demonstrated, "has come to be constructed as a series of fictional meta narratives" in the Robinsonades written after Defoe, "as each . . . is always-already invested in the myth of its ür-textual forbears—the original Robinsonade, and the imaginary island as constructed in Defoe's text. Each Robinsonade must necessarily situate itself within a cultural tradition that will always compare and contrast it with its textual predecessors."[18] In this sense, David's adventures in the Highlands—a land so much like an island with its unique and isolated sociocultural-historical setting only six years after the Jacobite rebellion of 1745—do not simply describe a particularly dark period in the history of Scotland but also reconstruct some of the structural elements and motifs in *Robinson Crusoe* that Stevenson could use, not merely for the sake of entertaining his readers, but for producing a "many-faceted story"[19] of depth for a political purpose. The "island" metanarrative of *Kidnapped* shows that it is a counter-Robinsonade, for instead of sanctioning and promoting colonialism, it reveals the destructive nature of British conquest in the Highlands and offers an explanation to the resistance that issued in the wake of the Jacobite rebellion, probing the different layers of national identity and raising questions about the possibilities of reconciliation between Highlanders, Lowlanders, and the English.

Before examining the trope of the island in *Kidnapped* more closely, it is useful to look at some of the "common set of motifs"[20] typical of Robinsonades that Stevenson uses to meet the requirements of a Scottish romance, or Scottish counter-Robinsonade. Some of the characteristics, in which Stevenson is following in Defoe's footprints, can be found in the technical details and form. *Kidnapped*, besides being a historical novel of adventure, is also a fictitious memoir or autobiography. The long subtitle of *Kidnapped* is a spoiler title in the eighteenth-century mode, reminding readers of Defoe's mariner who is the purported author of his own life story: "*Kidnapped*, being the Adventures of David Balfour in the Year 1751: How he was Kidnapped and Cast away; his Sufferings in a Desert Isle; his Journey in the Wild Highlands; his Acquaintance with Alan Breck Stewart and other notorious Highland Jacobites; with all that he Suffered at the hands of his Uncle, Ebenezer Balfour of Shaws, falsely so-called: Written by Himself, and now set forth by Robert Louis Stevenson" (1). Stevenson, however, also includes his own name as the editor who "now set forth" the memoir to readers, which Defoe refrained from doing in order to make his readers believe in the authenticity of Crusoe's personal narrative. He even supplies a map of the Highlands on the prefatory page tracking David's journey, just as Defoe did in order to designate the location of the desert island for the fourth edition of *Robinson Crusoe*.[21] Stevenson attributes the success and "charm" of *Robinson Crusoe* to the romance of the story that is created by Defoe to meet the "deeply seated" desire in men "for fit and striking incident,"[22] simultaneously "show[ing] us the realisation and the apotheosis of the day-dreams of common men."[23] The success of Defoe's effort to meet this internal demand in readers is best attested by *Robinson Crusoe*'s publication history in the Victorian era; by the end of the nineteenth century the mariner's story would be published in more than two hundred editions.[24] In order to show the value and importance of incident in a novel, Stevenson compares *Robinson Crusoe*'s afterlife to Richardson's *Clarissa*, which is lacking in such romance: "And yet a little story of a shipwrecked sailor, with not tenth part of the style nor a thousandth part of the wisdom, exploring none of the arcana of humanity and deprived from the perennial interest of love, goes on from edition to edition, ever young, while *Clarissa* lies upon the shelves unread."[25]

If "*Robinson* depends, for the most part and with the overwhelming majority of its readers, on the charm of circumstance,"[26] as Stevenson claimed, then so does *Kidnapped*. The major part of *Robinson Crusoe* describes the mariner's existence as a castaway on a desert island, situated between adventures that lie outside this experience. *Kidnapped* is also constructed in a frame-like structure, in which David's visit to his treacherous uncle and his return to claim his rightful inheritance forms the frame narrative to the story. David's kidnapping, the forced voyage on the brig *Covenant*, his shipwreck, and the journey with Alan across the Highlands compose the major part of the book. As opposed to Crusoe, however, who hungers for adventure, David is more pragmatic and wishes to discover if he is entitled to any inheritance at all, only in order to be able to plan his future. Chapter 14, "The Islet," is a Robinsonade "in miniature," as J. R. Hammond observed, in which David's narrative is reminiscent of "Defoe's terse, matter-of-fact documentary style: his technique of narrating events with the circumstantiality of a factual account."[27] The details of his survival are illustrated in Crusoe-like vivid detail as in the passage when David, tormented by hunger, is searching for live fish to eat in the incessant chilly and rainy weather of the island: "I knew indeed that shell-fish were counted good to eat; and among the rocks of the isle I found a great plenty of limpets, which at first I could scarcely strike from their places, not knowing quickness to be needful. There were, besides, some of the little shells that we call buckies; I think periwinkle is the English name. Of these two I made my whole diet, devouring them cold and raw as I found them; and so hungry was I, that at first they seemed to me delicious" (83–84).

David's trials and tribulations, however, are not limited to starvation, exposure to cold rain, and fever on the isles of the Inner Hebrides. Throughout his inland travels across the exotic Highlands and the more familiar Lowlands, David's life is also threatened by the occupying British troops. In all of his adventures David is a wavering young fellow, also reminding readers of Scott's Edward Waverley. It is, however, through the friendship of the more self-assertive Jacobite Highlander Alan Breck Stewart, a Catholic, and a real historical personage who comes from "the more savage places of the Highlands" (99), that David can survive the ordeal, reach maturity, and experience a Crusoe-like spiritual rebirth. The friendship with Alan makes it possible for David to become acquainted with Highland culture. Their close alliance begins on the *Covenant* when David saves Alan's life against Captain Hoseason and the mercenary crew who wish to seize Alan's gold and take his life. David and Alan are outnumbered, defending their lives against the crew (chapter 10). They find themselves isolated on a ship, which in itself forms a small island in the middle of the sea. If, as Foucault suggests, the ship itself can be regarded as a heterotopia, a place of otherness, a "floating piece of space, a place without a place, that exists by itself, that is self-enclosed and at the same time is given over to the infinity of the sea,"[28] it is a suitable meeting ground for David's first encounter with the "other," wild culture of the Highlands, which, nevertheless, also forms a part of Scotland. David's shipwreck on Erraid and his stepping ashore on the "rugged and trackless" (90) Ross of Mull can also be interpreted as stages in a journey that act as "transitional passage[s]" and "cultural contact zone[s]"[29] leading to the metaphorical "island" of the Highlands.

Defoe's Crusoe, the exile of the desert island, enters the "cultural contact zone" when he first glimpses the solitary footprint of a native on the beach. Much later he encounters "savages" and rescues Friday from a cannibal culture, which, as a Christian, he wholeheartedly rejects, but later begins to tolerate. Friday eventually learns to identify with European culture after Crusoe colonizes him by converting him and teaching him English. The initial realization, however, that the island may be visited occasionally by "savages," makes Crusoe "terrify'd to the last Degree" (112). In *Kidnapped* it is the red-coated English who are the cause of fear. In the sparsely populated, impoverished, and terrorized country that still speaks Gaelic, a tongue that the young Scotsman does not speak, "David is a Lowlander, an exile in his own land," as Julia Reid emphasized, and "his Lallans speech and Covenanting ways alienate him from Highlanders as much as Englishmen."[30] In his journey across the Isle of Mull David observes the consequences of British military presence after the rebellion: the forced changes in Highlander costume and weaponry, the poverty of attire, food, and low standard of living:

> The Highland dress being forbidden by law since the rebellion, and the people condemned to the lowland habit, which they much disliked, it was strange to see the variety of their array. Some went bare, only for a hanging cloak or great coat, and carried their trousers on their backs like a useless burthen: some had made an imitation of the tartan with little parti-coloured stripes patched together like an old wife's quilt; others, again, still wore the Highland philabeg, but by putting a few stitches between the legs, transformed it into a pair of trousers like a Dutchmen's. All those makeshifts were condemned and punished, for the law was harshly applied, in hopes to break up the clan spirit; but in that out-of-the-way, sea-bound isle, there were few to make remarks and fewer to tell tales. (91)

All the prohibitions and reprisals would gradually lead to the disappearance of clan culture, as Stevenson and Sir Walter Scott before him well knew. Stevenson was just as fascinated by the history of Scotland as Scott and especially by the period of the Jacobite rebellion and its aftermath. Using historical sources for writing *Kidnapped*, especially the document *The Trial of James Stewart for the Murder of Colin Campbell of Glenure* (1753), he fictionalizes the famous Appin murder of the Red Fox in 1752, setting it one year earlier in the novel than when it actually took place.[31] Although Alan Breck Stewart was one of the accused in the case, his relative, James of the Glen Stewart, had to hang (in all probability innocently) for the assassination. Like David, Alan is eyewitness to the bloody murder of Colin Campbell. Both of them have to escape—Alan has been considered an outlaw ever since the Jacobite rebellion—although neither of them can be considered guilty for what happened.

The most important moral decision that David as a loyal subject of King George has to make is whether to follow Alan in the flight from the red coats. David is at first incredulous when Alan informs him that the idea of proving his innocence to the authorities is naïve and will not get him anywhere in the Highlands. "This is a Campbell that's been killed," Alan explains, "Justice, David? The same justice, by all the world, as Glenure found a while ago at the road-side" (111). In other words, there is no alternative for David, as Alan wisely points out: "Either take to the heather with me, or else hang" (112). It comes as a shock to David, as an Anglicized Lowlander, that there is no means to prove his innocence; British political oppression in the Highlands prevents the democratic function of judicial institutions. At the beginning of his adventures he is bursting with pride at the sight of English soldiers: "The pride of life seemed to mount into my brain at the sight of the red coats and the hearing of that merry music" (11). After the murder, however, the sight of the English soldiers fills him with fear: "Yet we could see the soldiers pike their bayonets among the heather, which sent a cold thrill into my vitals; and they would sometimes hang about our rock so that we scarce dared to breathe" (125). It comes as a bitter surprise to David that although he is a "Whig," as Alan calls him, he has become a wanted person, hunted by the English (54). Thus David's political allegiance to the British Crown is put to the test throughout the journey, the most dangerous part of which lies across the Western Highlands. Lying flat on a rock burning with heat and observing the movements of the red coats in Glencoe, hiding out and living in a cave near the Heugh of Corrynakiegh, or escaping through the heather, David shares the status of an outlaw with Alan in their exile. When not in flight, David and Alan live the life of Robinson Crusoe in the wilds of the Scottish Highlands:

> We slept in the cave, making our bed of heather bushes which we cut for that purpose, and covering ourselves with Alan's great coat. There was a low concealed place, in a turning of the glen, where we were so bold as to make fire: so that we could warm ourselves when the clouds set in, and cook hot porridge, and grill the little trouts that we caught with our hands under the stones and overhanging the banks of the burn. This was indeed our chief pleasure and business; and not only to save our meal against

worse times, but with a rivalry that much amused us, we spent a great part of our days at the water side, stripped to the waist and groping about or (as they say) guddling for these fish. (129)

The idyllic scenes of temporary respite strengthen the bond of friendship between David and Alan and increase their awareness of approaching danger.

Unlike Victorian Robinsonades, David's adventures on land from Erraid to Appin and from Appin to Edinburgh (in the company of Alan) bring to the fore the negative effects of the British occupation rather than its benefits; their dangerous journey is more like a covert reaction against it. The arduous trek of the Lowlander and Highlander across the geographical territory of the Highlands is a way of reappropriating it, as Nathalie Jaëck suggests: "Indeed, Alan and David's active occupation of the Highlands, and their constant escaping the vigilance of the Red Coats, amount to an underlying commentary on English imperialist behaviour in Scotland: it is a way to reappropriate the colonised territory of the Highlands, to walk over it and physically occupy the land that had been lost to English Rule."[32] In other words, David not only begins to see the political situation in the Highlands through the perspective of the colonized, rather than the colonizer, but symbolically reacts against it by joining Alan in reconquering Scotland, unified together against the English. The cultural and linguistic differences between the Lowlander David and Highlander Alan are thus diminished and they become allies in resisting the English conquest.

In the wilds David comes into contact with Alan's kinsmen and ordinary Highlanders. David encounters historical figures, such as Cluny Macpherson and the son of Rob Roy. Through his contact with Alan and the Highlanders, David comes to accept and admire their dedication to "feudal values of honor and unswerving loyalty to [their] clans."[33] As a strict Presbyterian he is ready to concede that the Highlanders' perennial attachment to communal identity above individual interests is acceptable in Christian terms, albeit with reservations: "Alan's morals were all tail-first; but he was ready to give his life for them, such as they were.... 'I'll not say it's the good Christianity as I understand it, but it's good enough'" (110). There is, however, also a Robinsonian spiritual journey that is awaiting David that parallels the physical flight across the Highlands in his search for maturity and self-knowledge.

In a recent study, Wolfram Schmidgen reconsiders traditional colonialist interpretations of *Robinson Crusoe*, emphasizing that Defoe "grasps the island scenario as an opportunity to unsettle established assumptions"; and rather than seeing it "as comprehension, reduction, and domination," he regards it "as the transcendence of limits and the multiplication of the forms of life . . . ," urging us

ISLANDS IN ROBERT LOUIS STEVENSON'S *KIDNAPPED* (1886)

"to open up . . . toward limitless variety."[34] David in *Kidnapped*, who starts out as a "Low-country bod[y]" and "ha[s] no clear idea of what's right and wrong" (111), learns to "open up" through the "island scenario" toward Highlanders and Highland culture, questioning the validity of the reduced perspective of imperial "domination" that England exercises in the conquered land by preventing its "variety" to surface. The idea of "opening up" and learning to understand and tolerate a different culture in David's case produces a more expanded or Robinsonian fluid sense of identity. According to Schmidgen, "If *Robinson Crusoe* is a parable of the colonizing process, the success of this process depends not on seeing one thing or name as singular and same, but on seeing one thing or name as several and different. Identity is not singular, but plural."[35]

If the island in Defoe's *Robinson Crusoe* is the place of rebirth for Crusoe, the Highlands for David are the place where he begins to interpret and understand the "savage" culture of the Highlanders from a broader and more objective perspective. He becomes immersed in it, eventually even identifying with it.[36] In this sense, his contact with the island and islanders (the Highlands and Highlanders) makes his identity more fluid, "not singular, but plural." Ian Kinane also suggests that the island motif of the Robinsonades is the locus of personal development "representative of the metaphoric return of the individual to a greater sense of egoic completion, whereby 'island' and 'ego' become symbiotically entwined with one another."[37] Thus the geographical territory of the Highlands becomes similar to the islands of traditional Robinsonades for David; they are transformed into a place of "rebirth, reformulation, renewal."[38] Before David's rebirth becomes possible, however, trials have to be suffered, temptations have to be repelled, and transgressions have to be forgiven.

Crusoe's initial act of transgression lies in his disobedience to his father. All of his misfortunes originate in this rebellious filial act. David's transgression can be found in the internal pressure to rebel against his friend. He refuses to play cards with his host Cluny Macpherson on moral grounds owing to his Presbyterian upbringing and blames Alan for gambling and losing the little money they possess. He remains cold and unyielding to Alan's entreaties to be forgiven. When he provokes a quarrel with Alan (chapter 21), the differences in Catholic and Presbyterian upbringing and attitudes toward life and morality surface. David is still suffering from the aftereffects of illness, feeling miserable and exhausted from the flight in the heather. He is thus tempted to separate from his friend and tell Alan that his "friendship is a burden," and he should "take [his] risks and bear [his] hardships alone" (149). David's moral justifications seemingly derive from his strict Presbyterian background, but are mainly prompted by his exhaustion and cowardice. Disappointed in himself and ashamed of his disloyal feelings, however, he refrains from abandoning Alan. Instead, he insults the proud Highlander in an unpardonable manner: "Both the Campbells and the Whigs have beaten you; you have run before them like a hare. It behoves you to speak of them as of your betters" (155). Although David in this scene is provoking a duel, Alan shows true signs of friendship by not willing to engage in a sword fight with the younger and inexperienced David. He forgives David, just as David wishes to forgive Alan by this time, regretting his scathing words. The quarrel scene, which Henry James called a "real stroke of genius" on Stevenson's part, ends with David's repentance and his reconciliation with Alan.[39] David's repentance leads to the affirmation and reinforcement of the bond of friendship. This is the final stage in his moral development and in the road to conversion from boyhood to maturity and responsible manhood, distantly mirroring Crusoe's repentance and redemption.[40]

Through the physical and spiritual journey across the Highlands back to his home in the Lowlands of Scotland, David can see a "savage" culture that is worth preserving and is in many ways even more civilized than the one he knows, with its staunch belief in moral values of honor and loyalty. As David comments, "If these are the wild Highlanders, I could wish my own folk wilder" (91). David and Alan's friendship is symbolic; with their friendship the Highlands and the Lowlands form one heterogeneous "island," suggesting that the unique characteristics of each "island" nation, besides England's, can live side by side and survive. The counter-Robinsonade motifs and the metanarrative of Stevenson's *Kidnapped* also underline that it is together that the two friends can reappropriate the land of their ancestors, the island that has become a "colonized" part of the United Kingdom.[41] Stevenson, looking back at the end of the nineteenth century on the historical possibilities that were offered to Scotland a century and half before, sees a lost opportunity in having failed to create a healthy union between the two culturally, religiously, and politically divided Scottish peoples. In David and Alan's friendship Stevenson describes a historical opportunity that, had it been recognized in time, may have resisted the politics of assimilation and helped preserve the cultural diversities of Scotland. Stevenson's literary islands in *Kidnapped* thus help re-create the lost moment in history and examine the extent to which political resistance and cultural preservation might have been possible even after the Jacobite rebellion. By employing the island trope of traditional Robinsonades and imaginatively displaying the many thematic possibilities it offers, Stevenson creates a counter-Robinsonade out of *Kidnapped*, exposing it as more than simply a novel of adventure for boys or a historical romance, but rather as one that lays bare for many readers the politically provocative and unresolved problems existing between England and Scotland in the eighteenth century, as well as in the late Victorian period.

NOTES

1. Robert Louis Stevenson, *Kidnapped*, ed. Ian Duncan (Oxford: Oxford University Press, 2014). Further references are to this edition and are given parenthetically.
2. Robert Louis Stevenson, "A Gossip on Romance," in *Memories and Portraits* (London: Heinemann, 1928), 123.
3. Ibid., 123.
4. Paul Maixner, ed., *Robert Louis Stevenson: The Critical Heritage* (London: Routledge, 1998), 233.
5. Quoted after John Robert Moore, "Defoe, Stevenson, and the Pirates," *English Literary History* 10.1 (1943): 36. Moore's excellent article provides a thorough discussion of Defoe's literary influence on Stevenson.
6. Ibid., 40.
7. J. R. Hammond, *A Robert Louis Stevenson Companion* (London: Macmillan, 1984), 130.
8. Rebecca Weaver-Hightower, *Empire Islands: Castaways, Cannibals, and Fantasies of Conquest* (Minneapolis: University of Minnesota Press, 2007), 233.
9. Quoted after Richard Phillips, *Mapping Men and Empire: A Geography of Adventure* (London and New York: Routledge, 1997), 33.
10. Ibid., 34.
11. Ibid., 22.
12. Andrew O'Malley, for instance, regards *Treasure Island* as one of the "notable examples" of Victorian Robinsonades in *Children's Literature, Popular Culture, and "Robinson Crusoe"* (Houndmills: Palgrave Macmillan, 2012), 50. Richard Phillips refers to Stevenson's boys' classic as a Robinsonade "to a lesser extent" in *Mapping Men and Empire*, 5.
13. Diana Loxley, *Problematic Shores: The Literature of Islands* (Houndmills: Palgrave Macmillan, 1990), 169.
14. Julia Reid, *Robert Louis Stevenson, Science, and the Fin de Siècle* (Houndmills: Palgrave Macmillan, 2006), 125.
15. Nathalie Jaëck, "Kidnapping the Historical Novel in *Kidnapped*: An Act of Literary and Political Resistance," *Journal of Stevenson Studies* 11 (2014): 89.
16. Ibid., 101.
17. Janet Bertsch, *Storytelling in the Works of Bunyan, Grimmelshausen, Defoe, and Schnabel* (Rochester, NY: Camden House, 2004), 79.
18. Ian Kinane, *Theorising Literary Islands: The Island Trope in Contemporary Robinsonade Narratives* (London: Rowman & Littlefield, 2017), 30.
19. Hammond, *Robert Louis Stevenson Companion*, 134.
20. Bertsch, *Storytelling in the Works of Bunyan, Grimmelshausen, Defoe, and Schnabel*, 79.
21. Ian Duncan, "Introduction," in Robert Louis Stevenson, *Kidnapped*, ed. Duncan (Oxford: Oxford University Press, 2014), xxi.
22. Stevenson, "Gossip on Romance," 122.
23. Ibid., 123.
24. Phillips, *Mapping Men and Empire*, 23.
25. Stevenson, "Gossip on Romance," 125.
26. Ibid., 125.
27. Hammond, *Robert Louis Stevenson Companion*, 130.
28. Quoted after Kinane, *Theorising Literary Islands*, 65.
29. Kinane, *Theorising Literary Islands*, 68, 67. As Kinane argues, "To approach the island, one must necessarily navigate this transitional passage, negotiating as one does one's imagined preconceptions of space, as one crosses the indeterminate boundary between sea and land" (67).
30. Reid, *Robert Louis Stevenson*, 126.

31. Duncan, "Introduction," xv.
32. Jaëck, "Kidnapping the Historical Novel in *Kidnapped*," 88.
33. Jefferson A. Singer, *The Proper Pirate: Robert Louis Stevenson's Quest for Identity* (New York: Oxford University Press, 2017), 141.
34. Wolfram Schmidgen, "The Metaphysics of *Robinson Crusoe*," *English Literary History* 83.1 (Spring 2016): 106.
35. Ibid., 115.
36. Reid, *Robert Louis Stevenson*, 128.
37. Kinane, *Theorising Literary Islands*, 18.
38. Ibid., 9.
39. Quoted after Paul Maixner, "Introduction," in Maixner, *Robert Louis Stevenson*, 28.
40. David and Alan return in adventures that are discussed in Stevenson's sequel to *Kidnapped*, titled *Catriona* (*David Balfour* in the American edition).
41. Jaëck, "Kidnapping the Historical Novel in *Kidnapped*," 101.

Part Three

ECOCRITICAL READINGS

7

STORMY WEATHER AND THE GENTLE ISLE

Apprehending the Environment of Three Robinsonades

Lora E. Geriguis

Daniel Defoe's exposure as an eyewitness (and almost victim) to the Storm of 1703 that cut a three-hundred-mile-wide swath of destruction across England on the night of 26 November nearly cost him his life, but also jump-started his publishing career.[1] Defoe's first long-form publication, *The Storm* (1704),[2] is a series of generically diverse pseudo-journalistic pieces written about the "extratropical cyclone of unusual ferocity . . . [that] remains the worst storm in British History."[3] To varying degrees in all of his subsequent novels, Defoe harnessed his experiences with weather, deploying them both materially and metaphorically, to shape the action of the narratives and reveal his characters' interiority.[4] Apprehension about the weather erupts early in *Robinson Crusoe* (1719), when Young Robinson Crusoe boards a ship for the first time to have a taste of the sea life he has been craving, without his parents' knowledge and against their explicit wishes. As soon as the ship enters stormy waters off the east coast of England, Crusoe becomes "inexpressibly sick in Body, and terrified in my Mind" (8). Yet, the friend who had conspired to get him on board mocks his anxieties: "*I warrant you were frighted, wa'n't you, last Night, when it blew but a Cap full of Wind? A Cap full d'you call it?* Said I, *'twas a terrible Storm: A Storm, you Fool you*, replies he, *do you call that a Storm, why it was nothing at all*" (8). Being handed a bowl of punch to calm his fears, Young Crusoe in "that one Night's Wickedness . . . drowned all [his] Repentance" (8). The next day, this act of impiety is followed by a second, larger storm, one that strikes "Terror and Amazement in the Faces even of the Seamen themselves" (9) and actually sinks the ship close to shore; the crew and passengers barely escape with their lives. The ship's master attributes the stormy weather and the loss of the ship to Crusoe's disobedience, "like Jonah in the Ship of Tarshish" (12). Despite this cautionary experience, Crusoe continues to resist repentance and to persist in his wanderlust, which confirms him in the

[93]

path of another storm that eventually leaves him famously stranded on an Atlantic island for the better part of three decades.

Defoe's narrative harnessing of stormy weather reflects a sea change that was taking place in England regarding the way weather was being perceived, not only as evidence of God's will or power but also as an object of scientific study; in fact, "British researchers led the world in this kind of regular recording [of weather conditions]."[5] Picking up on these cues regarding data gathering, Defoe contrived for *The Storm* a "Table of Degrees" for identifying wind strengths, from "Stark Calm" to "A fresh Gale" to "A Tempest" with a dozen levels in total, to organize and authenticate the eyewitness reports he collected regarding the 1703 storm, an idea he later adapted to comic effect in *Robinson Crusoe* while describing the characters' competing perceptions of weather ("a Cap full of Wind" versus a "terrible Storm").[6] Daniel Defoe, though not himself a fellow of London's Royal Society for the Improvement of Natural Knowledge, was brought "into contact with the basic aims of the Royal Society in the way of verified accounts of places, things, and events" in the course of his education.[7] Defoe's "lively interest in science, and [Charles] Morton's theories can be found in . . . the early *Storm*,"[8] as is exemplified by Defoe's attempt to count the number of trees felled by the 1703 storm, an effort he gave up after reaching seventeen thousand.[9] Both by training and by artistic inclinations, Defoe was drawn to the power of details and attuned to the practices of documentation, elements of what Novak calls his "imagined reality";[10] these scientifically inflected qualities of Defoe's writing contributed to his reputation for "realistic narrative method," for which *Robinson Crusoe* came to be recognized as a pivotal example.[11]

The Royal Society's fostering of the long-term collection of weather data, as Golinski outlines, "informed public discourse about the national climate," and led to a perception of England's moderate climate as a national blessing, given its "good quantity of fertilizing, healthy rain" and being "almost never inflicted [with] excessive heat or cold" and only seldom suffering from violent storms; the British "concluded that they had been blessed by a benevolent providence with a climate well adapted to sustain the nation's prosperity and well-being."[12] Hence, the outcome of weather observation during the eighteenth century fed the superiority complex that undergird the nation's colonial ideology. England's "specter'd isle"[13] came to be perceived by many as home to an "island race" of people destined to leave their "indelible imprint on the globe" through colonialism.[14] The "emerging consciousness of the British national climate [allowed] for comparison between the climates of places that were quite distant from one another, such as the homeland and colonial settlements overseas," questions that became increasingly important since "they potentially determined the fate of conquest and settlement."[15] In essence, weather consciousness both justified and intensified England's colonial ambitions, an atmosphere in which Defoe's own worldview was shaped and his novels were written.

The storms that blow through *Robinson Crusoe* gather into a weather pattern visible within the Robinsonades, forming a three-hundred-year record of human apprehension and scientific perception of the environment. The various geographical locations, climate conditions, and historical contexts of these Robinsonades could easily be minimized as simply new window dressing framing the same old view, merely interchangeable backgrounds for the retelling of the original story. However, the climate of the setting (accurate or fanciful) as well as the people belonging to the location (acknowledged or erased) should instead be observed and measured for what they reveal about the ideology of each work, both in conversation with Defoe's text and independently. The way characters respond to storms or other climatic events, given the weather's association with Providence and fate, on the one hand, and its use as a plot device, on the other, become important lenses through which to ascertain each text's ideology.

The geographical contours of the body of Robinsonade texts are outlined in J. A. Cuddon's definition of what he alternatively termed "desert island fiction": "[Desert island fiction is a] form of fiction in which a remote and 'uncivilized' island is used as the venue of the story and action. It has a particular attraction because it can be placed right outside the 'real' world and may be an image of the ideal, the unspoilt and the primitive. . . . The publication of Defoe's *Robinson Crusoe* in 1719 marked the inception of a literary genre which has attained universal popularity."[16] Cuddon's dual binaries, of a "remote" island versus a perceived center, and that of a "'real' world" that is contrasted to an "unspoilt" and "primitive" ideal world, define the literary form in terms that clearly land it within a geography of colonial ideology, although inexplicably Cuddon does not acknowledge the form's link with colonialism. In most Robinsonades, the centered "real world" has frequently been England (or another European country) during its long reign as an imperial power, and increasingly America since its rise to dominance as a world power in the postindustrial age.[17] Further, Cuddon's definition also lacks any reference to two additional components integral to Defoe's *Robinson Crusoe* and fundamental to the recognition of any text as a Robinsonade:[18] namely, the forces of weather and the encounters with "the Other." The examination of three selected Robinsonades will demonstrate the importance of correcting Cuddon's critical breach, particularly for any reading that seeks to measure the colonial ideology operating within the environment of each work.

Three Robinsonades—one novel, *The Female American* (1767), and two films, *Daniel Defoe's Robinson Crusoe* (1997) and *Cast Away* (2000)—will be explicated to determine the natural, social, and political environments that render these texts as more than mere adaptations of the *Robinson Crusoe* myth, but also as commentary on their own times, places, and people, which in turn challenge, invert, or put a modern twist on the ideology of Defoe's own text. These Robinsonades span two centuries (the eighteenth and twentieth), two oceans (the Atlantic and Pacific), and two mediums (novel and film). The genre of the novel, which allows the author's imagination full reign to determine, order, and contain the natural elements, enables the creation of a mild Atlantic island as the setting for *The Female American*, in which violent natural forces make only a few dramatic cameo appearances in the plot, but which otherwise depicts this female Robinsonade tale within a nurturing environment. The primarily gentle island of *The Female American* will be examined for how those conditions relate to England's perception of itself in the eighteenth century as an island blessed with a benevolent climate, and for how that political trope sustains what Edward Simon describes as the text's "fantasy of noncolonial conversion."[19] In contrast, the two Robinsonades set in the Pacific Ocean are shaped by the fact that they are told through the collaborative medium of film, a form in which the people and physical environment depicted are no longer solely the figment of the godlike novelist's imagination and subject entirely to his or her articulation. Rather, film locations and actors, whether foregrounded or sublimated, play a decisive role in the collaborative nature of film production and reception. As a consequence, the climates of *Daniel Defoe's Robinson Crusoe* and *Cast Away* will be measured for how the weather and human elements are contended with by the crews, the actors, and subsequently the viewers themselves, all of whom become challenged to recognize what it means to produce/perform/picture or "modernize" a colonial myth at the end of the twentieth century, and to do so within a curated depiction of what is nevertheless a material environment. The colonial ideology that is the Robinsonade form's inescapable heritage from *Robinson Crusoe* is either reproduced or challenged in each example of the form, often decipherable by whether the ecology, climate, and people of each Robinsonade text are erased or acknowledged.

THE GENTLE ISLE ROBINSONADE:
THE FEMALE AMERICAN (1767)

In 1767, "the intellectual salons of Europe [were set] buzzing with accounts of Polynesia isles" by news of the "'discovery' of Otaheita (Tahiti) by Captain Wallis of the Dolphin" and Louis de Bougainville's report of naming an island after himself on the northern end of the Solomon Islands in the South Pacific.[20] The Gulf

Stream also brought the New World to England in the persons of two Native Americans, Cherokee Ostenaca and Samson Occom, a Moghegan preacher, who famously visited London in the 1760s.[21] In the midst of all this contact, two circulating libraries in London received copies of a new book with an increasingly familiar Atlantic setting.[22] *The Female American; or, The Adventures of Unca Eliza Winkfield* (anonymous, 1767) tells the tale of a biracial heroine, Unca Eliza, daughter of an Algonquian ("Indian") princess of Wingandacoa (Virginia), Unca, and an Englishman, William Winkfield, whose romance resembles the Pocahontas myth.[23] After the death of the parents, the daughter is castaway on an island off the coast of Virginia, a liminal space positioned between her American "Indian" and British identities. In what Edward Simon has called the "carnivalesque space of the desert island," which can be made to support a masculinist myth or coalesce with the topsy-turvy "conventions of the female Robinsonade," Unca Eliza is allowed greater scope of movement and freedom of action than her gender would otherwise have allowed her within an eighteenth-century novel set entirely in England and solely within the interior spaces of the domestic sphere.[24] The gender-role defiance and biraciality of *The Female American*'s plotline is facilitated by its simultaneously liminal and "remote" island setting.

Yet, from its inception *The Female American* was associated with, but also contested, the primacy of Defoe's 1719 castaway narrative. In fact, the narrator/"authoress" of *The Female American* specifically asserted precedence and authenticity over any similar castaway story, such as *Robinson Crusoe*, that might claim to predate and regender her tale.[25] The "Editor's note" included in the original London edition drives home the point: "Our authoress here seems to please herself, with the thoughts of the immortality of her history, and to prophesy of that of Robinson Crusoe, which only is inferior to her own, as fiction is to truth" (113). These claims of priority and reality were soundly rejected by the book's initial reviewers.[26] One of the two notices of the novel to appear in the London periodicals in 1767 diminished the work specifically as a "sort of second *Robinson Crusoe*; full of wonders." Another review sneers that the subject involves a "lady" who "is a most strange adventurer," and one whose tale is "calculated only for the wild Indians to whom she is so closely allied," and concludes by describing the reading of the work as "six hours very disagreeable employment."[27] These reviews must be understood in the context of the ongoing dominance of *Robinson Crusoe*'s popularity, seen in the successful London staging of the tale for the first time in 1781, the show's appeal being at least partially based on the storyline's perceived link with the "'real' experiences of shipwrecked mariner Alexander Selkirk" and Defoe's profound influence on "voyagers' tales and travel writing as well as fiction over the [eighteenth] century."[28] In contrast to such white male icons, Unca Eliza

Winkfield simply was not seen as "incarnating 'the whole Anglo-Saxon spirit'" as was Robinson Crusoe on the fictional page, and as did Captain James Cook, whose circumnavigation feats between 1768 and 1780 caused him to be seen as the "longed-for, real-life embodiment of many of [the] same myths and mystifications of Englishness" Robinson Crusoe continued to represent in the years immediately following the publication of *The Female American*.[29]

The scholarly debates over *The Female American*'s relationship to colonial ideology suggest that the text's "contradictions make it possible to read [it] as both imperialist and anti-imperialist."[30] However, Kvande ultimately determines that *The Female American* "offers a radical contribution to the debate on empire, property and Native peoples: by removing much of what marks her as English, the novel implies a rejection of English colonial power and even points towards social justice."[31] Edward Simon positions the work "in a liminal ideological space" but asserts that it narrates a "myth of non-colonial conversion," which he defines as a "depiction of religious conversion within a colonial context that is freely and rationally chosen by the faithful and where the conversion does not have any hidden colonial purpose despite the colonial environment."[32] Simon further clarifies the "myth of non-colonial conversion" as reliant on "certain theological positions of the eighteenth century that do not associate religion directly with human culture and social constructions" but rather with the alternative framework of "natural reason" so that "the adoption of [Christianity] . . . is not a forced imposition on a group of conquered people but rather an organic outgrowth of universal human thought."[33] Though neither Kvande's identification of the text's impulses toward "social justice" nor Simon's analysis of the "myth of non-colonial conversion" takes into consideration the island's climate, both elements can be seen as enabled by the island's gentle, nurturing environment. The author of *The Female American* engages with the geographical trope of Britain's beneficial climate justifying its positive national self-image when Unca Eliza's efforts to protect and convert the people who visit her island appear to be supported by an environment that sustains her physically and thereby enables her missionary work to proceed nonviolently.

Before Unca Eliza can appeal to the "natural reason" of her audience and convert them, she must first overcome her own irrationality, associated with her gendered emotions. Significantly, the island's climate and environmental conditions serve to calm her fears over time. Notably, Unca Eliza is castaway not by a storm but rather by the intentional cruelty of her ship's captain, whose greed is frustrated by her refusal to be coerced into signing a marriage agreement. However, though "put on shore" rather than cast there violently by a storm, and therefore physically unharmed, she faints on the sand—"My grief was too great for my spirits to bear; I sunk in a swoon on the ground" (65). When she is awakened by a wave washing over her, she takes a few steps on the shore and finds "the ruins of a building," which proves to be what she "wished for, an asylum" (65). Her fears of the island are shown to be unwarranted, in this case and others, when her every need is met with the conditions she finds. Yet the forming of her more rational mind takes several episodes to develop.

Unca Eliza's primary near-death experience is prompted, again, by unfounded fear of the island's climate, rather than an actual, realized threat. The hermit's journal, left behind by the island's earlier (and briefly simultaneous) inhabitant, provides her with clear instructions for how to subsist on the island year around (67).[34] Despite the advantages provided by having this information, Unca Eliza develops a fear of the coming raining season, which she defines as "answerable to winter in Europe" (128).[35] "How shall I, during the inclemency of it, procure the means of subsistence? . . . The rain perhaps may continue for many days, nay weeks, and confine me entirely to my cell . . . so greatly was my mind afflicted, that it brought on a violent fever, attended with a delirium. I raved, I cried, I laughed by turns. I soon became so weak, that I was scare able to crawl from my bed to get some water, of which I happened to have plenty" (74). Unca Eliza's excessive fears prompt a physical incapacitation that nearly proves fatal. To recover she must, as Burnham and Freitas summarize, "literally crawl, like an infant, in order to reach water and shelter. After undergoing a kind of inadvertent baptism in the island's river, she recovers her strength by nursing from the dugs of a she-goat"; this experience has been described as a "rebirth [which] increasingly resembles something more like a resurrection."[36] This event marks the turning point in her development of more rational thinking, which in turn serves to support "her subsequent development into a powerful and influential religious leader."[37] Marta Kvande reads this episode for its colonial ideological implications when she suggests Unca Eliza's "despair breaks down her English codes of behavior, and her baptism allows her to be reborn to into another, less British way of living."[38] It is the natural resources of plentiful fresh water, a favorable shade-tree topography, and accommodating animals that return her to life, after which she "could not but condemn [the] folly [of her fears] . . . and heartily repent" (77).

Aside from the earthquakes she witnesses but cause her no personal harm, Unca Eliza never really faces any significant danger while on her gentle isle. In fact, the three storms and three earthquakes depicted in the novel are situated in the story as serving useful purposes,[39] or at least as not ultimately harmful.[40] Further, the destruction caused by the hurricanes and earthquakes is shown as damaging only to the island itself;[41] however, no reports of Unca Eliza suffering as a result of lost resources, or even the need to clean things up afterward, are recorded in the text. For the most part, she is an observer of the weather that comes to the island, but not particularly a victim of it. "Defoe sees violence at the foundational moment of civilization and sovereignty," as witnessed in Crusoe's gun-shooting tendencies.[42] In contrast, the author of *The Female American* offers a "fantasy of non-colonial conversion" that does not require violence but is instead naturalized and rationalized, in part, by Unca Eliza's gender and biraciality, but also by the island's conducive ecology. As compared to the harsher contrasts and bolder colors of *Robinson Crusoe*, *The Female American* paints its narrative in pastel shades and gentler strokes; both texts' settings are well matched to the ideological action in their foregrounds. For the reader of the 1760s and 1770s, Unca Eliza's gentle Robinsonade seemed a pale shadow of the more favored original, masculine troupes pantomimed by Alexander Selkirk, Robinson Crusoe, and Captain James Cook.

Transitioning westward from the Atlantic to the Pacific and forward from eighteenth-century mercantile colonialism to the post/neocolonial twentieth century will evoke the new geographies and histories of the next two Robinsonades to be considered. The choice to film both movies on location in the South Pacific in the 1990s creates a detectable environmental and historical context through which these Robinsonades should be viewed. A particular irony is lent by the fact that the decade of 1990 to 2000 was declared by the United Nations General Assembly as the first International Decade for the Eradication of Colonialism, with the stated goal of adopting "an action plan aimed at ushering in the twenty-first century, a world free from colonialism."[43] The extent to which these two Robinsonades participated in that postcolonial discourse will be measured.

THE RAINY REVERSAL ROBINSONADE:
DANIEL DEFOE'S ROBINSON CRUSOE (1997)

Ostensibly not a Robinsonade at all, but rather claiming in the title to be a faithful rendition of Defoe's original novel, *Daniel Defoe's Robinson Crusoe* (1997) is legible as a twentieth-century post–civil rights era reinterpretation on the order of a Robinsonade, easily matching Cuddon's definition of "desert island fiction," with only a minimalist "period-costume" nod toward the source text and a great deal of filmic license taken with Defoe's plot and politics. Originally intended as a made-for-television Hallmark Channel production, the film was purchased by Miramax for theatrical distribution upon the news that Pierce Brosnan had just been selected as the latest actor to play the titular role in the James Bond film franchise.[44] However, the film, never released in U.S. or U.K. theaters, was largely panned by those who saw it on television or DVD. Reviews have described Brosnan's performance as Robinson Crusoe as "syrupy" and "unpersuasive," and the film itself as "laughable . . . briefly promising, mostly forgettable."[45] The film's "much more difficult" performance, according to another critic, is given by William Takaku, who plays Friday and renders the film "watchable."[46] The Bougainville Island–born actor's performance as Friday, as well as the South Pacific setting of this film, particularly its rainy climate and the contexts of its history of European exploration and 1990s anticolonial movement, will be read as constituting an active element in the ecology of the film's production and reception and therefore as critical to any assessment of its representation of colonial ideology.

Long before Brosnan and Takaku met on their film set, the South Pacific had been a coveted site within Western imagination, with the Spaniards, the Dutch, and the English competitively exploring the South Seas from the sixteenth century to the eighteenth. The French were latecomers, when Louis-Antoine, Comte de Bougainville (1729–1811) finally took his three-year journey (1766–1769), including passage through the South Pacific, to become the first Frenchman to circumnavigate the globe. Like the other Europeans before him, Bougainville left his name in the region when he christened one of the larger islands, positioned on the northern end of the Solomon Islands and eastern edge of what would later be deemed Papua New Guinea, after himself. Bougainville asserted that "I think we have well acquired the right of naming these parts,"[47] based presumably on the amount of effort and suffering required of the journey, during which scurvy and near starvation vexed the crew and officers alike. As Regis Stella puts it, "By their acts of naming lands they 'discovered,' Europeans began to assert control over their representation and incorporate them into their own history."[48] Locating the setting of the *Daniel Defoe's Robinson Crusoe* film in the South Pacific is just one more in a long line of examples of such appropriation of the South Pacific for Westerner self-expression.

Louis de Bougainville solidified his feat of circumnavigation by penning *A Voyage Round the World Performed by Order of His Most Christian Majesty, in the Years 1766, 1767, 1768, and 1769*, the English translation of which was published in London by John Forester, and dedicated to the Royal Society president, in 1772.[49] In addition to remarking on the significant threats posed by hunger and disease, Bougainville routinely comments on the local weather and the indigenous people they meet as additional challenges to be managed. Regarding the weather, the epic scale of the rainy season is registered in almost biblical tones: "One tempest comes on before the other is gone off, it thunders continually, and the nights are fit to convey an idea of chaotic darkness."[50] Hence, the South Pacific's climate becomes a factor for the Europeans to surmount, as much as the starvation, disease, and islands' inhabitants they confront.

Bougainville describes the various native peoples of the South Pacific his crew encounter as varying in posture from cautious curiosity to open aggression

[101]

or an air of indifference, which the Frenchman found most perplexing of all. An example of the latter occurred in the waters of the vicinity of what the Spaniards had previously named the Solomon Islands, one of which Bougainville later named for himself.[51]

> [The ship] had landed on two isles, where our people had found no signs of habitation, or cultivation, and not even any kind of fruits. They were going to return, when, to their great surprise, they saw a negro, quite by himself, coming towards them in a periagua, with two outriggers. In one ear he had a golden ring, and his arms were two lances. He came up to our boat without shewing any marks of fear or surprize. Our people asked him for something to eat and to drink, and he offered them water, and a small quantity of a sort of flour, which seemed to be his ordinary food. Our men gave him a handkerchief, a looking-glass, and some other trifles of that sort. He laughed when he received these presents, and did not admire them.[52]

In this exchange, the Europeans, who are in a desperate condition regarding their food supplies, are in the position of receiving aid, while the man in the boat remains free to laugh both at the Frenchmen in the ship and at their "trifles." The power dynamic of this scene clearly challenges the superiority complex of colonial ideology that the Frenchman carried with him to the South Pacific. For just a moment at least, the seascape of Bougainville's book is navigated by a person who manages to circumvent its colonialist paradigm.

The behavior and physical description of this "laughing" man in Bougainville's book corresponds to the long-held reputation of the people of (the so-named) Bougainville Island, as explained by Marilyn Havini and Josie Sirvi, two Bougainvillean scholars and activists of the 1980s and 1990s: "Bougainvilleans . . . never perceived themselves as inferior to white people. While the colonial administration maintained its paternal attitude, which treated the local population like children and assumed for themselves superiority as their right, Bougainvilleans retained their dignity, even as they appeared to comply. They were biding their time while they worked out how best to rise above the domination of their land and their lives."[53] This description as well as the episode of the laughing man in Bougainville's book provide an important critical context for viewing the performance of the Bougainvillean actor, director, and social activist William Takaku as Friday in *Daniel Defoe's Robinson Crusoe*.

The film's location is identified in the press only as Papua New Guinea (henceforth PNG),[54] though PNG is a nation-state composed of several land masses, including Bougainville Island, Takaku's birthplace. Bougainville Island, while bound by international law and UN mandate as a part of the PNG nation, has made several efforts to declare its independence.[55] Given their linguistic, cultural, and ethnic links, the people of Bougainville assert their commonality with the Solomon Island, rather than PNG. Yet since Louis de Bougainville chose to name the island after himself in the late 1760s, right up through the 1990s when *Daniel Defoe's Robinson Crusoe* was being filmed, the people of Bougainville Island have had to content with one kind of colonization after another.[56] In 1988 the national government of PNG, the Bougainville Copper Limited (a subsidiary of Rio Tinoto, an Australian-British corporation), and the Australian government conspired together to force Bougainville to accept mining of the island on a scale that produced the largest man-made hole in the southern hemisphere, and displaced people from their home villages to be rounded up in crowded corporate housing far from their traditional sources of food.[57] Bougainville activists and rebels staged a significant resistance movement; hostilities claimed the lives of between fifteen and twenty thousand people during the decade of 1988 to 1997, before New Zealand helped to broker a peace treaty.[58] During what came to be known as the Battle for Bougainville,[59] William Takaku left Bougainville to pursue this theater and film career.[60] Given the ongoing violence taking place on Bougainville during the shooting of *Daniel Defoe's Robinson Crusoe*, it is unlikely that the film's location, identified as Papua New Guinea, would have included Takaku's home island. However, the dialog's references to "Friday's island" in the film, both as a place from which Friday is exiled and as the destination for the pair's eventual escape, and where after a safe homecoming Friday is killed by the Europeans who arrive to capture additional slaves and also rescue Crusoe, certainly evoke the contemporary politics of Bougainville Island during the 1990s.

Takaku's Friday shows strong resistance to the enslavement of body and the tyranny of names that Brosnan's Crusoe at first deploys against him. Two of the most iconic and most illustrated moments in Defoe's novel involve the scenes that occur just shortly after Crusoe has rescued Friday from being eaten by the cannibals, only to become his named property instead. The first occurs when Friday, in apparent gratitude for his life being spared, "kneel'd down again, kiss'd the Ground, and laid his Head upon the Ground, and taking me by the Foot, set my Foot upon his Head; this it seems was in token of searing to be my Slave for ever" (147). This scene is also staged in the film, but with a significant twist at the end: when Takaku lifts Brosnan's foot, he places it not on his head but on his shoulder while looking up toward Brosnan-Crusoe and the camera; with a sudden move Takaku rotates Brosnan's foot so that "James Bond" falls on the ground disarmed of his gun by Takaku. Although this powerful move is slightly deflated by the fact that Takaku is shown holding Brosnan's gun backward, the reversal of Defoe's original scene clearly signals that Takaku's performance of Friday will be dramatically different from Defoe's imagined character.

The revised head-food gesture scene is followed closely in the film by the second iconic moment found in Defoe's novel related to Crusoe's intended reeducation of Friday. Shortly after their initial meeting, Crusoe makes a demonstration for Friday of shooting a parrot in order to teach Friday a lesson about the power that Crusoe's gun affords him: "Pointing to the Parrot, and to my Gun, and to the Ground under the Parrot, to let him see I would make it fall, I made him understand that I would shoot and kill the Bird; according I fir'd and bad him look, and immediately he saw the Parrot fall, he stood like one frightened . . . if I would have let him, he would have worshipp'd me and my Gun" (153). Brosnan's performance of this demonstration plays out much like Defoe describes, but Takaku's response to the killing of (not a parrot but) the bat with his gun is certainly not one of "worship." Instead, after Brosnan congratulates himself for having successfully demonstrated his gun, Takaku picks up an object off the ground and throws it expertly into the trees, felling a second bat himself. He then walks over, picks up to the two dead bats, and holds them up side by side in an unspoken gesture of "so what, anyone can do that," reminiscent of the indifference of the "laughing" man Bougainville describes in his 1772 book. The combined effect of these two scenes, in which Defoe's gestures of colonial domination are subject to significant reversal through Takaku's embodiment, is to render ironic the insistence of the film's full title (for its U.S. release at least) of *Daniel Defoe's Robinson Crusoe*, because the politics of the Crusoe-Friday relationship are clearly *not* Defoe's.

While these pivotal scenes of human interactions are dramatically reversed in the film, the island as location of the action is similarly transformed by Takaku's performance. The film significantly truncates the time that Crusoe is alone on the island as compared to how that time period is depicted in the novel, which likely contributed to the criticism that the "film's main flaw is its pacing . . . Crusoe's shipwreck and his first days, weeks, and months on the island are skimmed over in about fifteen minutes of on-screen time."[61] While perhaps unsatisfactory to some critics, the consequence of the artistic choice to limit Crusoe's solo screen time is to bring the ratio of screen time between Friday and Crusoe into greater balance, minimizing the valorization of Crusoe and increasing the viewers' exposure to Friday's point of view. As a result, the island as location comes to serve less of a platform for a performance focused on the solo castaway idiom that has been used by some critics, such as Cuddon, to demarcate a work as a Robinsonade. Instead, the island as location in the 1997 film functions more as a testing ground for the relationship between the two men; this shift means the film spends less time glamorizing the a priori colonial myth and more time scrutinizing the racial politics that undergird colonialism. The island's climate and environmental factors demand little of the two men, a "gentle isle" scenario similar to *The Female American* and that facilitates the film's ideological work, which is directed as the reeducation of Crusoe away from his initial racism, toward the ability to see Friday as a friend. The artistry and politics of the film, in this regard, reflect Hollywood values from post–civil rights America, in a stark contrast to the neocolonial, postindustrial, corporate globalist politics actively scaring South Pacific islands of the 1990s.

As the catalyst needed to initiate Crusoe's transformation, a fissure in the two men's relationship emerges when Takaku's Friday comes to understand the meaning of the name "master" that Brosnan's Crusoe has taught Friday to use. Extrapolating the implications for himself, Takaku-Friday declares forcefully, "I am not a slave," before walking out of the camp he has been sharing with Brosnan-Crusoe. The next several images involve some panoramic sweeps of the island, cut in by shots of Friday and Crusoe living independently from one another, and Takaku-Friday in particular being shown as competent in his own survival skills within the landscape. The island is shown to be fully capable of sustaining both men, each using their own differing survival techniques (indigenous and imported), with plenty of room for both. Takaku-Friday appears comfortable in his independence and isolation (or at least the film does not examine the separation from his point of view). In contrast, Brosnan's Crusoe is troubled by the division. Crusoe declares, "Something had to be done," words that are spoken over the image of Crusoe walking out of the trees toward the beach where Friday is fishing, using what appears to be his own cultural techniques. In the scene's climax, Friday stands up from the fire he is tending on the beach and hands Crusoe a piece of cooked fish in a gesture that positions Friday as the generous provider to Crusoe's grateful recipient—a gesture that recalls Louis de Bougainville's "laughing" man feeding the starving French sailors. The fireside beach scene also reverses an earlier scene in the film that took place when Friday brought breakfast to Crusoe while wearing the chains that had been placed on his legs by a suspicious and fearful Crusoe—itself a gesture reminiscent of the description Havini and Sirvi provide of the coping mechanism employed during "colonial times [when] Bougainvilleans retained their dignity, even as they appeared to comply."[62] With the echo of that earlier food-focused scene in mind, the moment of reconciliation staged on the beach as the freely generous gifting of fish by Takaku-Friday to Brosnan-Crusoe not only is legible as a reunion of two people but reads like a dismantling of the racial hierarchy previously depicted. Takaku's Friday is able to offer the bounty of the sea to Brosnan's Crusoe on his own terms. In this way, the island has served both Friday's and Crusoe's needs individually, but also provided the conduit for their reconciliation.

LORA E. GERIGUIS

Up to this point in the film, the weather has been mild and sunny, sustaining rather than challenging, in a "gentle isle" format that demands little narrative attention. However, that changes suddenly when the reconciliation process described above is concluded in a scene that is staged in a downpour. As the two men shake hands, the rain is used to emotive effect as it runs down both of their smiling faces and elicits their laughter. The slow-motion footage represents the highest point in the evolution of their relationship from master-servant to equal humans. During that scene Takaku-Friday also tells Brosnan-Crusoe his "spirit name," thereby exorcising the possessive nature of the name given to him by Crusoe. After the handshake scene, Takaku-Friday and Brosnan-Crusoe recognize the rain they are standing in indicates that the rainy season has begun and therefore escape from the island to the sea is unwise; in response, they determine to stay on the island and prepare to fight the "cannibals" who will inevitably return. *Daniel Defoe's Robinson Crusoe* portrays the rainy season precipitation as part of the island's naturally occurring weather cycles during which human events simply take place, instead of partaking in the colonial discourse that frequently treats weather (particularly storms and rain) as a hostile force intent on challenging the colonialists' survival in a foreign landscape (reminiscent of Unca's fear of the rainy season, but which does not materialize in that "gentle isle" Robinsonade). Hence, Brosnan-Crusoe's *acceptance of* Takaku-Friday's humanity coincides with Crusoe's *adaptation to* the climate of the island that Friday already apprehends.

With Crusoe's racism seemly resolved, the dynamics of the newly equalized relationship in *Daniel Defoe's Robinson Crusoe* play out in flashes of merriment and cooperation, scenes that are all staged in fair weather. This episode is cut short, however, by the return of the neighboring people to the island for another cannibal feast. In preparation for their battle, both Brosnan-Crusoe and Takaku-Friday are shown praying according to their different religions in tandem with one another. Further, both men are shown wearing facial paint of a similar design as each other, and successfully pairing up to battle the cannibals by setting off explosions that systemically destroy the camp Crusoe built. During the battle, Crusoe is injured, which forces Friday to evacuate Crusoe to his home island for healing.

While on Friday's island European slavers suddenly appear and kill Friday and kidnap members of his community, in fact the rescue of Crusoe is enabled by these ongoing activities of the slave trade. Despite the film's portrayal of Crusoe's growth toward recognizing Friday's humanity, the emotional and political complication of the mechanism of Crusoe's rescue is hurried over in the rush toward the film's more convenient heterosexual romantic denouement. Friday's death in the film, not portrayed by Defoe until *The Farther Adventures of Robinson* Crusoe

(1719), leaves Crusoe to return home alone, to find Mary, the woman he fought a dual over that precipitated his travels in the first place, faithfully tending the flowers outside of an idealized, domestic cottage, seemingly awaiting his return. Nevertheless, despite the fact that the film's arc leads to Crusoe's return to Brosnan's native Scotland (not England) to be reunited with Mary, and despite having included a portrayal of Friday's death, the final pairing viewed in the film is not Crusoe-Mary but Crusoe-Friday. The film actually concludes with a reprised image of that rainy reversal handshake between Takaku and Crusoe, set in slow motion and augmented with a voice-over by Crusoe: "For the rest of my days, I would think often and long of the man who gave me the greatest gift of all, my life when I had all but lost it, and his friendship unto death." Allowing the rain of the South Pacific to supersede the differently wet British climate reframes the film's true climax away from the gain of homecoming to the loss of friendship caused by slavery and racism. When this final emotional cost accounting in the film is compared to the wealth accumulation measured at the conclusion of Defoe's novel, we can see again the difference in the ideological positions of Daniel Defoe's *Robinson Crusoe* (1719, novel) and *Daniel Defoe's Robinson Crusoe* (1997, film).

Just four years after the film's release, which coincided with the end of the hostilities known as the Battle for Bougainville, the island was granted status as the Autonomous Region of Bougainville within that nation of Papua New Guinea in 2001.[63] Takaku, in his narration of a video about the 2009 Bougainville Reeds Festival at Kieta, one event in a series of reconciliation and cultural revitalization efforts that continued in the decade after hostilities ceased, put such efforts into the even broader historical context of industrialized global corporate imperialism: "At this times [sic] when the world is facing great change and uncertainty, many indigenous people of the world are challenged whether to keep our culture or allow it to die as we follow our developmental efforts that are based on the powerful western orientations and influences that sooner or later might surely see the demise of our Melanesian languages and cultures."[64] Through his performances, we can glimpse Takaku's aspirations for human reconciliation and a reversal of the cultural demise forecast by the storm clouds perpetually forming over the horizon of his home island.[65] While some critics have described Brosnan's performance as "laughable" or "forgettable,"[66] when Takaku's involvement in the film and the Friday-Crusoe relationship are put center stage and attention is paid to both the place and time contexts of the production, the film's significance becomes elevated and dignified. Without accounting for William Takaku's breakout performance as the embodiment of the personhood of the Friday character (as a type for the unnumbered victims of colonial domination) augmented by the depiction of the natural environment and climate of the location, the antiracist gestures made in this Robinsonade and its significant reversals of Defoe's own colonial ideology cannot be fully appreciated.

THE NO-FOOTPRINT NEOCOLONIAL ROBINSONADE: *CAST AWAY* (2000)

In contrast to the traces of Bougainvillean culture detectable in the Takaku-Brosnan Robinsonade, the island episodes of *Cast Away* (2000),[67] though shot in Fiji, manage to appear completely removed from any specific time or place. Tom Hanks plays Chuck Noland, in the Crusoesque role and performs opposite the "Wilson" volleyball, the Friday substitute. Even more so than in Defoe's novel, *The Female American*, and the 1997 Miramax *Robinson Crusoe* film, the island of *Cast Away* is stripped of all indication of any prior or neighboring human civilization. Noland's island bears evidence of no indigenous inhabitants or even previous visitors. After a computer-generated special-effects storm snatches Noland's plane from the sky and deposits him on the island, the flotsam he gathers from the wreck serves as synecdoche of the "real" world of global commerce, which Noland is shown dominating in the opening of the film, but nothing more proximate to the island itself than that is seen. As a result, Noland's island serves as a better model of the "remote" quality emphasized in Cuddon's definition of "desert island fiction" than do the islands of *The Female American* or the 1997 *Daniel Defoe's Robinson Crusoe*, both of which are demonstrably adjacent to other islands and even include evidence of preexisting cultures and peoples.

Why did the late 1990s produce a second Robinsonade film set in the South Pacific? Tom Hanks is quoted as saying he wanted to make the film to "reinvent the 'stuck on a desert island' concept. He felt that up to that point, most people's association of the idea was limited to either 'Robinson Crusoe' or 'Gilligan's Island' and that there was room for a new take, one rooted in the modern day."[68] The resulting "modern" take portrayed by the DreamWorks production equates to an erasure of indigenous people in favor of a world where Western global commerce is contrasted to scenes of empty, "virgin" spaces devoid of any people with prior claims to the land. What is old is neocolonial again. To underscore this point, Hanks was repeatedly praised by critics for the "superb" acting skills he demonstrated by being able to "carry *Cast Away* all by himself for about two-thirds of its running time."[69] Noland is altered by the island's environment both mentally and physically. Noland adapts to the rhythms and routines of his new environment, marking out time on trees and rocks; he moves from measuring time in minutes before the plane crash to measuring time on the island in months, years, and seasons.[70] Noland's relationship to the island, its climate, and other challenging environmental conditions makes demands on the castaway that are also written visibly on the actor's body by the loss of fifty pounds he famously endured in the course of production.[71] This physical transformation, seen by many as important for his performance, linked his initial pudgy appearance at the beginning of the film with the excesses of the "real" and "remote" world he has left. The revelation of his lean physique (introduced in the film by a "four years later" indicator written over shot of shimmering water) is a tribute to the demands of survival that the narrow range of resources available on the island have required of him.

Aside from the visually spectacular storm scene that perpetuates the plane crash, Noland's direct exposure to wet weather on the island is minimized by his discovery of the cave, where he rides out the one or two other storms that are depicted; however, a point is made to show that the sounds of rain and the flashes of lightening are stimuli to which he becomes sufficiently accustomed to sleep through toward the end of the island episode. The film's memorable rain scene occurs after he is back in Memphis. Noland and Kathy Frears (played by Helen Hunt) have their long-anticipated reunion/goodbye kiss in a rainstorm on a dark night, but there the rain comes across as little more than the heavy-handed metaphor for the tragedy of their doomed love affair.[72] The Memphis rain serves as a rather blunt pathetic fallacy in *Cast Away*, while the weather on the South Pacific island is little more than an unfortunate inconvenience mostly avoided in tourist fashion. The option to use weather conditions on the island to suggest a realism in the man-against-nature focus of the island episode is largely sacrificed in the film, in favor of focusing on the development of the Noland-Wilson relationship, which forms the heart of this modern repackaging of the colonial myth.

Though the solo human on the island, Noland does have a helpmate: Wilson's creation aids Noland's survival on the island, just as Wilson's loss at sea materially aids Noland's reentry into civilization. Wilson-Friday is a perfect reflection and fulfillment of Noland-Crusoe's inner psyche; as such he only laughs when told to and knows to exit the stage prior to Noland's rescue/return to the "real" world. The Wilson-Friday function is to serve Noland-Crusoe as long as he is needed and then be lost at sea when his ongoing presence would make an awkward accessory for Noland's homecoming TV appearances—a plot line for the disposable "other" that is rooted in the *early* modern day. While a shiny new, in-the-box, faceless Wilson volleyball appears again at the end of the film on the passenger seat of the car, the effect is comfortably humorous and the viewer is left assuming Noland will find a more appropriate conversation partner now that he has returned. In those terms, *Cast Away* has achieved the status Tom Hanks sought: this "modern" neocolonial, postindustrial myth has devised a "better mouse trap" for packaging and monetizing the "other" as a friendly piece of sporting equipment.[73] The Noland-Wilson bond has gone on to highly recognizable pop-cultural status, with unnumbered references made to the famous "Wilson!" line made in advertisements and other outlets.[74] Given its recasting of the troubling racial politics represented by Friday in Defoe's text, with the convenient plastic-wrapped Wilson substitute, *Cast Away* invites its twenty-first-century Western audience to indulge in the colonial myth—like so many colonially inflected tropical travel advertisements—seemly freed of any of its racist baggage because no person is shown being colonized. However, the film's erasure of the human (colonial and other) history that has played out on the islands of the South Pacific, including Fiji, amounts to a fantasy built on an imaginative genocide and a special-effects-simulated land grab.

Once Noland returns to Memphis and has been given a haircut, a shave, and a new set of clothes, his look is one of tanned fitness, as though he has returned home after a rejuvenating vacation in a tropical paradise. The film's final image is a close-up of Noland's face searching the empty, desert horizon. Unlike the Miramax *Daniel Defoe's Robinson Crusoe* film, no memory of the island episode interrupts the climax of the DreamWorks film, which instead focuses on Noland's future alone. This "modern" Robinsonade keeps Robinson Crusoe center stage, and the margins strikingly void, as if there are worlds yet for him to discover. The (neo)colonial ideology is heavy in the air as the credits roll. While the film reveals no traces of an indigenous presence on the island, the *Cast Away* credits include the following message of thanks to "The Matagali of Mosesi Namomo of the Village of Yanuya, The Native Land Trust Board of Fiji, Fiji Visitor's Bureau." Further, we are told, "the production employed several local Fiji islanders in the surrounding archipelago, including the neighboring Mana Island about a mile away. The locals were allowed to keep some of the supplies and tools as tokens of their help."[75] Whether these gifts were of value to the recipients or mere "trinkets" of the sort scoffed at by the "laughing" man of Louis de Bougainville's *Voyage* is unknown.

Any impact that the Matagali people may have had on the final product of *Cast Away* is illegible. The film's ideological gunpowder is reserved instead for questions pertinent only to the world-weary, Western tourist who vacations on Fiji and hopes that rain will not spoil his holiday; the film completely erases those people who have lived and died on those islands for centuries by learning to adapt to the climate. In comparison to the palpable fingerprints William Takaku left on the celluloid that recorded his performance as Friday, the Matagali people of Fiji were not permitted to leave any traceable footprints on Noland's island.

SUSTAINED WINDS: THE LONGEVITY AND PLIABILITY OF THE ROBINSONADE

What Louis de Bougainville wrote in the eighteenth century of the rainy seasons he experienced in the South Pacific—"one tempest comes on before the other is gone off"[76]—can also be said of the oppression and exploitation that persists along the continuum of early modern European colonialism to contemporary corporate global neocolonialism. The people of the Autonomous Region of Bougainville continue to fight for self-determination. After setting several dates for a referendum vote on the island's political future, which the PNG government made contingent on the complete disposal of weapons dating back to the civil war of the 1990s, a nonbinding vote to choose between either "greater autonomy from PNG" or complete "independence" was staged beginning on November 23, 2019. When the counting was done and the vote certified, a "97.7 percent majority voted for option two, in a voter turnout of 87.4 percent which was a national electoral record."[77] However, that vote by the Bougainvillean people is dependent on ratification by the PNG government, which to date has not yet occurred. The unfinished work of the UN International Decade for the Eradication of Colonialism, first declared in 1990, has necessitated its renewal for two additional decades (2001–2011 and 2011–2020), thereby creating an overlap between those decolonizing efforts and the 2019 tercentennial commemoration of the 1719 publication of *Robinson Crusoe* and the subsequent three-hundred-year history of the Robinsonade.[78]

The pliability of the Robinsonade, in its varying levels of acclimatization to its diverse historical contexts, allows the form to either reproduce or challenge the colonial ideology that Defoe's *Robinson Crusoe* has so long evoked. When a Robinsonade is read for both its relationship to Defoe's themes and its own particular time and place contexts, it becomes possible to discern conspicuous and telling gaps in the foundational colonial myth. When a Robinsonade narrates those gaps or a scholar explicates them, newly recovered voices can be made to be heard over the din of destructive storms that have blown for centuries across the landscapes of both real and imagined islands.

NOTES

1. At the time of the 1703 storm, Defoe "was in a well-built brick House . . . but opening the door to attempt an Escape into a Garden, the Danger was so apparent, that they all thought fit to surrender to the Disposal of Almighty Providence, and expect their Graves in the Ruins of the House, rather than to meet most certain Destruction in the open Garden." Daniel Defoe ("The Storm: or a Collection of the Most Remarkable Causalities and Disasters Which Happen'd in the Late Dreadful Tempest, Both by Sea and Land," 1704),

The Storm, ed. Richard Hamblyn (London: Penguin, 2003), 30–31. All references to *The Storm* are to this edition.
2. Defoe wrote three texts that were originally titled and published individually: "The Lay-Man's Sermon upon the Late Storm" (February 1704, prose), "The Storm: or a Collection of the Most Remarkable Casualties and Disasters Which Happen'd in the Late Dreadful Tempest, Both by Sea and Land" (July 1704, prose), and "An Essay on the Late Storm" (August 1704, poetry). See Defoe, *The Storm*. Defoe's earlier short-form publications were *The Shortest-Way with the Dissenters* (1702) and *Hymn to the Pillory* (1703).
3. Hamblyn, "Introduction," in *The Storm*, x.
4. For example, the weather terminology of *Moll Flanders* (1722) is predominantly metaphorical (e.g., "I saw the cloud, though I did not foresee the storm"; 50) or else is used in descriptions of uncomplicated sea travel or climate observations (e.g., she suggests settling in Carolina based on its "warm weather"; 553). Daniel Defoe, *Moll Flanders: A Norton Critical Edition*, ed. Albert J. Rivero (New York: Norton, 2003). *Roxana* (1724) is littered with many metaphorical uses of weather, but also with nearly as many actual weather episodes as in the travel-based works of *Robinson Crusoe* and *Captain Singleton* (1720); Roxana and Amy play contrasting roles in their responses to the fear of death raised by the threat of drowning during a storm at sea. Daniel Defoe, *Roxana*, ed. John Mullan (Oxford: Oxford University Press, 1996), 148–151. In *Captain Singleton*, the mutineers turned pirates have "their motions dictated by the petulance of weather . . . [and the] nature and impact of the weather are described in great detail in the text." Lora Geriguis, "'A Vast Howling Wilderness': The Persistence of Space and Placelessness in Daniel Defoe's *Captain Singleton*," in *Topographies of the Imagination: New Approaches to Daniel Defoe*, ed. Kit Kincaid, Katherine Ellison, and Holly Faith Nelson (New York: AMS Press, 2014), 191.
5. "Understandings and experiences of the weather figured in the process of enlightenment and modernization." Jan Golinski, *British Weather and the Climate of Enlightenment* (Chicago: University of Chicago Press, 2007), xii, 4.
6. Defoe, *The Storm*, 24.
7. Maximillian E. Novak, *Daniel Defoe: Master of Fictions, His Life and Ideas* (Oxford: Oxford University Press, 2001), 220.
8. Charles Morton made a point of including the discoveries of Royal Society members in his textbook for students, *Compendium Physicae* (ca. 1686). I. Bernard Cohen, "The Compendium Physicae of Charles Morton (1627–1698)," *Isis* 33.6 (June 1942): 658. See also Paula Backscheider, *Daniel Defoe: His Life* (Baltimore: Johns Hopkins University Press, 1989), 15–16.
9. Novak, *Daniel Defoe*, 222.
10. Ibid., 87.
11. Ibid., 536.
12. Golinski, *British Weather*, 4.
13. William Shakespeare, *Richard II* (II:i) (1595). John Guant's lines are often referred to as the "specter'd isle" speech.
14. Kathleen Wilson, *The Island Race: Englishness, Empire and Gender in the Eighteenth Century* (London: Routledge, 2003), 55–56.
15. Golinski, *British Weather*, 6, 5.
16. J. A. Cuddon (revised by C. E. Preston), "Desert Island Fiction," in *The Penguin Dictionary of Literary Terms and Literary Theory*, 4th ed. (London: Penguin, 1998), 215–216. Earlier editions of this work were produced by Cuddon only and titled *A Dictionary of Literary Terms* (London: Penguin, 1977, 1979, 1991).
17. For an excellent study of an example of a Robinsonade that makes its "central" world a European country other than the more typical England, Germany, France, or America,

see Lina Lamanauskaite Geriguis, "Discovering the Lithuanian Reinscription of *Robinson Crusoe*," *Lituanus: Lithuanian Quarterly Journal of Arts and Sciences* 54.4 (Winter 2008): 61–75.

18. While "Robinsonade" does not appear as an entry in the 1979 edition of Cuddon's work, it was added in the 1998 fourth edition "revised" by C. E. Preston following the death of Cuddon in 1996. What is unclear is whether the idea for adding "Robinsonade" as an entry to the 1998 edition was Cuddon's or Preston's given that Cuddon "also left proposals for many new entries which he could not himself finish" (C. E. Preston, "Preface to the Fourth Edition," xviii). In any case, the "Robinsonade" entry added is brief and focused primarily on identifying the term as German, along with listing a few exemplary German titles; the entry concludes with a cross-reference back to the long-standing "desert island fiction" entry. As a consequence, the Penguin publication limits the term "Robinsonade" to a far more narrowly national meaning than is employed here, where "desert island fiction" and "Robinsonade" are used basically interchangeably.

19. Edward Simon, "Unca Eliza Winkfield and the Fantasy of Non-colonial Conversion in *The Female American*," *Women's Studies* 45.7 (2016): 649–659.

20. Patrick Vinton Krick and Jean-Louis Rallu, eds., *The Growth and Collapse of Pacific Island Societies: Archaeological and Demographic Perspectives* (Honolulu: University of Hawaii Press, 2007), 1.

21. Marta Kvande, "'Had You No Lands of Your Own?' Seeking Justice in *The Female American* (1767)," *Women's Studies* 45.7 (2016): 685.

22. The London edition title page of *The Female American*, which lists the two lending libraries the novel was printed for as owned by Francis Nobel and John Nobel, is included in Michelle Burnham and James Freitas's second edition of *The Female American* (Peterborough: Broadview, 2014), 41. Further references are to this edition and are given parenthetically.

23. For the source of the Pocahontas myth, see John Smith, *A Generall Historie of Virginia* (1624), in *Captain John Smith's America: Selections from His Writings*, ed. John Lankford (New York: Harper & Row, 1967).

24. Simon, "Unca Eliza Winkfield," 650.

25. The plots of both *The Female American* and *Robinson Crusoe* are set in the seventeenth century, which makes Unca Eliza's claim of priority (if not reality) at least plausible. Unca Eliza indicates that her parents met at the time of the 1622 massacre of the English colonists at Jamestown. The couple were married about six months after meeting, and Princess Unca "prov[ed] with child from the night of their marriage" (55). Therefore, since Unca Elza notes that she was "four and twenty" (62) at the time of her arrival on her island, that would date her island episode as beginning in approximately 1646, about a dozen years prior what Crusoe's journal records the date of his being castaway on "the Island of Despair," 30 September 1659.

26. Kvande has correctly observed that "we should not take the dismissive reviews [in 1767 London periodicals] as definitive of the novel's reception" more broadly. Kvande, "'Had You No Lands of Your Own?," 686. Burnham and Freitas note that text crossed the Atlantic to reach the book sellers in Massachusetts by 1800 and Vermont in 1814 (39), but about which they "have located no reviews . . . in American periodicals" (9).

27. Excerpts taken from the *Monthly Review; or, Literary Journal* 36 (1767), and the *Critical Review; or, Annals of Literature* 23 (1767), both quoted in an appendix by Burnham and Freitas (249).

28. Wilson, *Island Race*, 88.

29. Ibid., 90. "The vast troves of information on distant lands and peoples garnered on the voyages [of Cook, Bougainville, and Hawkesworth] swelled the seven lines devoted to the

South Pacific in the [1768] first edition of the *Encyclopaedia Britannica* to forty double-column pages in the third edition of 1788–97." Ibid., 58–59.
30. Kvande, "'Had You No Lands of Your Own?,'" 684.
31. Ibid., 684.
32. Simon, "Unca Eliza Winkfield," 649.
33. Ibid., 650.
34. In contrast, Crusoe has to determine the threats on his island by trial and error and then painstakingly write his own journal.
35. Even later in the text when she fears she has been trapped in the underground tunnels of the temple by an earthquake, she instead finds that her fears were unfounded in that the latch of the hatch simply was not pulled back far enough (97).
36. Burnham and Freitas, "Introduction," 20.
37. Ibid., 20.
38. Kvande, "'Had You No Lands of Your Own?,'" 692.
39. For example, the waves of the first storm she experiences dash open the chest, thereby rendering the contents of clothing inside, which otherwise might have remained unusable, accessible to her (71).
40. See the episode of the later storm and earthquake, which she thought at first had buried her in the underground cavern before she realized the bolt of the hatch simply needed further sliding, after which she was freed (89–90).
41. "My way was frequently obstructed by trees torn up with their roots, and scattered here and there, and the earth in many places covered with the bodies of dead bird, goats, &c. and the carcasses of other small animals, whose names I knew not. . . . Many of the rocks were rent in pieces, and their broken fragments made an horrid appearance" (89).
42. Christopher Loar, "How to Say Things with Guns: Military Technology and the Politics of *Robinson Crusoe*," *Eighteenth-Century Fiction* 19.1–2 (2006): 5.
43. From the minutes of the fifty-ninth plenary meeting of the United Nations General Assembly, 22 November 1988. See United Nations, "The United Nations and Decolonization," https://www.un.org/dppa/decolonization/en/history/international-decades.
44. *Daniel Defoe's Robinson Crusoe* (1997); film by Miramax; directed by Rod Hardy and George T. Miller; staring Pierce Brosnan as Robinson Crusoe and William Takaku as Friday, Polly Walker as Mary, Ian Hart as Daniel Defoe, James Frain as Robert, the publisher; executive produced by Bob Weinstein; edited by Greg Feather.
45. Clark Douglas, "Robinson Crusoe," *365movieguy.com*, 22 March 2015, www.365movieguy.com/review/3/22/robinson-crusoe. Doc Ezra also calls the movie "laughable" and urges that "if you must watch a movie about a guy on an island, rent Cast Away (at your own risk) instead." Doc Ezra, "Robinson Crusoe (2001)," *Needcoffee.com*, 7 December 2003, www.needcoffee.com/2003/12/07/robinson-crusoe-2001-dvd-review/.
46. Barbara Shulgasser-Parker, "Robinson Crusoe (1997)," www.commonsensemedia.org/movie-reviews/robinson-crusoe-1997.
47. Louis de Bougainville, *A Voyage Round the World Performed by Order of His Most Christian Majesty, in the Years 1766, 1767, 1768, and 1769* (1772), trans. John Reinhold Forster (Cambridge: Cambridge University Press, 2011), 312.
48. Regis Tove Stella, *Imagining the Other: The Representation of the Papua New Guinean Subject* (Honolulu: University of Hawaii Press, 2007), 2.
49. Forster also amends Bougainville's text with footnote "corrections," including an expansion of the list of prior circumnavigations.
50. Bougainville, *Voyage Round the World*, 335–336.
51. James E. Cormack, *Isle of Solomon* (Washington, DC: Review and Herald, 1944).
52. Bougainville, *Voyage Round the World*, 360.

53. Marilyn Taleo Havini and Josie Tankuanani Sirvi, eds., *As Mothers of the Land: The Birth of Bougainville Women for Peace and Freedom* (Canberra: Pandanus Books, 2003), xv–xvi. The authors of this work are themselves Bougainvilleans who participated in the Bougainvillean resistance movement of the late 1980s and 1990s.
54. "Trivia: Robinson Crusoe (1997)," *IMDb*, www.imdb.com/title/tt0117496/trivia?ref_=tt_trv_trv.
55. The modern era of Bougainville's efforts for self-determination can be dated to the United Nations' Resolution 1514 of 14 December 1960, namely the Declaration on Granting of Independence to Colonial Countries and Peoples, which treated "Papua New Guinea" as the umbrella political entity that encompassed several neighboring islands, including New Britain and Bougainville. "A Bougainvillean submission to the 1964 UN Visiting Mission on Decolonization objected to the alignment of Bougainville with the Territories of Papua and New Guinea. The submission, which was part of a continuing cry to be reunited with the Solomon Islands, was ignored by all the political players. . . . In 1975, PNG received independence (16 Sept), but Bougainville preempted this with its own declaration of independence on Sept 1, 1975." Havini and Sirvi, *As Mothers of the Land*, xvi–xvii.
56. The island was occupied by Germany in the late nineteenth century. See Charles D. Rowley, *The Australians in German New Guinea, 1914–1921* (Melbourne: Melbourne University Press, 1959). The people of Bougainville were prey to the "black-birders" who forced people from Bougainvillea into indentured work agreements to provide the manpower to run the sugar cane fields of North Queensland from 1870 to 1905 and invaded by the Japanese in World War II (1942).
57. Havini and Sirvi, *As Mothers of the Land*, xv. See also Sinclair Dinnen, Ron May, Anthony J. Regan, eds., *Challenging the State: The Sandline Affair in Papua New Guinea* (Canberra: National Center for Development Studies, 1997).
58. See *Experience Bougainville*, a (21 January 2014) video sponsored by the Christensen Fund (Palo Alto, CA), which includes interviews with combatants in the civil war discussing the politics that precipitated the conflict and the after math. www.youtube.com/watch?v=_sCxL0oF0rs.
59. Havini and Sirvi, *As Mothers of the Land*, xx.
60. For a brief biography of William Takaku (died 2011), see "William Takaku." *Alchetron*, 24 March 2018, https://alchetron.com/William-Takaku. See also Nancy Sullivan's "Interview with Albert Toro," in *Cultural Producers in Perilous State: Editing Events, Documenting Change*, ed. George E. Marcus (Chicago: University of Chicago Press, 1997), 347.
61. Holly E. Ordway, "Robinson Crusoe" (re: Walt Disney Studies Home Entertainment release 2002), *Dvdtalk.com*, 17 February 2002, www.dvdtalk.com/reviews/3419/robinson-crusoe/.
62. Havini and Sirvi, *As Mothers of the Land*, xvi.
63. See the full text of the Bougainville Peace Agreement (30 August 2001) here: https://peacemaker.un.org/png-bougainville-agreement2001.
64. William Takaku, narrator, "Bougainville Reed Festival at Kieta" (1:11–1:38), https://youtu.be/jX2_BinvFNc.
65. William Takaku died in January 2011. An obituary, "Farewell Takaku, You Were Truly a Legend" (7 February 2011) by Margaret Munjin, published in the *National* (PNG) newspaper, described his death as "a huge loss to the nation." She went on to chastise the PNG government for staying "silent over his death [which amounted to] a slap in the face of the people of the Autonomous Region of Bougainville."
66. Douglas, "Robinson Crusoe."
67. *Cast Away* (DreamWorks and 20th Century Fox, 2000), starring Tom Hanks and Helen Hunt; directed by Robert Zemeckis; written by William Broyles Jr.

68. "Trivia: *Cast Away* (2000)," *IMDb*, www.imdb.com/title/tt0162222/trivia.
69. Roger Ebert, "Cast Away," *Rogerebert.com*, 22 December 2000, www.rogerebert.com/reviews/cast-away-2000. Tom Hanks has said that playing so many scenes alone was "rough," significantly more so than the requirement to lose weight. "You're not sharing the storytelling lifting with someone you can react off of. It's almost like making a silent movie; you have to tell every aspect of the story physically, being totally alone." James Poniewozik, "Saving Tom Hanks," *Time Europe* 157.1 (8 January 2001), http://content.time.com/time/world/article/0,8599,2056298,00.html.
70. For an analysis of time in the film, see Carol Kaufman-Scarborough, "Two Perspectives on the Tyranny of Time: Polychronicity and Monochronicity as Depicted in *Cast Away*," *Journal of American Culture* 26.1 (March 2003): 87–95.
71. "Trivia: *Cast Away* (2000)."
72. One popular conspiracy theory argues that Kelly was already having an affair with Dr. Jerry Lovett (played by Chris North) based on the age of her child when Noland returns home after only "50 months." Pete Elmst, "The Secret Affair in Cast Away: Kelly Frears Should Be Ashamed of Herself," *Applaudience*, 25 November 2016, https://medium.com/applaudience/the-secret-affair-of-cast-away-7b7f9999a303.
73. Replica "Wilson Cast Away" volleyballs are available for sale at Walmart, on Amazon.com, and at other retailers for about $15.25, a roughly 50 percent markup from regular volleyballs of similar quality.
74. During the summer of 2018, "Flo" of the long-running Progressive insurance company advertisement campaign had a spot running on U.S. television based on a *Cast Away* motif, including the famous "Wilson!" line.
75. "Trivia: *Cast Away* (2000)."
76. Bougainville, *Voyage Round the World*, 336.
77. "Bougainville Referendum Process Electoral Process Formally Ends," Radio New Zealand, 23 January 2020, www.rnz.co.nz/international/pacific-news/407953/bougainville-referendum-electoral-process-formally-ends. For a timeline of the referendum campaign and voting process as well as arguments and predictions about the outcome of the vote, see Henzy Yakham, "Stage Set for Referendum on Bougainville's Future," *Papua New Guinea Post-Courier*, 18 January 2019, https://postcourier.com.pg/stage-set-referendum-bougainvilles-future/. See also "Ball Rolling on Bougainville Referendum," Radio New Zealand, 23 May 2016, www.radionz.co.nz/international/pacific-news/304534/ball-rolling-on-bougainville-referendum.
78. See United Nations, "United Nations and Decolonization."

8

ROBINSON'S BECOMING-EARTH IN MICHEL TOURNIER'S *VENDREDI OU LES LIMBES DU PACIFIQUE* (1967)

Krzysztof Skonieczny

MICHEL TOURNIER'S FIRST NOVEL, *VENDREDI ou les Limbes du Pacifique* (1967), is famously multifaceted. As Susan Petit enumerates, *Friday*, among other topics, "rewrites the familiar story of Robinson Crusoe, imagines a non-Oedipal path to psychological wholeness, reinterprets Christianity, sums up a historical dialectic, replies to a famous debate between Lévi-Strauss and Sartre, and develops a philosophical theory of knowledge."[1]

Appreciative of the richness of *Vendredi*, I set a more humble task in this article, aiming only to tackle one subject, namely the question of Robinson's (and, to a lesser extent, Friday's) relationship with the island Speranza. While for Defoe's Robinson his island is an unnamed object of conquest and rational management, in Tournier's case it plays an altogether different role. Indeed, as Gilles Deleuze indicates, "The isle is as much the hero of the novel as Robinson or Friday."[2] In this essay I show that this is more than a metaphor and that throughout the novel the island Speranza plays an active part in the story, provoking philosophical questions about its subjectivity and agency, and invites Robinson to enter a process that, using Rosi Braidotti's concept, I refer to as becoming-Earth.

I proceed by first indicating the relationship of Tournier's book with Defoe's *Robinson* as understood by the author himself and by several critics. I then show its place in the context of the ecological movement, which flourished in the late 1960s and 1970s, leading to a reexamination of our attitude to Earth as such, after which I comment on how the later development of this movement—of which, of course, Tournier could not have known at the moment of writing *Vendredi*—and especially the introduction of the term "Anthropocene," can lead to a more nuanced reading of the novel. I then summarize Braidotti's views, introducing her understanding of the posthuman, as well as presenting the notion of becoming-Earth. Finally, I show how Tournier's book can be seen as an exemplification of becoming-

Earth and an attempt at reinterpretation of the relationship between the (post)-human and (what is left of) nature.

ROBINSON AND VENDREDI

In his intellectual autobiography *Le vent Paraclet*, Tournier acknowledges the importance of Crusoe's story, claiming that Robinson is "one of the constitutive elements of the western man's soul."[3] This statement needs to be understood in the wider context of Tournier's development as a writer or, more precisely, the shift from wanting to become a philosopher—a dream thwarted by not receiving his *aggregation* at the Sorbonne in 1949—to finding a new vocation. For Tournier, since a philosopher deals with the fundamentals of the human condition (for example through constructing a metaphysics), the question was, how does a writer approach these fundamentals? The answer is through engaging with myths. While Tournier's approach to myths and mythology is an immense topic, which has been dealt with extensively by others, notably Melissa Barchi Panek,[4] I point to two aspects of myth that are crucial to the understanding of *Vendredi*.

First, "myth is a fundamental story,"[5] which means that it encompasses—in a single story so simple that it could well be recounted to children—all the levels of philosophical thinking, from epistemology and metaphysics to ethics. It is from this belief that *Friday* seems to derive the complexity I indicated in the first sentence of this essay; it is also because of this that it is, all things considered, an engaging and imaginative story that was easily transformable into a children's book, which Tournier did in his 1971 adaptation of the novel *Vendredi ou la Vie sauvage*. For Tournier, these fundamental stories form a cultural background against which the subject can situate himself or herself to establish an orientation in the world. To use the author's own imagery, "the human soul forms itself from the mythology which is in the air."[6]

Second, "a myth is a story that everybody already knows."[7] In *Friday*, Tournier seems to have remained quite faithful to this part of the definition, as, at face value, he proposes very few changes to Defoe's narrative—for example, he pushes the events one century forward, making the shipwreck happen on 30 September 1759, describes Robinson as a married man, and moves the island from the Atlantic to the Pacific (which actually puts it closer to the actual island where Alexander Selkirk, the person whom Defoe based his story on, was stranded).[8]

But the actual point of writing as retelling a story everybody knows is not simple repetition. As Tournier says, the writer's "ambition is to enrich or at least modify this mythological 'hum,' this bath of images in which their contemporaries live and which is the oxygen of the soul."[9] This individual ambition is accompanied by a social or even historical role—the writer's task is to renew the myth so that it remains relevant to the "human soul" and does not turn into simple "allegory."[10]

True to this program, Tournier reinterprets Robinson's story in the light of social changes he witnessed in his time. The 1967 book is inspired equally by the author's tenure at the Musée de l'homme (Museum of Man) under the direction of Claude Lévi-Strauss and the political and social tumult of the 1950s and 1960s France, caused, among other factors, by the dismantling of the French colonial empire—especially in the aftermath of Algeria gaining independence five years earlier. One of the effects of these changes was the influx of migrant workers into France, people who—as Tournier remarks—received no thanks or voice for enriching their new country in a cultural as well as economic sense. Indeed, as the writer admits in *Le vent Paraclet*, he would have liked to dedicate *Friday* to "the enormous and silent mass of immigrant workers in France, all those Fridays sent to us by the third world, the three million Algerians, Moroccans, Tunisians, Senegalese and Portuguese, on whom our society depends, but who we never see, who we never listen to, and who cannot cast a ballot, and do not have a syndicate, or a spokesperson, the only real proletariat that exists in France."[11]

While Tournier does not employ a shift of perspective from Robinson to Friday, which would seem a logical way to go about creating what amounts to a postcolonial version of the story—as Gérard Genette remarks, "no Robinson, however well-meaning, can hope to write that particular *Friday*"—he does engage in what Genette calls "transvaluation,"[12] a process involving the devaluation of one character (Robinson) and (counter)valuation of another (Friday).[13] The stakes of this process are perhaps best summarized by Tournier himself, who sees Defoe's Robinson as representing (the only possible) civilization, while his own Robinson represents only *a* civilization, one that—at least in the circumstances of the island—is greatly inferior to Friday's. Tournier seeks to remedy the original book's great flaw, which is to have made Robinson blind to the fact that instead of trying to teach Friday anything, he should instead learn from his companion, who is much more at home in the environment they share.

Mindful of these "postcolonial" readings of *Vendredi*, the soundness of which seems to have been confirmed by the author himself, I would like to focus—as I already indicated—on a problem that is seemingly more insular in the novel, but perhaps equally important for the construction of the "soul" of today's man, namely the ecological themes in Tournier's text.

KRZYSZTOF SKONIECZNY

TOURNIER IN THE ANTHROPOCENE

The political turmoil Tournier mentions as one of the inspirations for his book was not the only important change that came to pass at the time *Vendredi* was published. Another important context is the growing awareness of the ecological crisis. Books such as Rachel Carson's *Silent Spring* (1963) highlighted the havoc wreaked by agriculture and industry in the environment, and scientific reports—most famously *The Limits of Growth* prepared for the Club of Rome in 1972—heralded an imminent collapse of the environment and fossil-fuel-based economy within the next fifty years. The late 1960s also witnessed the first photographs of Earth from space, which radically changed the perspective from which the world was seen.

In this general atmosphere, it is worthwhile to note a famous text that was first published in *Science* in the year of the publication of *Vendredi*, namely Lynn White Jr.'s "The Historical Roots of Our Ecological Crisis." Seeing that while we cannot point to the exact moment when humans started altering their environment, we can certainly point to modern technology and science and their nineteenth-century success as a pivotal point in the character of these alterations, White proposes to start "by looking, in some historical depth, at the presuppositions that underlie modern technology and science."[14] After a short inquiry, he notices that the voluntaristic Western Christian theology of the Middle Ages—a time when the West first emerged as a technological power, if not yet a scientific one—was fertile ground for what was to become modern science. In his own words, "Modern Western science was cast in a matrix of Christian theology."[15] While this does not mean that more pro-ecological currents cannot be found within Western Christianity—the author himself points to Saint Francis of Assisi—according to White, no other belief system has separated man and nature by such a great abyss.

It is this conglomerate of Christianity and modern technology that Robinson—both Crusoe's and Tournier's—brings with him to the island; the duet is joined (more explicitly in Tournier's case) by a third partner, namely accumulative capitalism. It is also this belief system that forces Crusoe's Robinson to see himself as the only hero of the story, reducing the island to a place to be tamed and profited from. It is, finally, Christianity and modernity that stand as the first and most important points of criticism for Tournier in his retelling of the story.

Much as *Vendredi* may well be read as a purely postmodern reaction to its staunchly modernist predecessor—as it is indeed read, for example, by Melissa Barchi Panek—I believe that the interpretative possibilities the book gives are far from exhausted in such a reading. According to Panek, "*Vendredi* and his incarnation of Nature represent a postmodern attribute: the impossibility of conforming Nature into a categorical and controllable system."[16] However, in this "postmodern" understanding, Nature remains an irrational, impersonal, and inhuman force that can be only enslaved (as the "modern" Robinson would have it) or yielded to. The vision of Robinson's final relationship to Nature—or to Speranza—as simple submission in fact reinforces the view that the two sides of the relationship (man and Nature) are Others who cannot find a way to coexist within a master-slave dialectic, which is kept intact as a force organizing the relationship.

It is therefore not the modernist enslavement of Nature that should be undermined but the very dialectic that enables it—the criticism needs to be more fundamental than the "postmodern" model proposes. The need for such criticism became all the more dire as our understanding of the extent of human impact on Nature changed in the decades that followed the sixties and seventies, leading to the redefinition of our current predicament as the Anthropocene.

First proposed in 2000 as a new geological epoch, whose temporal extent, legitimacy and scientific usefulness are still under debate,[17] the idea of the Anthropocene has been adopted in the humanities and arts, leading to a wide array of interdisciplinary projects seeking to make sense of our current place in the world.[18] While I cannot even approach a summary of this field of study—for whose vastness intellectual importance and intellectual fashion bear equal responsibility—I would like to point out a feature of the change in the relationship between man and Nature of which the proclamation of Anthropocene is a symptom, and which will be an important point of reference in my interpretation of *Vendredi*.

Man's becoming a geological force is a pivotal moment in the dialectical relationship described above. It is especially so if the Anthropocene is interpreted (perhaps with a slight exaggeration with respect to the scientific meaning of the term) as a state in which man controls or at the least has a decisive impact on Earth or Nature as a whole. Effectively, this means that one of the terms of the dialectic (man) has swallowed the other (Earth), or, Ulrich Beck claims, somewhat anticipating this meaning of the Anthropocene, "modernization has *consumed and lost its other* [i.e., Nature]."[19]

What the above seems to indicate is the need to rediscover the difference between man and Nature or Earth in a way that would refrain from framing their relationship in dialectical terms of mastery and slavery, but would still allow for actual relating, precluded if one frames the relationship in terms of otherness. If, as Deleuze says in an early text, "islands are either from before or for after humankind,"[20] then even the most antimodern Robinson could never actually achieve the intensity and intimacy he does with Speranza.

KRZYSZTOF SKONIECZNY

BRAIDOTTI, BECOMING-EARTH, AND AGENCY

Such a rediscovery, I believe, can be found in Rosi Braidotti's version of posthumanism. Braidotti develops a wide interdisciplinary perspective aiming to unwork the rational-white-male-centric humanism embodied in the Vitruvian man and a specific reading of Protagoras's formula "man is the measure of all things."[21] Instead of such a vision of subjectivity, she proposes a more nuanced view of "posthuman subjectivity [that] reshapes the identity of humanistic practices, by stressing heteronomy and multi-faceted relationality, instead of autonomy."[22]

For Braidotti, such a reshaping needs to include the thesis that "subjectivity is not the exclusive prerogative of *anthropos*."[23] Among the many elaborations of this thesis, Braidotti proposes the notion of becoming-Earth, which is thought as a positive "reconfiguring [of] the relationship to our complex habitat, which we used to call 'nature.'"[24] As the author of *The Posthuman* explicitly claims, one of her goals is a "post-anthropocentric configuration of knowledge that grants the earth the same role and agency as the human subjects that inhabit it."[25]

The idea of Earth's agency is, at face value, a preposterous claim that seems to ignore simple biological and psychological facts, such as the notion that specific cognitive functions (and especially consciousness) are needed for actual agency and no organism without a complex brain structure can actually have it. Even within perhaps the most ambitious scientific (or borderline-scientific) hypothesis of Earth as an organism, namely the hypothesis of Gaia (also cited by Braidotti as an influence), according to which "life defines the material conditions needed for its survival and makes sure that they stay there,"[26] no claim of agency in this sense is made.

Such a psychological understanding of agency is, of course, not the only possible one. With the emergence of theories such as Bruno Latour's actor-network theory (ANT), treating all human and nonhuman entities participating in a given event as equal actors, the notion has been used in a much wider manner. However, even if such attempts are certainly refreshing reactions to rampant anthropocentrism, they do not seem to include the ethical dimension that I see as important for Braidotti in her reconfiguration of our understanding of the man-earth relationship—even if not explicitly stated as such.

A useful way to understand this dimension can come from an unlikely source—namely, a Wittgenstein-inspired philosopher. When analyzing consciousness, Alva Noë points out experiments conducted by psychologists Fritz Heider and Marianne Simmel, who showed the participants animated films in which circles and triangles moved on a screen. Even though the shapes' movement was entirely random, the subjects tended to "attribute to them ... goals, intentions, and mental attitudes such as fear."[27] For Noë, this points to the fact that consciousness is first and foremost an attribution. More importantly, it is an attribution that has important consequences for the way we treat beings that we see as possessing or not possessing it.

Noë calls this the moral character of consciousness: "The question of whether a person is in fact a conscious person is always a moral question before it is a question about our justification to believe."[28] I believe the same can be said about agency. Having goals and intentions—as were attributed to the circles and triangles in the above experiment—and trying to achieve them is the very core of agency. The attribution of agency also has moral overtones and is predominantly a practical question, and it is these factors that, in my understanding, underpin the ideas behind Earth's subjectivity or agency.

What matters, then, is not whether Earth is objectively an agent or not, but what changes in our practical and moral treatment of it when we choose to treat or understand it *as if* it were to have agency. It seems that only through such an understanding of agency can we actually comprehend the stakes and ideas embedded in Braidotti's conception of becoming-Earth.

The inspiration for this notion is clearly Deleuzian—becoming-Earth can be situated next to such well-known themes as becoming-intense, becoming-woman, becoming-imperceptible, or becoming-animal. The last notion may be especially informative in this context, not only because Braidotti herself analyzes both of these concepts in terms of "life beyond the species," but also because of a certain type of agency required for becoming-animal, also on the part of the animal.

As described in *A Thousand Plateaus*, becoming-animal sweeps up the animal as well man (even if the animal is not actually "real").[29] What is more, both of the parties need to be active in the process—to take Deleuze and Guattari's example, Moby Dick is leading Ahab as much as Ahab is pursuing the whale.[30]

It is in this context that I propose to read Braidotti's notion of becoming-Earth. One does not become-Earth without the participation of Earth as an agent in the process. While this notion might seem to raise the question of what Earth becomes, it seems that we should follow the authors of *A Thousand Plateaus* and focus on the entire "block" of becoming (man and Earth, Robinson and Speranza) rather than the fate of the given individual. What is at stake is not the thanatological becoming-soil of man, but a redefinition of the relationship between a (living) man and a (living) Earth.

KRZYSZTOF SKONIECZNY

ROBINSON'S BECOMINGS (I)—CASTAWAY TO CAPITALIST

In Tournier's novel, Robinson's relationship with the island can be divided into several stages. The castaway first decides to leave for Chile as soon as possible and sets about building a boat he dubs *Escape*. It is then that he first encounters the dog Tenn, the only other being to survive the shipwreck of *Virginia*—the animal however runs away at the sight of Robinson, probably perceiving inhumanity in the task-consumed human. Unable to get the *Escape* to the ocean shore—the boat was too heavy to lift or drag to the water—Robinson gives up and retreats to the mire, where he lies, half-submerged and half-conscious, for the better part of the time, this being the first time he allows himself to be smothered by the isle in a motherly (if muddy) embrace. After seeing a hallucination of his sister aboard a Spanish galleon heading for the island, Robinson snaps out of his depression and decides to make the island a place to live for himself, engaging in meticulous planning, intense goat herding, and—later—crop cultivation, thus making a one-man civilizational jump from hunting and gathering to accumulative capitalism; he also gets back Tenn, who this time readily accepts him as his master. It is during this period of his sojourn on the island—the only one whose logic seems to coincide with Crusoe's version of the story—that Robinson inadvertently saves Friday, who at first seems seamlessly integrated into the capitalist machine as a precarious laborer, working six days a week (and participating in worship on Sunday), and given only enough money to purchase a half-day off every once in a while.

But it is also in this period that Robinson starts coming into contact with "*another* island behind the one where he had labored so long in solitude, a place more alive, warmer and more fraternal, which his mundane preoccupations had concealed from him" (90).[31] This contact comes in two most important forms, namely when Robinson climbs down to the bottom of the cave whose first room he uses as his place of storage and enters a mother-child relationship with Speranza, and then when he and the island become lovers (or even husband and wife), as Robinson fathers mandrakes in the pink coomb.

Yet the island will turn out to be an unfaithful wife when Friday is found to copulate with it in the same way Robinson does, which leads to a serious beating of Friday by Robinson, who only relents when "a few words gasped by Friday penetrat[e] his blanket of godlike wrath—'Master, don't kill me'" (167). Shortly after, Friday, nearly caught smoking his master's pipe, tries to hide his transgression by throwing it into the cave, in which Robinson kept several barrels of gunpowder scavenged from the shipwreck. The explosion destroys nearly all of Robinson's settlement, seemingly returning him to his castaway status; it also kills Tenn. The new beginning changes the relationship between the former master and the former slave, and it is now Robinson who is forced to learn a new way of living, which in turn allows him—freed of the capitalist accumulation burden he forced upon himself—to enter into a newer and more active relationship with Speranza, which will last until the ship *Whitebird* comes to the island, finally taking Friday (but not Robinson, who stays with Speranza and finds a new companion in Thursday, a cabin boy who flees the ship) with it.

Along the lines of Braidotti's notion of becoming-Earth, every phase of Robinson's relationship to Speranza needs to be analyzed from the point of view of both parties, taking into account their respective agency. In the capitalist phase Robinson manages to extricate himself as a subject from the zone of indiscernibility that he has already had time to appreciate during his time in the mire;[32] it is a state where, as he writes in his journal, "Robinson is Speranza. He is conscious of himself only in the stir of myrtle leaves with the sun's rays breaking through, he knows himself only in the white crest of a wave running up the yellow sun" (93). Robinson sees it as his duty—or at least as a necessity—to change this state of things and impose a subject-object logic, needed for the "rationalization of the world" (94). He is well aware that such a relationship—the dialectical master-slave relationship between subject and object—means the destruction of the object in its uniqueness ("My eye is the corpse of light and color. . . . My hand refutes the thing it holds"; 95). However, he sees the careful negotiation (a "subtle and pure equilibrium"; 95) of this relationship as the only way for "salvation, at least a kind of salvation—that of a fruitful and harmonious island, flawlessly cultivated and administered" (95). It seems that what Robinson is after is a relationship between a master and a slave that would be just liberal enough to keep the latter functioning.

In such circumstances, the only way for the slave to react is by submission or rebellion, and it seems that Speranza entertains both possibilities. Initially, the island answers with fecundity—all of Robinson's crops seem to take on, his herding operation moves flawlessly, and he even manages to rid himself of the plague of rats from the *Virginia* shipwreck thanks to the island's own strain. His only problem—the overaccumulation of agricultural produce—is due to the constraints of his own system rather than any defiance on the part of Speranza.

The mire, and then especially the five-foot recess beneath the darkest room of Robinson's cave, can be understood as the attempts of the island to break the vicious circle of accumulation and reinstate the indiscernibility between Robinson (subject) and Speranza (object). Since the relationship, at this point, has already been defined as that of master and slave, it seems that the only struggle—as we know from Hegel, and more importantly in the French context, Kojève—can be that of life or death. In the crevice, Robinson is reminded of his mother, of an idyllic mother-child relationship, and feels himself as a "bean, caught in the massive, indestructible flesh of Speranza" (105). But—as Freud would have it—the relationless peace inside the mother's womb, the place to which all men seek to return, is in fact as close to the beginning of life as it is to its end. Robinson understands all this perfectly without having read *Beyond the Pleasure Principle*: "Life and death were so close to one another in this luminous place that with only a moment of inattention, of relaxation in his will to live, he could slip from one into the other" (105). After this experience, which may or may not have been a death and rebirth in itself,[33] Crusoe decides to exercise more caution in his journeys to the recess, thus foiling Speranza's attempt to reset their relationship in the most radical—if motherly—way. What is more, Robinson learns to use the time in the recess in his favor, draining the island's energy in another attempt to negotiate the subject-object relationship.

What finally drives Robinson out of the recess is the change his abuse of it has brought to the relationship. Not able to withstand the readiness to serve as fecund mother to Robinson's crops and herds and to Crusoe himself, Speranza loses her ability to support the rich growth that allowed for its cultivation and the castaway's capitalist success. Streams dry up, crops fail and goats bear stillborn children. Robinson realizes that the isle "was being exhausted by the monstrous maternal role he has imposed on her" (109). This alone, however, is not enough.

What finally drives Robinson away from the recess is his realization that as an adult man he cannot simply return to the womb as if nothing has changed since the innocent days of his early childhood. He sees his Oedipal situation for what it is only when he barely escapes impregnating the island-mother ("My semen escaped me. I had only time to place my hand, for its protection, over the narrow crevice, no more than two fingers broad, at the very bottom of the womb of Speranza"; 109)—and decides to return to the recess only when the time comes for him to die.

After the unfortunate event Robinson and Speranza quickly find a fragile equilibrium between use and abuse in the husband-and-wife relationship that starts when Robinson first visits the coomb, and then realizes his union with the island is a fertile one. The white mandrakes that are born from this relationship are a proof that both parties seem to have found their role in the capitalist system imposed by Crusoe (for, as we know at least since Marx, the familial relation and capitalism are closely intertwined).

This part of the novel, where Tournier skillfully balances between the humorous and the scandalous, the perverse and the absurd, opens itself to numerous interpretations. According to Ronald Bogue, whose interpretation focuses on Tournier's critique of various facets of Western racism and colonialism, "Tournier provides an analysis and critique of the eros of exoticism through his exploration of Robinson's libidinal engagement with Speranza."[34] For Panek, the sexual union is easily interpreted in terms of the modern/postmodern distinction, which governs her reading from the start: "This hyperbolization and perversion of nature's femininity proves to be a postmodern approach to undoing an established norm which is the Romantic's ideological conception of Nature's beauty."[35] Finally, for Petit, the question is first and foremost psychoanalytical: "The important, non-Freudian point in this development is that Robinson has no Oedipal conflict because there is no father figure to compete with him for his 'mother's' attentions."[36]

While all of these readings certainly have merit and show important points of Tournier's thinking, they do not seem to take into account the isle itself and its own agency (and how it was negotiated with Robinson) in the logic of the book. From this point of view, the most important point is the transformation of Speranza in the process of the sexual union—Robinson "had humanized her whom he could henceforth call his wife" (130). He will later regretfully acknowledge, "My love affair with Speranza was still largely human in its nature; I fecundated her soil as though I were lying with a wife" (212). This is perhaps Robinson's most Anthropocenic moment. The island is drawn so deep inside the union with the human that it loses its island-ness and is encompassed by the human world. Contrary to Panek, I would say that it is here that the modern, capitalist Robinson finally colonizes the island in its entirety; he manages to accommodate it just enough for it not to lose its fecundity. But it seems that the mandrake children—as it were, deformed, monstrous hybrids of the vegetal and the human—can be understood as the first indicators of the wrongness of this relationship; it is not their "unnatural" character that is unnerving (one of the key traits of Braidotti's posthumanist approach is the problematization of the natural/cultural/unnatural distinction) but rather the fact that they are a mechanical, "averaged sum" of their parents and not actual, unique beings in themselves. As monstrosities, the children are a synecdoche of Robinson's relation to Speranza, seemingly efficient and flourishing, but actually absurd in its grandiosity.

ROBINSON'S BECOMINGS (II)—FRIDAY'S APPRENTICE TO SOLAR BEING

The fact that another change in Robinson and Speranza's relationship can come about only after an intrusion from the outside might in itself be read as evidence of the fullness of the modern man's victory. At first, the arrival of Friday—who was saved by Robinson only because Tenn made him miss his shot and kill one of Friday's pursuers—does not seem to change the accumulative habits of the island's governor; it even offers a way to speed the process up thanks to the 100 percent increase in the labor force. But Friday is soon observed to be a destructive force ("Beneath the shadow of submissiveness, Friday possessed a mind of his own and what came out of it was profoundly shocking and subversive of discipline on the island"; 154). Friday's exploits will soon prove revolutionary after the pipe incident, but even before that one can observe in his actions a method that will serve as revelatory for Robinson himself.

When, seeing that Robinson took his "vacation" (stopping the water clock and his daily, productive occupations), Friday takes Tenn to roam around the island, he not only causes the rice field to dry up (to save the dog) and dresses up Robinson's cacti with clothes and precious stones from the *Virginia*, but also replants some willow-like shrubs upside down. When Robinson, looking for Friday (who is indeed hiding among them, painted in a leafy pattern), notices the effects of his work, he is most puzzled by the fact not that his companion did this but that the shrubs—and Speranza—have accepted this strange state of affairs, grown green shoots on the roots, and (most probably) started using their buried branches as roots.

Christy Wampole thus comments upon this passage: "When Crusoe comes across Friday's shrine, he is shocked to find that nature has accepted the inversion imposed upon it. Because Friday has made his own body into that of a plant, he illustrates even more clearly to Crusoe that the inverted plants are not simply figures for themselves but figures for human convertibility. By analogizing his own body as plant, he makes clear that the human is a changeable creature."[37] Wampole seeks to see this as another stage in Robinson's path to transcendence (symbolized by his union with the sun); however, I pursue a slightly different interpretation. Even if Friday's masquerade shows human changeability, it would be a mistake to treat inverted plants as mere symbols or figures of something that they are not—Deleuze and Guattari repeatedly warn us of the perils of treating becoming-animal as a symbolic process, and it seems we should exercise the same caution when it comes to becoming-Earth. This event is to be read at face value: Friday shows Robinson a process of experimentation, whence he introduces a change that utterly escapes the prevailing utilitarian logic of Crusoe's capitalism, and, in return, Speranza accepts this change as a welcome diversion, and instead of monstrous man-Earth hybrids produces plants that offer Friday a chance to produce his own nonlethal zone of indiscernibility, thus forming a framework for a very basic understanding of becoming-Speranza of Friday and Speranza's becoming-Friday.

While this moment does give Robinson pause, it does not seem to shake him enough to abandon his accumulative ways; nor does the even more evident situation, when Crusoe finds Friday fornicating with Speranza in the coomb.

Contrary to Petit's take on the matter, it seems that this situation is Oedipal to the core—Robinson sees in Friday a rival in the conquest of his mother-wife; it is only logical that he would try to kill the intruder (no matter if Friday was the father or the son in this scenario). What is telling is that after Friday succumbs to Robinson's attack, begging for his life and thus agreeing to play the slave in their dialectic relation, Robinson goes back to his fortress and reads from the book of Joseph, realizing that his jealousy was a mistake. Friday's deed is to be understood not as an attempt to supplant Robinson as the husband of Speranza but as another experiment. As with the shrubs that he planted upside down, Friday tried, and indeed he failed—Robinson will later (after the explosion) admit that "the earth repelled him" (209), for Friday (as his later experiments, and the final boarding of the *Whitebird*, seem to ascertain) is a creature of the sky, and not of the earth.

Friday's experiments are so successful not because they follow a specific logic or plan, as did Robinson's early experiments with Speranza. Crusoe did follow the path of experimentation and sought Speranza's agreement, but all his projects were aimed at humanizing the island, even though he felt that another island was possible beyond that which he knew. The change that came with Friday's initial experiments was that they were utterly pointless from an anthropocentric point of view, hence their perceived whimsical and absurd nature. Interestingly, when Friday starts to follow a more rational plan to make the goat Andoar fly by turning its skin into a kite, thus proving his interest in the matters of air, he seems to be set upon a clear path that will lead him to leave Speranza along with the crew of the *Whitebird*, through which, in a sense, he supplants Robinson, who decides to stay with his island.

The desperation of aloneness quickly leaves Robinson, not only because he finds the boy Thursday (or Sunday, strangely found in the English translation), but especially because he finally can find himself one with Speranza. Seeing the sunrise, Robinson feels the full impact of the "sun-god" bestowing him with "an armor" against his prior desperation, and yet does not yield to simple transcendence but remains rooted in the isle: "His feet were solidly planted on the rock, and his legs sturdy and unshakable as columns of stone" (235). Thus "going solar" is for Robinson not a mystic gesture of seeking an otherworldly connection with a Western-type deity, but rather a manner to become-Earth without imposing the burden of his humanity on Speranza. In other words, instead of treating the island as an unknown "other," who can be known only insofar as she is subjugated to the knower's rules of knowing, he just becomes "another"[38] being next to Speranza, growing, as she does, in the sun's warmth, according to its rhythm. Not untouched by the passing of time, he nevertheless aligns himself with the circular logic of the passing days, shedding the linear logic of capitalist accumulation and finding an eternity, a zone of indiscernibility with the island that is not maternal, not thanatic, and—most of all—not human.

CONCLUSIONS

According to Braidotti, one of the most important tasks for critical theory and the (post)humanities in our current ecological predicament is to "fin[d] an adequate language for post-anthropocentrism. [The] resources of the imagination, as well as the tools of critical intelligence, need to be enlisted for this task."[39] While Robinson's eventual becoming-Speranza surely does not provide any obvious recipes, his shifting relationship with the island does help to propose a few pointers concerning the redefinition of the theoretical relationship between humans and Earth or Nature that could stem from a posthumanist position inspired by Braidotti. The most important seem to be the precariousness of the communication (or feedback) in such a relationship and the precariousness of the posthuman state (if it is at all possible).

While Robinson tends to "listen" to Speranza from the very beginning, and she seems to answer with what might be interpreted as agreement—from the ease with which he grows crops to the strength he gets from staying in her "womb"—as I have tried to show, what Robinson unwittingly does is try to humanize the island, and at the end of his period of solitude he even achieves his own "Anthropocene," making the isle into his own image. All of this happens while he works to find his own peace with Speranza, to foster what he understands as a good relationship. In this final, husband-and-wife period, what is needed is an intervention from outside—the coming of Friday—to break the humanist stalemate and move on to another form of subjectivity. The end product, however, the solar Robinson, while certainly not human anymore, and "having-become-Speranza," while having a lot in common with the island, seems to have lost any direct relationship with it (if he ever had one in the first place).

Perhaps more importantly, the posthuman state, while Robinson was actively seeking it throughout what I have called his "becomings," revealed itself to be fleeting and precarious in itself. From his modernist, Christian, and capitalist beginnings, through the almost lethal period of lethargy, to the Freudian slips of his Oedipal adventures, and finally the quasi-pagan times of sun worship that finally provide him with something to root his newfound posthumanity in, Robinson keeps going back and forth between the modern and the postmodern, the anthropocentric (or Anthropocenic) and the Earth-centric, from human to posthuman. In light of these vacillations, it seems that if posthumanism creates a chance to rethink our relationship to Earth (and, conversely, to our own humanity), then it must be seen not as a state but as a fleeting horizon, a task to be thought and rethought, while constantly letting ourselves be reminded that we are, indeed, still all-too-human.

NOTES

1. Susan Petit, *Michel Tournier's Metaphysical Fictions* (Amsterdam: John Benjamins, 1991), 2.
2. Gilles Deleuze, "Michel Tournier and the World without Others," in *Logic of Sense*, trans. Mark Lester and Charles Stivale (New York: Columbia University Press, 1990), 302.
3. Michel Tournier, *Le vent Paraclet* (Paris: Gallimard, 1977), 221.
4. Melissa Barchi Panek, *The Postmodern Mythology of Michel Tournier* (Newcastle upon Tyne: Cambridge Scholars, 2012).
5. Tournier, *Le vent Paraclet*, 188.
6. Ibid., 191.
7. Ibid., 189.
8. These—and other—changes are enumerated in, among others, Gérard Genette, *Palimpsests: Literature in the Second Degree*, trans. Channa Newman and Claude Doubinsky (Lincoln: University of Nebraska Press, 1997), 368–372.
9. Tournier, *Le vent Paraclet*, 192.
10. Ibid., 193.
11. Ibid., 236–237.
12. Genette, *Palimpsests*, 367.
13. This way of thinking about *Vendredi* situates the novel alongside other transvaluations of the Robinsonade and the Enlightenment values its original installment promotes, such as Sven Delblanc's *Speranza* or Barry Unsworth's *Sacred Hunger*. For a full comparison, see Susan C. Brantly, "Engaging the Enlightenment: Tournier's *Friday*, Delblanc's *Speranza*, and Unsworth's *Sacred Hunger*," *Comparative Literature* 61.2 (2009): 128–141.
14. Lynn White Jr., "The Historical Roots of Our Ecological Crisis," in *The Ecocriticism Reader: Landmarks in Literary Ecology*, ed. Cheryll Glotfelty and Harold Fromm (Athens: University of Georgia Press, 1996), 5.
15. Ibid., 11.
16. Panek, *Postmodern Mythology of Michel Tournier*, 88–89.
17. See, e.g., Richard Monastersky, "Anthropocene: The Human Age," *Nature* 519.7542 (2015): 144–147.
18. See, e.g., Heather Davis and Etienne Turpin, eds., *Art in the Anthropocene: Encounters Among Aesthetics, Politics, Environments and Epistemologies* (London: Open Humanities Press, 2015).
19. Ulrich Beck, *Risk Society: Toward a New Modernity*, trans. Mark Ritter (London: Sage, 1992), 10.
20. Gilles Deleuze, "Desert Islands," in *Desert Islands and Other Texts (1953–1974)*, trans. Michael Taormina (New York: Semiotext(e), 2004), 9.
21. Rosi Braidotti, *The Posthuman* (Cambridge: Polity, 2013), 13.
22. Ibid., 145.
23. Ibid., 82.
24. Ibid., 81.
25. Ibid., 160.
26. James Lovelock and Sidney Epton, "The Quest for Gaia," *New Scientist* 65.935 (6 February 1975): 304.

27. Alva Noë, *Out of Our Heads* (New York: Hill & Wang, 2010).
28. Ibid.
29. See, e.g., Gilles Deleuze and Felix Guattari, *A Thousand Plateaus*, trans. Brian Massumi (Minneapolis: University of Minnesota Press, 1987), 305.
30. Ibid., 248.
31. Michel Tournier, *Friday*, trans. Norman Denny (Baltimore: Johns Hopkins University Press, 1997). Further references are to this edition and are given parenthetically.
32. This Deleuzian term is discussed at length in, among others, Matthew Calarco, *Thinking through Animals: Identity. Difference. Indistinction* (Stanford, CA: Stanford University Press, 2015), esp. 48–69.
33. See, e.g., Rick Dolphijn, "Undercurrents and the Desert(ed): Negarestani, Tournier and Deleuze Map the Polytics of a 'New Earth,'" in *Postcolonial Literatures and Deleuze: Colonial Pasts, Differential Futures*, ed. Lorna Burns and Birgit M. Kaiser (Houndmills: Palgrave Macmillan, 2012), 211; and Petit, *Michel Tournier's Metaphysical Fictions*, 6.
34. Ronald Bogue, "Speranza, the Wandering Island," *Deleuze Studies* 3.1 (June 2009): 129.
35. Panek, *Postmodern Mythology of Michel Tournier*, 79.
36. Petit, *Michel Tournier's Metaphysical Fictions*, 6.
37. Christy Wampole, *Rootedness: The Ramifications of a Metaphor* (Chicago: University of Chicago Press, 2016), 108.
38. For a different take on "anotherness," see Dolphijn, "Undercurrents and the Desert(ed)."
39. Braidotti, *Posthuman*, 82.

Part Four

THE ROBINSONADE AND THE PRESENT CONDITION

9

"THE TRUE STATE OF OUR CONDITION"

The Twenty-First-Century Worker as Castaway

Jennifer Preston Wilson

THE FILM ROBINSONADE OF THE twenty-first century restages Robinson Crusoe's confrontation with the emptiness that emerges from his own ambition and restlessness; he feels trapped by consequences as he realizes "that in this desolate Place, and in this desolate Manner I should end my Life" (47). *Cast Away* (2000), *Moon* (2009), and *The Martian* (2015) all transpose Crusoe's headlong pursuit of adventure and sovereign ascendancy into a twenty-first-century professional world that consumes the protagonist's existence. Through a crisis situation that places an isolated engineer in estrangement from his usual modes of being, these films explore how we might awaken to a new sense of self and revaluation of time. Each hero's survival depends upon an ironic frontiersmanship requiring his deliberate sabotage of corporate assets to purely personal ends in order to effect a dramatic self-rescue. Together, these three Robinsonades reenvision Defoe's eighteenth-century portrayal of how a man might ask himself, "Why is it *that thou wert not long ago destroy'd*?" (68) in order to grapple with the same question in a modern world where the ideologies of individual freedom and corporate work have intertwined to render people replaceable at every level.

The work environments depicted in recent film Robinsonades detail the ever-expanding demands upon personal time that crowd out the idea of a private sphere and instrumentalize institutional success at its expense. This reduction of family life and private time occurs in each case under the banner of corporate excellence. Chuck Noland, a systems engineer at FedEx in *Cast Away*, knows that he is ridiculous for allowing his pager to dictate his life, and yet his job consists of increasing company productivity. As Paula M. Rayman notes, this conflicted double consciousness has become ubiquitous to the global economy. Caught in "a never-ending cycle of overwork, pressured consumption, and exhaustion from trying to get ahead and to find time . . . we wind up living in ways we would prefer to change but we feel we have no choice."[1] Noland is sufficiently aware of the paradox posed by his work to give his girlfriend her very own pager as a mock Christmas present before handing over her real gift, an engagement ring, but he does not realign his life due to this realization. The opening of the ring's box and offering of the marriage proposal must wait because he is yet again at the airport, leaving in the midst of holiday celebrations to obey the summons of his pager to relentless work.[2]

Sam Bell in *Moon* is even more deeply indentured to corporate control in a three-year term of mining moon rock for Lunar Industries. His contract reduces him almost entirely to his economic value, and his existence is managed and minimalized to extract that value. His managers patronize him in video conferences, talking to him with condescension as they call him "buddy" and speak in slow, exaggerated intonations.[3] This belittling attitude suggests that Lunar Industries adheres to the "scientific management" principles of Frederick Taylor, who advocated "reducing worker skill and knowledge to simple and discrete formulas, so that production can be performed by 'men who are of smaller caliber and attainments and who are therefore cheaper than those required under the old system.'"[4] To this end, the supervisors have put Bell, the sole human employee at the base, under the care of a nanny-like robot named GERTY who mirrors his charge's moods with projected emoticons. If uncertain about how to handle a situation, GERTY falls back upon posing the most basic of questions in a way that confirms Bell's simplified status, such as asking, "Are you hungry?"[5] To further contain their employee, Lunar Industries has designed the Sarang station living quarters to encourage passive compliance, including an easy chair, video screen, model town, houseplants, ping-pong table, exercise equipment, and bunk. Even the few extras Bell is allowed, such as chewing gum, a stress ball, and an eyepiece for hobbyist pursuits, are symbols of dispersed energy and tunnel vision. Unlike Noland in *Cast Away*, Bell does not consciously register objections to his work, but his log entries and talk with GERTY reiterate his weariness after three years of solitary labor. Bell's sleep and daydreaming do, however, access an unconscious awareness of his own exploitation. In one waking vision, Bell takes a break from watching recorded television sitcoms to refill his mug. When he looks back at his chair, he is astonished to see it filled by a teenaged girl in a yellow dress.[6] Unnerved, he accidentally burns his hand, and when he looks back, she is gone. This manifestation marks the first of several psychic disturbances that alert Bell to the fact that more time than three years has gone by.

While Noland refuses to stand up to overwork and Bell passively follows orders, *The Martian*'s Mark Watney embraces the unceasing demands of NASA as the culmination of his training as a botanist and mechanical engineer. Even when it seems that the dangers of his job will kill him, he reveres science as a big idea worthy of self-sacrifice.[7] Watney willingly defines himself through his work, and the utopian perspective of the film idealizes NASA as governed by beneficent leaders who tolerate reasoned mutiny by risk-taking teams. Since NASA's rule breakers in the film always turn out to be right, *The Martian* obscures the limits of human reason and efficacy to construct an improbable depiction of a government agency. With his combined content knowledge and problem-solving skills, Watney is the ideal employee for such an agency, representing the *ur*-engineer who can cobble together a solution to anything, with the forces of time or chance never catching up to him. At the end of the movie he is shown proselytizing new astronaut recruits, having been subsumed into the apparatus of NASA itself.[8] Unlike the two previous Crusoe figures, Watney by choice merges with his occupation.

Despite their different workplaces, Chuck Noland, Sam Bell, and Mark Watney are all complicit in entering into their extreme and life-dominating work environments, much as Robinson Crusoe's decisions lead him into island exile. As Pat Rogers asserts, "[Crusoe's] story is clearly that of an adventurer *rejecting* the bourgeois comforts held out to him by his father."[9] Similarly, none of these recent film Crusoes seek work that will be merely safe and sufficient. Noland's quick-wittedness and taste for adventure (witnessed in photos of active, outdoorsy vacations) bring him to FedEx, where work is fast-paced and involves travel. Bell's grueling assignment with Lunar Industries is linked to his desire to impress his wife after a period of estrangement. Watney, in turn, holds idealistic ideas about being an astronaut and regards the foundation of the Jet Propulsion Lab at Caltech as a momentous historic event.

Amid these all-encompassing workplace cultures, the three films enact *Robinson Crusoe*'s allegory of his literal shipwreck as a spiritual and material crisis that must be overcome, thus causing the hero to reassess his values. Following the central plot event, we see an isolated protagonist coping with a new day-to-day existence by salvaging aspects of his old reality to survive. The shipwreck itself is understood by Crusoe as stemming from his original sin, and while he has moments of deep spiritual questioning, he also rouses himself to bodily self-preservation, such as when he finds the tide has washed the remains of his ship within reach. He rationalizes that "as there was little Relief in [tears], I resolv'd, if possible, to get to the Ship . . . with a great deal of Labour and Pains, but hope of furnishing my self with Necessaries" (37). Crusoe's coping ultimately balances between his spirit and substance, and he stands "'divided between earth and heaven, between accumulation and renunciation, action and contemplation.'"[10] While none of the Robinsonades replicate the intensity of Crusoe's doubled crisis of body and soul and instead replace his Christian faith with a post-Enlightenment interest in the individual, *Cast Away* most nearly approaches the novel's complexity; *Moon* emphasizes psychological trauma, and *The Martian* explores intellectual pride, yet all strive to make their audiences wonder, "How would I hold myself together in such a trial?"

The Martian's Mark Watney has little reason for spiritual self-questioning as his "wreck" is merely an accident and might have happened to anyone else on his team. Like Crusoe, though, he faces a severe likelihood of death and displays incredible stamina and resourcefulness in the face of danger. To this end, he raids the abundant supplies either abandoned or predelivered from Mars missions past, present, and future. When Watney begins to think long term about how he might adapt the rover to get to the Schiaparelli Crater to meet the next Ares landing, he resolves, "I'm going to have to science the shit out of this"[11] and digs up a buried radioisotope thermonuclear generator to provide heat for his vehicle. He makes this hazardous move because he simply has to in order to survive; as he sums it up, "The point is . . . I'm not cold anymore."[12] This sort of deadpan mockery of risk occurs repeatedly as Watney frames his experience. His other verbal release, swearing, expresses his frustration at mistakes or circumstances that get in his way, but he always tries again. As a follower of science and reason, he is depicted as persistent and nonemotional. Like Crusoe, he seems designed to represent *homo faber*, man the maker, who discovers himself through what he builds.[13]

In *Cast Away* and *Moon*, the heroes also must scavenge for their physical survival, but their efforts are more symbolic acts than elaborate feats of engineering. While Watney adapts one sort of survival supplies into another, Noland and Bell have few materials to utilize and these items narrowly represent the corporate interests they serve. The use values they find in these materials in fact overtly sabotage the aims of FedEx and Lunar Industries, respectively, and subvert the role of complacent employee. Noland's earlier fanatic pursuit of procedure disappears when he tears open packages stamped with the motto "The World on Time," ensuring that they will never be delivered.[14] Likewise, Sam Bell uses his woodworking tools—implements designed to keep him pacified and occupied in amateur pursuits—to slash hoses on the base. He thus manufactures a false crisis that will allow him to override the corporate orders forbidding him to venture outside.[15] These moments of finding new applications for familiar things are characteristic not just of these two films but of *The Martian* as well, with the qualification that NASA fully supports the repurposing of its assets.

While Watney's fully corporatized self anticipates his final shift into becoming a human representative for NASA recruitment,[16] Noland and Bell rebel against the utilitarian aims of their employers and struggle to assert their individuality and sustain their sense of uniqueness. We overhear Noland, four years into his island sojourn, mockingly quoting his earlier self about the "sin" of losing track of time now that time is all he has.[17] Noland uses his boundless new existence to construct elaborate cave paintings of his lost love, Kelly Frears, not caring for anything else other than return to her. In *Moon*, Bell also has to confront the idea of earlier versions of himself, but he must work through the trauma of learning that Lunar Industries has cloned him against his will and incinerates each increasingly decrepit "Sam Bell" at three-year intervals. These two films thus skillfully adapt *Robinson Crusoe*'s Christian allegory of a soul struggling to repent and reform into a contemporary psychological drama of the personality disintegrating. By doing so, they raise crucial questions about the self tormented by its own previous complacency.

All three film protagonists resemble Crusoe in his capacities for persistence and tinkering, and their more formalized depictions of a hero as problem solver thematize a broader human desire for control. Chuck Noland offers the most compelling study of an engineer who endures heart-wrenching personal loss and yet maintains his intelligent tracking of the seasonal tide and wind conditions to be ready to make an informed escape should he have the chance. Against Noland's clear preference for an ordered existence, he learns to "just keep breathing" and accept the random nature of life. Noland's story might be taken as an allegory of awakening to the ills of the twentieth-century workplace, which had "degraded the ancient ideal of the active life into something meager—a mere hunt for efficiency."[18] Leaving behind the self he had cultivated at FedEx, Noland channels his mathematical and conceptualizing skills to await the most hopeful moment for a new beginning. Even though his chances are slim, Noland has come to appreciate the potentiality of human action. As Hannah Arendt theorizes, "The life span of man running toward death would inevitably carry everything human to ruin and destruction if it were not for the faculty of interrupting it and beginning something new. . . . Men, though they must die, are not born in order to die but in order to begin."[19] The physical and behavioral transformation of Noland as he enters back into American life supports the idea that he is not returning but beginning. Unlike his earlier mannerisms, the new Noland is slow to speak and allows others the time and space to make their own decisions. He keeps his analytical engineering mind-set but now operates with empathy for the subjective and independent realities of others.

Sam Bell, by contrast, is an engineer manqué, held back by numerous factors including his stultifying work where he merely monitors the machines that fulfill all the important procedures. When an error occurs in the cloning sequence and Bell_2 meets Bell_1,[20] we see the difference between the two in a clear mapping of the film's argument that positive change has occurred in Bell_1's three years of service. This development will soon be cut short by his imminent death. Through physical suffering and the steadying influence of GERTY's programmed kindness, the older Sam clone has become less angry and more philosophic about human limitations during his contracted term. His portrayal represents the tragedy of human potential that will be lost with his destruction and thus a truncated vision of human mortality itself. The film establishes his growing capacity to develop an engineer's traditional abilities—technical expertise and reasoned problem solving—but that promise is crushed by the secretive corporation's abuse of the related field of bioengineering. The clones of Sam make the best of a very bad situation, but the briefness of their lives and the uncertainty of their identities underline the dangers of powerful technology placed in the hands of a corporation answering to financial rather than ethical demands. As Rev. Stanley S. Harakas remarks, "Cloning would deliberately deny by design the cloned human being a set of loving and caring parents. The cloned human being would not be the product of love, but of scientific procedures. Rather than being considered persons, the likelihood is that these cloned human beings would be considered 'objects' to be used."[21] This latter scenario most certainly is the main factor in Lunar Industries' utilitarian approach to its labor problems; rather than go to the great trouble and expense to send a new worker to the moon every three years, the company has created its own efficient labor pool ready for quick transitioning when needed. The initial Sam Bell thus becomes a natural resource to be mined, parallel to the helium-3 extracted from the lunar surface.

While the analytical capacities of Noland and Bell are gradually revealed as their ordeals worsen, *The Martian* opens with an immediately positive depiction of engineering, offering a detailed portrayal of the multiple, overlapping problems Watney must solve in his life-or-death situation. As the film goes on, however, its didacticism, untempered by side plots or character development, undermines its utopian theme. The nuanced portrayal of engineering as a field in ethical flux under its corporate use that we see in *Cast Away* and *Moon* shifts to scientist dogma immortalizing NASA in *The Martian*. Scientism holds that "all interesting questions can either be answered by science or not answered at all, and that the methods of (natural) science should prevail everywhere."[22] We see the limitations of this mode of thought in the sequential plotting of the film that privileges a linear, problem-solving perspective. The more general, philosophical and moral questions raised by *The Martian* go undeveloped: Are the billions of dollars used to rescue Watney best spent in this way (as opposed to applying them to public education or health crises, for example)? How should we view the leader of NASA, Teddy Sanders, when he retains staff who have openly flaunted his orders? How much is NASA using Watney-mania to magnify its own funding? Will Watney's life after rescue be worth living after his near starvation and long-term exposure to radiation? These and other pertinent questions outside the exclusive purview of science are ignored, although it would be quite possible to simultaneously present a heroic view of science and pursue wider themes that inform its practice. In "Two Cheers for Scientism," Taner Edis argues that science best flourishes alongside other fields of knowledge. To abet that coexistence, he distinguishes "philistine scientism" from a respectable scientism that "concerns continuities in our forms of knowledge . . . including not just the natural and social sciences but those aspects of mathematics, philosophy, and the humanities most concerned with investigation and explanation."[23] If this juxtaposition had occurred in *The Martian* and its meticulous attention to scientific process had extended to psychological and philosophical nuance, the film might answer author Samuel C. Florman's call for art that depicts engineering as engaging "humanity's deepest impulses."[24]

The issues of order and control that infuse the portrayals of engineers in these films come to a climax in adaptations of Crusoe's relationship with Friday. "Wilson" fills this role in *Cast Away*, and his muteness and malleability differ significantly from the questioning eagerness of Defoe's Friday, who wants to understand everything, including *"why God no kill the Devil, so make him no more do wicked?"* (158). While Wilson cannot serve in Friday's role of reverse anthropologist, some critics see the volleyball/interlocutor as engaging a critique of cultural assumptions nonetheless. Robert Mayer reads Wilson as "a projection of the film's Crusoe" but finds ambiguity in whether this process "removes the non-Western other" or turns the Friday figure with its increasingly wild appearance "into a true object . . . subjected to Noland's will."[25] Rebecca Weaver-Hightower interprets Wilson as being about Noland's needs, fears, and limitations and argues that his obsessive focus on his inanimate companion blocks his ability to interact with the living whale that travels alongside the hero.[26] Because Wilson is born of Noland's anger and displays the bloody handprint from this outburst, we might rather interpret Wilson more as a blood-brother equivalent to the protagonist. When Wilson floats away, Noland regards himself as lost as well. The two are inextricably bound, as can be seen near the end of the movie when Noland is driving through Texas with a new version of Wilson by his side.

If the Friday figure in *Cast Away* is a totemic blood-brother, in *Moon* he is an even closer relation—another Sam Bell. *Moon* intertwines the surreal terror of Crusoe's sighting of the footprint and the ethical problem of his treatment of Friday into the crisis of meeting one's own clone. After Sam Bell_2 rescues Sam Bell_1 from the rover crash,[27] the two warily begin interacting and expressing paranoid thoughts about the other. Even though he very well knows the answer, Bell_1 disturbedly whispers to GERTY, "Who's the guy in the rec room?"[28] The denial continues when Bell_1 yells in a confrontation, "I'm the original Sam!," asserting his own claim to authenticity and full selfhood and diminishing Bell_2 as a mere clone.[29] Forced to open his mind to the logic that perhaps he, too, is not original, Bell_1 has to grapple with the fact that his main solace, the idea of his wife Tess, is shared by Bell_2. Like Crusoe's building trust in Friday, Bell_1 uses a commonality to bond with his clone and proudly confides the news of their daughter Eve, born during his first year at the Sarang station. As the plot develops, the clones learn to care for each other without hierarchy and several times change out their roles in plans to thwart Lunar Industries. They see each other as one and interchangeable, unlike *Robinson Crusoe* where the hero rises over his subjects to become their ruler.

At first glance, no one seems to fit the role of Friday in *The Martian* because the culture at NASA is so insular. The exclusive focus on the space agency is so strong, however, that it functions as another island, and when Mark Watney is rescued from his Martian exile he still remains apart from wider society. The film posits the general world outside of NASA as its other—an audience and bankroll for its endeavors, as seen in the footage of regular CNN reports about Watney and crowds that gather to view his rescue. The nonscientists of the earth thus collectively signify Friday's submissive approval and fawning support of the film's Crusoe. In the DVD of *The Martian*, an "Extras" reel makes this divide between scientists/nonscientists even clearer, featuring a segment titled "The Right Stuff" where a psychologist interviews each of the Ares III crew members. This skit is a satire on the psychologist as pseudo-scientist who wastes the team's time with useless questions and then at the end of it all has to ask Johannsen for the low-down on each of his subjects to come up with his report.[30] The film thus mocks the field of psychology as lacking rigorous methodology at the same time that it idolizes the natural sciences, replicating the cultural imperialism of Defoe's Crusoe.

The enduring fascination with and remaking of Defoe's 1719 *Robinson Crusoe* comes in part from its genre hybridity. The work combines the abundance of factual detail of the early novel with the circular plotline of the romance.[31] As such, it becomes a barometer with which to assess the current intricate state of human strivings and wider spiritual shortcomings at any point in time. Like *Robinson Crusoe*, which begins and ends with the urge to wander and its connection to colonial conquest, these three films all come full circle to their initial idea to emphasize theme. *Cast Away*, for instance, begins at a crossroads in Texas as a FedEx truck picks up a box at the Petersons' ranch; following the progress of this package, the camera takes us to Russia where we meet up with Chuck Noland on assignment. The film ends at the same crossroads where it began, suggesting that perhaps fate all along had been drawing Noland to this very spot and to the newly divorced or widowed Bettina Peterson. The symbolic meaning making Noland had carried out in his cave paintings while on the island now seems magical; even though the love he paid homage to, Kelly Frears, has married another man, Noland's more general hope for reunion and love seems to have been granted in his meeting with Bettina. *Moon* shares the circular plot form, beginning with a grandiose advertisement for Lunar Industries and ending with media reporting on Sam Bell_2's testimony against that energy conglomerate. The clash of truths set up between corporate marketing and journalism goes unresolved; one person's ability to confront large-scale corruption is thus questioned, especially given that the last words of the film are from a news host who slanders Bell_2 without knowing anything about him. *The Martian*'s plot also follows a circular pattern, beginning with the Ares III work on Mars and concluding with the launch of Ares IV. This emphasis highlights the film's heroic portrayal of science and validates the indefatigable efforts of human intelligence.

Because they bring us round to reconsider the beginning sequence, the circular plotlines in these twenty-first-century film adaptations emphasize problems and solutions. This pattern seems particularly fitting for works that feature engineer heroes. *Cast Away* initially follows the viewpoint of Bettina Peterson's FedEx box adorned with her personal insignia, a pair of encircled wings. In returning a similarly marked box to sender after his island captivity, Noland takes it out of circulation and gives it agency with his written explanation that "this package saved my life."[32] With this remark, Noland reveals the complete turnaround from his initial obsession with time to growing attentiveness to that which makes life meaningful. The symbolism of the wings prompts Noland to infuse this particular box with meaning, and in rescuing it, it rescues him. The symmetry of the winged emblem further seems to portend that the broken gateway to the Texas ranch will soon be mended so that it reads Chuck and Bettina. Theirs will not be a world without FedEx, but it will be in an environment where "a whole lot of nothing" allows for artistic and existential freedom.[33] The film signifies that their homestead will not be a clichéd version of the West as clear from Bettina's break with her adulterous, cowboy husband. Instead, the artist and the survivor will come together to make a new world based on their shared appreciation of the deeply symbolic and mysterious nature of life. The film strengthens this theme by the subtlety of its ending, which leaves Noland at the crossroads, asking the audience to interpret the symbolism of the story they have just viewed.

Moon likewise pursues a circular plot pattern, beginning and ending with Earth media coverage. Although 99 percent of the film is set on the moon, this bookending emphasizes that the problem is not with technological advancement, but with the craven human impulse to maximize profits, enabled by false narratives spread via the communications network. Sam Bell_2, as he returns to Earth, faces numerous challenges including his hypershort lifespan, his inevitable meeting with the original Sam Bell, and the trauma of testifying against Lunar Industries in public. In making himself into a news story, Bell_2 sacrifices his independence out of hope for eventual justice. The film does not oversimplify the activist's attack on corporate corruption, in that the final words are voiced by a talk show host who, without even knowing the evidence, asserts that Bell_2 is a sham. However, while immediate change might not occur due to the propaganda of those in power, Bell_2's inspiration to knock down the communications blackout for his successor clone on the moon may hold hope for the future. Thus, the hypocritical message about a clean-energy future in Lunar Industries' film-opening commercial is replaced by a real story of the possibility for change when one person acts to protect others. Like *Cast Away*'s conclusion, hope is built upon an agonizing realization that one is replaceable. While Chuck Noland loses "the love of his life,"[34] he continues on new roads and finds new potential in his future. Sam Bell, in realizing his cloned state of being, suffers greatly but ultimately finds support as the multiplicity of his selves take collective action against the perpetrator of wrongs against him.

In *The Martian*, the plot begins and ends with NASA's work as we see different iterations of the Mars Ares project in action. Scientific discovery itself is thus elevated as what most matters and what must carry on. Watney's heroism is based upon his ability to jerry-rig the specialized knowledge of his teammates and serve as a scientific jack-of-all-trades. This prospect does not daunt him; in fact, we hear ambition in Watney's eager anticipation of how his accidental abandonment on Mars "is going to be a research effort, with a bunch of experimentation. I'll have to become my own little NASA, figuring out how to explore far from the Hab."[35] Likewise, Crusoe preens with satisfaction over his self-sufficiency; he marvels that having "never handled a Tool in my Life . . . yet in time by Labour, Application, and Contrivance, I found at last that I wanted nothing but I could have made it" (51). The rightful pride each man feels in purposeful work to counteract tragic circumstance becomes fraught with ethical problems once that pride is magnified into dominion over others' lives. Crusoe builds his own state, claiming that he has followed the guidance of divine providence in doing so. As he surveys his burgeoning domain, he notes, "My Island was now peopled, and I thought my self very rich in Subjects; and it was a merry Reflection which I frequently made, How like a King I look'd" (174). Watney is also surrounded by subjects at the end of his story, as admiring students swarm the new celebrity instructor at NASA, unanimously raising their hands with questions when granted the permission to do so. In each plotline, the castaway incorporates others under his authority without engaging debate or dissent. Watney becomes a one-man NASA and Crusoe becomes the one person who encompasses a whole nation, the king. *The Martian*'s ending sequence of the Ares IV launch thus comes to resemble Crusoe's final tallying of the considerable assets of his kingdom, as the media blitz on Watney has clearly won over billions of dollars of reinvestment in NASA to expedite this mission.

Considered together, these recent Robinsonades all utilize the genre hybridity of Defoe's original text to propose solutions to the life-constricting modern workplace cultures they depict. *Cast Away* shares Defoe's engagement with the providence tradition, as seen in the large arc between the film's beginning and ending sequence at the crossroads. This unifying pattern suggests a guiding force has ordered events, directing Noland's path for a larger purpose. J. Paul Hunter reads Crusoe as likewise led by providence; he identifies Defoe's protagonist as an everyman "of ordinary capabilities who overcomes many of his limitations by a combination of divine guidance and enlightened effort."[36] Cultivating an attunement to the "secret Intimations of Providence" (127), Noland resembles Crusoe as he learns to take on aloneness and risk, trusting his safety to powers beyond his understanding. While Duncan Jones's *Moon* does not offer the comfort of a providential theme, it does trace its hero's spiritual biography as Sam Bell_1 faces significant struggles when his pride and coherent sense of self collapse. Just as *Robinson Crusoe* channels the seventeenth-century spiritual biography's "intimate relationship to . . . the personal diary and the funeral sermon,"[37] *Moon* details Bell's daily life as it unfolds in direct proximity to the cremation chamber. As the film progresses, Bell finds reason to care about his unique soul and changes the course of his life to call to account those who would reduce him to a disposable worker.

The Martian reverses this pattern of employee exploitation as Watney voluntarily surrenders his self in service of science. This last film develops a utopian message common to a number of Robinsonades,[38] suggesting that Watney never really leaves his island as his work and life merge together. While *Cast Away* and *Moon* close cut with their heroes still traveling, *The Martian* grounds Watney inside NASA's complex. This circumscribed conclusion, purportedly attempting to isolate the best of human intelligence, also ushers in a discordant dystopian note because such prioritization involves a large commitment of resources that cannot go elsewhere.[39] The film's scientific utopia depends upon others' willingness to advance the mission of NASA above the rights and needs of the wider populace. Helen Thompson identifies the root of this paradox in "The Crusoe Story," where she argues that "like a wife, Friday is loving, a passion that, by divesting his servitude of sullenness, performatively sustains its difference from a Lockean state of slavery."[40] In *The Martian*, Friday's spousal role is enacted by the nonscientist

[145]

public cheerfully wed to the advances of science. This "servitude" that is not enslavement is so taken for granted that the film does not develop a single character who works outside the space agency. Alternately, *Cast Away* and *Moon* stage Friday as an aspect of the Crusoe figure's self, and thus avoid the problem of positing advancement upon the willing subjugation of others. While all three works interact meaningfully with Defoe's story, the two that feature engineers humbly trying to work toward both personal and societal redemption offer a more profound consideration of the myths of labor and time by which we live.

NOTES

1. Paula M. Rayman, *Beyond the Bottom Line: The Search for Dignity at Work* (New York: Palgrave Macmillan, 2001), xvii.
2. Robert Zemeckis, dir., *Cast Away* (Los Angeles: 20th Century Fox and DreamWorks, 2000), DVD.
3. Duncan Jones, dir., *Moon* (Culver City, CA: Sony Pictures Classics, 2009), DVD.
4. Frederick Taylor, *Shop Management* (New York: Harper & Brothers, 1912), 105, quoted after Andrea Veltman, *Meaningful Work* (Oxford: Oxford University Press, 2016), 73.
5. Jones, *Moon*.
6. Ibid. In the DVD's special feature "Science Center Q&A with Director Duncan Jones," Bell's visions are linked to the ability of twins to tap into sensory input from each other. Jones speculates that clones would possess this capacity as well.
7. Ridley Scott, dir., *The Martian* (Los Angeles: 20th Century Fox, 2015), DVD.
8. Scott, *The Martian*. Andy Weir's novel, which provided the basis for the film's script, ends earlier, concluding with Watney's entry into the *Hermes* and reunion with his team. Andy Weir, *The Martian: A Novel* (New York: Crown, 2014), 366–369.
9. Pat Rogers, *Robinson Crusoe* (London: George Allen & Unwin, 1979), 76, emphasis original.
10. William H. Halewood, "Religion and Invention in *Robinson Crusoe*," *Essays in Criticism* 14 (1964): 339–351, quoted after Rogers, *Robinson Crusoe*, 79.
11. Scott, *The Martian*.
12. Ibid.
13. For an analysis of how Crusoe fits into the *homo faber* role, see David Blewett, "The Iconic Crusoe: Illustrations and Images of *Robinson Crusoe*," in *The Cambridge Companion to "Robinson Crusoe,"* ed. John Richetti (Cambridge: Cambridge University Press, 2018), 161.
14. Zemeckis, *Cast Away*.
15. Jones, *Moon*.
16. Kyle Pivetti argues that Watney's history goes beyond aggrandizement of NASA and scientific endeavor. He interprets the ending as establishing a new world order of "an interplanetary American empire." Pivetti, "The King of Mars: *The Martian*'s Scientific Empire and *Robinson Crusoe*," in *The Cinematic Eighteenth Century: History, Culture, and Adaptation*, ed. Srividhya Swaminathan and Steven W. Thomas (London: Routledge, 2018), 130.
17. Zemeckis, *Cast Away*.
18. Jennifer Summit and Blakey Vermeule, *Action versus Contemplation: Why an Ancient Debate Still Matters* (Chicago: University of Chicago Press, 2018), 44.
19. Hannah Arendt, *The Human Condition* (Chicago: University of Chicago Press, 1958), 246.
20. Jones, *Moon*. Sam Rockwell's performance in the film clearly distinguishes the two clones, one near the end of his lifespan and the other newly awakened. I refer to them as Bell_1

and Bell_2, respectively, to set them apart. Given the age of the original Sam Bell's daughter, they would more accurately be the fifth and sixth clones to be activated out of the hundreds in storage.
21. Rev. Stanley S. Harakas, "To Clone or Not to Clone?," in *Ethical Issues in Human Cloning: Cross-Disciplinary Perspectives*, ed. Michael C. Brannigan (New York: Seven Bridges Press, 2001), 89.
22. Maarten Boudry and Massimo Pigliucci, eds., *Science Unlimited? The Challenges of Scientism* (Chicago: University of Chicago Press, 2017), 4.
23. Taner Edis, "Two Cheers for Scientism," in Boudry and Pigliucci, *Science Unlimited?*, 89.
24. Samuel C. Florman, *The Introspective Engineer* (New York: Thomas Dunne, 1996), 123.
25. Robert Mayer, "*Robinson Crusoe* in Hollywood," in *Approaches to Teaching Defoe's* Robinson Crusoe, ed. Maximillian E. Novak and Carl Fisher (New York: MLA, 2005), 172–173.
26. Rebecca Weaver-Hightower, *Empire Islands: Castaways, Cannibals, and Fantasies of Conquest* (Minneapolis: University of Minnesota Press, 2007), 209.
27. Jones, *Moon*.
28. Ibid.
29. Ibid.
30. Scott, *The Martian*.
31. Clive Probyn describes these elements as a "linear/historical mode of narrative (the eponymous life-histories) and a circular, endlessly/recurrent narrative mode (departure/exile, initiation, and return)" in "Paradise and Cotton-mill: Rereading Eighteenth-Century Romance," in *A Companion to Romance: From Classical to Contemporary*, ed. Corinne Saunders (Malden, MA: Blackwell, 2004), 258.
32. Zemeckis, *Cast Away*.
33. Ibid.
34. Ibid.
35. Scott, *The Martian*.
36. J. Paul Hunter, *The Reluctant Pilgrim: Defoe's Emblematic Method and Quest for Form in* Robinson Crusoe (Baltimore: Johns Hopkins University Press, 1966), 176.
37. Ibid., 82.
38. Lyman Tower Sargent, *Utopianism: A Very Short Introduction* (Oxford: Oxford University Press, 2010), 24.
39. Sargent argues for the symbiotic relationship between utopian and dystopian visions. Ibid., 22.
40. Helen Thompson, "The Crusoe Story: Philosophical and Psychological Implications," in Richetti, *Cambridge Companion*, 124.

10

GILLIGAN'S WAKE, GILLIGAN'S ISLAND, AND HISTORIOGRAPHIZING AMERICAN POPULAR CULTURE

Ian Kinane

IN THIS CHAPTER I EXPLORE the ways in which Tom Carson's sprawling pastiche *Gilligan's Wake* (2003) provides a critical retrospective of modern American cultural history through the lens of the 1960s American situational comedy *Gilligan's Island* (CBS, 1964–1967). I argue that the neoimperialist cultural politics that Carson contends underpins modern America places the *Robinson Crusoe* story (and it associated heritage) at the heart of twentieth- and twenty-first-century popular culture in the United States. To this end, I propose to examine the transmedial relationships between Daniel Defoe's *The Life and Strange Surprizing Adventures of Robinson Crusoe* (1719), Carson's *Gilligan's Wake*, and the television series *Gilligan's Island*, and the ways in which cultural memory, literary culture, and popular culture coalesce to augment and authorize particular counter-canonical narratives of American cultural history.

First, I should, perhaps, nuance my claim by acknowledging upfront that the only explicit reference made to the ubiquitous figure of Robinson Crusoe in Tom Carson's *Gilligan's Wake* comes in the novel's third chapter, narrated by the sympathetic and buffoonish Thurston Howell III, who is a reimagining of one of Sherwood Schwartz's original characters from the sitcom *Gilligan's Island*. Almost in passing, Howell evokes Crusoe in a telling moment: during a brief reverie in which he is reflecting on the isolation he feels not upon a deserted island but within the increasingly estranged and loveless marriage to his wife Eunice, nicknamed "Lovey." Howell notes, "Given longevity, almost any marriage, I suppose, eventually evolves into the cozy story of Mr. and Mrs. Crusoe, who have built the signal in the same place, share pleasure in the promontories they have named together and the birds that they call pets, and know the offshore shipwreck's skeleton in their sleep" (71).[1] Though the passage ostensibly alludes to a couple happily ensconced in the comfort and routine of their aged union, Carson's reference to

Daniel Defoe's titular hero, as well as to a condensed account of some of that character's principal duties on his infamous island, belies Howell's ultimate loneliness: for on Defoe's island, of course, there was no Mrs. Crusoe. In fact, Lovey is engaged in an adulterous affair and is almost careless in her disregard for Howell's growing suspicion of that fact ("One desolate afternoon . . . I found her in a bower with our son's tutor. . . . Her makeup was disarranged"; 71). The novel's reference to Crusoe functions not merely as symbolic of Howell's loneliness but as an example of Carson's structuring principle. Thurston Howell is one of the novel's seven narrators; Lovey, too, picks up the narration in the chapter immediately following her husband's. Each of the novel's additional five narrators (who are allotted one chapter apiece) round out the cast of this recognizably loquacious gathering: the seven archetypal characters of *Gilligan's Island*. For in Carson's *Gilligan's Wake*—a portmanteau of Schwartz's rudimental sitcom and James Joyce's hermetic verbiage *Finnegans Wake* (1939)—oblique and passing references to American popular cultural memory are couched in a series of interlinking narratives that, taken together, recount a parodic vision of twentieth-century American cultural history. The implicit point of Carson's labored novel is that fictional characters (specifically those of *Gilligan's Island*) are not as marginal to cultural history as their roles within a mediocre television sitcom would initially suggest. Carson deliberately fleshes out his borrowed characters' lives, imbuing them with vitality, marking each of them out as essential, in some way or another, to a real moment or important juncture in American national history.

For example, throughout the course of the novel, the reinvented characters of *Gilligan's Island* interact with various American political, literary, and cultural figures, such as John F. Kennedy, Alger Hiss, Sammy Davis Jr., Henry Kissinger, and Frank Sinatra, to a name a few, and their associations with these real historical figures are presented as pertinent or as in some way influential to the course of American history. In Matthew Luter's words, Carson offers an "interpretation of American history defined by conflict between privileged movers-and-shakers and innocent, occasionally even oblivious outsiders."[2] Carson's intent, then, is to draw in from the cultural marginalia characters whose relative positions on the fringe of American history renders them inconsequential; he endows them with political and historical significance, reconstituting them and offering them up for the reader's reconsideration as central to historicized constructions of the American twentieth century. In so doing, Carson's narrative conflates high- and low-brow art forms, incorporating a plethora of popular cultural characters, references, and riffs within an equally labyrinthine frame of postmodernist meta-narration, wordplay, and self-referentiality. The result of such conflations is the dissolution of the arbitrary distinctions between historical memory and popular culture. Thus, the passing reference to Crusoe in the novel is demonstrative of the politics of Carson's contrapuntal form: it is the eponymous hero of Defoe's narrative, the protagonist of one of the earliest literary novels, who is islanded from, or made marginal to, the narrative of *Gilligan's Wake*, a novel inspired by a popular television sitcom, while the characters of *Gilligan's Island* are thus brought in from the margins of the pop-culture trash heap and made integral to Carson's revisioning of twentieth-century American history.

But the connection between Defoe's *Robinson Crusoe* and Carson's *Gilligan's Wake* is more than simply referential. Sherwood Schwartz, the creator and writer of *Gilligan's Island*, has openly acknowledged his debt to Defoe ("I can't deny the possible influence of *Robinson Crusoe*. It was one of my two favourite books when I was younger").[3] If *Robinson Crusoe* occupies a foundational place in English literary tradition and post-eighteenth-century Western culture, *Gilligan's Island*, which owes its origins to the Crusoe myth, "is one of the most ubiquitously comprehended references in American cultural history."[4] *Robinson Crusoe* was marketed on its initial publication as a work of nonfiction, and in the introduction to the *Serious Reflections of Robinson Crusoe* (1720), a series of essays ostensibly narrated by Crusoe himself, Crusoe claims that the events of *Robinson Crusoe* were not fictional inventions but historical events recounted in narration. In a sense, the reification of Defoe's novel as part of Britain's cultural and national mythology, and the extent to which questions about the narrative's authenticity still persist in the conflation of the character Crusoe with the historical figure Alexander Selkirk—a Scottish sailor who was marooned on Más a Tierra in the Juan Fernandez archipelago in 1704—is precisely the point Carson strives to make with *Gilligan's Wake*. Fiction adopts the aura of history, and, in turn, historical narrative reifies and elevates certain fiction as history—as something above fiction, above itself, as something of equal significance to historical narrative. In other words, it would be inaccurate to class *Robinson Crusoe* simply as a work of fiction; such categorization would fail to take into account the mythic proportions of the narrative, and the extent to which Defoe's novel became in the eighteenth century a foundational national, cultural, and political narrative within Britain's colonial enterprise—not to mention its equally foundational position within the canon of Western literature and in the development of the novel form. The novel has been reified (and, to a certain extent, has reified itself) within the cultural imaginary as a historical rather than fictional narrative; it is "almost universally known, almost universally thought of as at least half real."[5] That the Chilean government renamed Más a Tierra Robinson Crusoe Island and the largest of the Juan Fernandez islands Alexander Selkirk Island further suggests the power of fictional narrative to conflate, supersede, and become incorporated within narratives of history.[6]

GILLIGAN'S WAKE AND AMERICAN POPULAR CULTURE

What Carson achieves with *Gilligan's Wake*, I argue, is a disentangling of the means by which history is created through an assemblage of fictional narrative that is (often retroactively) reified within the cultural imagination and authorized as "fact." I contend that Carson's novel satirizes the ways in which the enterprise of writing history often replicates the enterprise of writing fiction. In *Gilligan's Wake*, Carson instructs his readers to recognize the ways in which such "ubiquitously comprehended references" within American national history can be decoded as products of narrative and narration and, equally, to recognize the ways in which such narratives are reified or augmented as history through the collective cultural memory and celebration of popular cultural forms. What Carson's *Gilligan's Wake* does is to shore up the complex intertextual weaving of personal and cultural memory that occurs within society and by which social, cultural, and political metanarratives become reified as national mythologies. By divesting his characters of their archetypes, by giving over to each of them their own stories and by making his characters absolutely essential to their various, interconnected strands of American history, Carson illustrates the ways in which historical myths originate as narrative, and the ways in which narrative itself is important in shaping and reshaping historical mythology and national identity. While Paul Cantor has argued that "if we want to see the end of history . . . we might well begin by turning on our televisions,"[7] Carson's approach in *Gilligan's Wake* very much suggests the opposite: namely, that popular cultural forms are inherently historical and inherently politicized, and that an understanding of the ways in which history is constructed begins and ends with comprehending the ways in which popular culture and the "mindlessness" of television functions (to quote Cantor from elsewhere, "popular culture offers us a window into ideological developments in America").[8] Carson's novel argues fervently that we take seriously the mechanisms by which fiction and history come to be so closely entwined through the memorialization of popular culture. For Carson, fiction cannot be viewed as separate from history, largely because the enterprise of history is much the same as the enterprising of writing narrative. As such, the novel deconstructs the authority of historical narrative by underlining the ways in which power itself is configured as a product of narrative mythmaking.

A further clue as to Carson's intent may be found in the novel's fourth chapter, narrated by Lovey Howell. As a result of her emotional disaffection for her husband, Lovey strikes up a friendship and, later, a physical relationship with Daisy Buchanan, the erstwhile ingénue of Fitzgerald's *The Great Gatsby*, which is fueled by Lovey's growing dependence on morphine, and which Daisy supplies in plenty. In his comingling of these two characters, in particular, Carson makes clear his heretical purpose: high and low art are forged together, as a secondary character from a mildly humorous but doltish prime-time network television sitcom and Fitzgerald's literary Hedone, his proxy for the vacuity of moral values and the cynical pursuit of wealth in America's roaring twenties, are reimagined as occupying the same conceptual plane. That Fitzgerald's Great American Novel should be placed at the literal center of Carson's novel (Lovey's is the middle of seven chapters) suggests that *Gilligan's Wake* is deconstructionist in intent; and given Carson's evident contempt for America's political and cultural biases (in the overly parodic chapter "Professor X," for instance), Fitzgerald's work, which cautions against the excesses of those decadent values that have now come to define contemporary America, is the ideal foil for Carson's project. The imbrication of different fictive worlds in *Gilligan's Wake* owes much to Carson's bricolage approach, which he applies throughout the entire novel, but which is expressly spelled out for the reader in Lovey's narration. Toward the end of her chapter, Lovey is shown to descend the staircase in her mother's household, noticing, as she reaches the telephone table, the visiting cards of two of her mother's friends, "Louise Merskine" and "Christina Caldwell." Taking a sudden fancy, Lovey tears both of the cards up and begins to "idly rearrange the fragments." She takes pause at one particular configuration of words, the reader is told, "because it seemed to make a sort of nonsensical, mysterious sense, and for the life of me I couldn't understand why" (128). The words that Lovey has fashioned now read "Erskine Caldwell" and "Tina Louise": the former the name of the American novelist and short-story writer whose work commonly dealt with issues of social inequality and poverty in the American South; and the latter the stage name of Tina Blacker, an actress who starred in the film version of Caldwell's novel *God's Little Acre* (1933), but whose most famous role was that of the Hollywood siren, Ginger Grant, in *Gilligan's Island*. Lovey's paradoxical, "nonsensical" familiarity with this configuration of names works on a number of levels. On the level of intratextual narrative, Lovey's chapter in the novel concludes shortly after this scene, and the narration is taken up in the next chapter by the character Ginger. So, in a sense, Lovey's "premonition" heralds the arrival of Ginger's narrative voice within the text. On another level, Carson's bricolage technique recalls the modernist poetics of *The Waste Land* (1922), which Eliot wrote in fragments and which Pound pieced together. At times the style of Carson's novel, though distinctly postmodernist in outlook, simultaneously depends upon and deliberately problematizes the poetics of literary high modernism. This should not be surprising. Of popular entertainment forms such as television, Luter notes that the medium "by nature requires a willingness to tolerate and interpret serendipitously juxtaposed appearances of unexpected imagery."[9] In *Gilligan's Wake*, Carson imitates the formal conventions of television's hyperimagery and the poetics of mass consumption; through the deluge of the

GILLIGAN'S WAKE AND AMERICAN POPULAR CULTURE

text's asystematic intertextuality, he employs the conventions of popular media (its insistence on hyper-referentiality) often through the formal sensibilities of literary modernism (Lovey's bricolage, for instance). As though they were transient ephemera, a series of images flashing by on a screen, so Carson's innumerable references and asides within the novel are issued and almost immediately overlaid by another, thereby merging the poetics of the literary novel with the mobility of television. Given the novel's emphasis on visuality and on the power of the remediated image, then, it is not for nothing that Brendan Driscoll refers to *Gilligan's Wake* as a "Technicolor pastiche."[10]

Luter notes that "Carson's novel may be a definitive post mortem on the idea of [*Gilligan's Island* . . .] serving as an archetypal American story that can speak to the idea of America in a meaningful way."[11] While Carson certainly takes his scalpel to the sitcom, Schwartz's creation by no means remains inert: unlike the figure of Robinson Crusoe, continually reinvigorated through the many imitations of Defoe's novel, Carson revivifies *Gilligan's Island* not in homage, nor as an effort to deconstruct the political allegory which purportedly underpins the series.[12] Rather, to understand Carson's intent in any meaningful way, we might look to the second half of his novel's title, to the novel's other notable intertext: *Finnegans Wake*. *Gilligan's Wake* is not simply a postmodernist meta-exercise in plundering American history and popular culture for satire; and nor is it, as Tim Cavanagh has misjudged, a compendium "to randomly dip into for weird-but-true historical tidbits and fictional-but-alarmingly-realistic inventions."[13] More accurately, Carson's novel might be thought of as an elegy to twentieth-century America; it is a novel that mourns the values and mores of the very society it lambasts; and it is a novel that is an indictment of its own cultural production. (*That* is the new Great American Novel.) This is not, of course, to suggest that Carson's bricolage approach is, in any way, a dehistoricizing one, nor one that, in its fractiousness, fashions for itself an ahistorical fictionality. Rather, the point of *Gilligan's Wake* is precisely that Carson wishes to return his reader to historicity, and to those moments in which fiction is reproduced *as* history. While Adorno and Horkheimer foretold in the mid-twentieth century of the cultural "sameness" that has come now to both erase and define the erasure of those once-divergent historical discourses of macrocosmic and microcosmic, the universal and the particular,[14] between them Jameson and Hutcheon have later attempted to return the postmodern to its historicist origins. For Jameson, postmodernism represents not a process of dehistoricization but "an attempt to think historically in an age that has forgotten how to think historically in the first place"; he sees the production of the postmodern itself as inextricably tied to a "crisis in historicity."[15] For Hutcheon, postmodernism is concerned entirely with the reinstatement of history at the empty modernist heart of early twentieth-century cultural discourse: "What the postmodern writing of both history and literature has taught us is that both history and fiction are discourses, that both constitute systems of signification by which we make sense of the past."[16]

Thus, in his fictional-historical pastiche, Carson denigrates neither fiction nor history but sees the osmotic exchange between both as the means by which he, and his readers, might be granted access to an unauthorized but far more authoritative (if rather unorthodox) vision of American cultural history—something betwixt and between historical fact and cultural memory. Such an approach is advocated by Hutcheon, who notes of the discourses of history and fiction that both "derive their force more from verisimilitude than from any objective truth"; that both are linguistic, narrative constructs void of structural transparency; and that both are equally intertextual.[17] The interrelationality Hutcheon identifies here is precisely what Carson achieves with *Gilligan's Wake*; American history is reconstituted by the exact terms of its own cultural logic: as a product of intersecting, intertextual references to popular cultural forms (television programs, books, films, music) and the ways in which such forms constitute a cultural, national memory.

But in addition to this, Carson's novel also serves to reorient the reader's critical awareness of the role such popular forms play in historicizing American culture; to borrow a phrase from Hutcheon, *Gilligan's Wake* acknowledges "the meaning-making function of human constructs."[18] In other words, while Carson's novel trades in the inter-referentiality of its many wordplays, its knowing in-jokes, and its riffs on popular culture, it is also decidedly cognizant of the ways in which such references take on iconographic status and, moreover, of the ways in which such cultural iconography has become, like *Robinson Crusoe*, invested with the power of myth. In essence, *Gilligan's Wake* is a tapestry-like history of twentieth-century American popular culture; or, to put that another way, *Gilligan's Wake* is a particular history of America. This history is a deliberate construct, a deliberate fiction, but Carson's novel nevertheless illustrates the powerful role of fictionality in making meaningful a particular vision of history that touches on, rubs up against, or has some basis in fact (again, much like the relationship between Alexander Selkirk and Robinson Crusoe). Luter has queried whether a "nostalgic pop history supplant[s] a more authentic history" or whether history is already replicated in popular culture.[19] For *Gilligan's Wake*, with its dissolution of the divisions between high and low culture, art and popular entertainment, and history and fiction, the history of the American twentieth century *is* the history of pop. Jameson's lamentation of contemporary culture's insatiable populism was prescient; he noted that society was "condemned to see History by way of [its] own pop images and simulacra of that history."[20] But Carson's novel is not a passive product of the cultural development Jameson identifies; rather, Carson keeps one eye trained at all times on the poetics of postmodernism: on the return to history. *Gilligan's Wake*, then, is a form of historiographic metafiction. If writing history is a process of uncovering and analyzing factual records, then Carson's novel constitutes the "imaginative reconstruction of that process."[21] Here is Hutcheon, once again: "Historiographic metafiction refutes the natural or common-sense methods of distinguishing between historical fact and fiction. It refuses the view that only history has a truth claim, both by questioning the ground of that claim in historiography and by asserting that both history and fiction are discourses, human constructs."[22] In revising American history vis-à-vis the elaborate conventions of its pop-culture pastiche, *Gilligan's Wake* dispels the myth of historical authenticity and distorts America's claim to its own historicized national narratives. In rewriting (or perhaps writing anew) America's fiction of itself, Carson opens up American history, precluding that narrative from being either "conclusive" or "teleological."[23] As Luter has noted of the novel's focus on *Gilligan's Island*, Carson is, on the whole, much less interested in "what the ubiquity of television tells us about American culture than in how that culture and its history can be depicted, questioned, and re-defined in literary fiction."[24] Carson's novel does not view history as teleologically static; on the contrary, history in *Gilligan's Wake* is made dynamically live. Take, for instance, Thurston Howell's unwitting sponsorship of one Alger Hiss for a government role in the U.S. State Department in chapter 3. In the course of American history, the real Alger Hiss was tried and convicted of perjury in 1950 with respect to his role as a Soviet spy and for his involvement in international espionage. In Carson's sardonic takeoff of American history, it is the witless but well-connected Howell who inadvertently grants Hiss access to the upper echelons of American power and who is shown to be initially responsible for Hiss's ascent. In the alternate history of America that Carson puts forward, it is no coincidence that the shortsighted, ignorant, vociferous, but wealthy conservative Howell should lead the nation to its potential undoing.

Moreover, it is through the postmodern poetics of Carson's novel and its particular dynamics of historical representation that notions of hegemonic power, and the power of mythmaking itself, come to be questioned. In the novel's first chapter, a deluge of stream of consciousness narrated by a character who identifies himself as Maynard G. Krebs (but who is, it is strongly implied, the titular Gilligan),[25] the reader witnesses a protest against the 1961 Bay of Pigs invasion by American forces. During the protest, another character (in reported speech) exclaims that "when governments write bad poetry, poets have to govern," and calls for government forces to "Free verse!" (4). Here, Carson conflates that antiwar protest of the enflamed American proletariat during U.S.-Cuban tensions with an exhortation to "free" literary verse from its constraints. Politics and poetry are aligned: Carson suggests that where the former (inevitably) fails the latter must prevail, thus underlining the symbiotic relationship between power and language. True political power, then, Carson proffers, consists of the ability not only to construct narrative (national, historical, mythological) but to govern people's interpretation of that narrative so adroitly that fiction becomes naturalized. With this in mind, Carson's narrative becomes analogous for the processes by which such historical mythmaking can be undone and then done over. The wordiness of *Gilligan's Wake*, confounding though it is to readers at first, is an integral part of the novel's politics: in its sheer verbiage, Carson's novel is a furious attempt to rewrite history and to disentangle the myths of nationalism upon which America is so dependent. A little further into the first chapter, Carson's narrator, the addled Krebs, urges the reader to "reverse the game" and to "rearrange everything . . . we knew—old songs, TV shows, other books, news of the day," in order that it might "refer to our shared text, and so to us" (15). Here, Carson is not only consolidating the premise of his novel, in signposting quite clearly the jumbled pastiche of his approach, and purposefully calling attention to his dizzying use of intertexts and pop culture references, but also underlining the fervent political drive at the heart of the novel: his incitement for the reader to "rearrange everything" she or he believes in. Like Eliot and Pound's bricolage in *The Waste Land*, Carson's form is one of protest, a provocation to view American national history as nothing more than an assemblage of narrative fragments. In crafting a narrative that is replete in commonplace, popular references, Carson conceives a "shared text" in which the narratives of history are not separate from or exclusive to mainstream fiction, but are a vital part and consequence of it. History, in *Gilligan's Wake*, is an egalitarian enterprise, something that, through the characters from *Gilligan's Island*, is made more socially accessible.

However, Carson also subtly demonstrates the ways in which hegemonic ideology operates upon American mainstream fictions, and the ways in which the atrocities of national history, committed ostensibly in the name of American self-betterment, are often deliberately occluded from, or sublimated within, national narratives. Take, for instance, the sudden appearance on Thurston Howell's doorstep of a series of comic books, the *Two-Fisted U.S. Adventures* series, instead of the morning newspaper. Howell notes that "a dozen different titles in all [appeared] until a second instalment of the first one I'd seen was delivered, at which point the whole cycle began over again," and that "as months and then years went by, if one adventure was retired, another would replace it" (74). The *Two-Fisted U.S. Adventures* comics showcase a number of all-American, aggressively masculinist, ultraconservative adventure narratives ("*Two-Fisted* Puts the White Back in the

Old Red, White and Blue"; 76), to which Howell becomes swiftly addicted, enshrining the comic collection in its own custom-built room within his home. Try as his son might to coax him into "the realm of literature" (74), Howell's addiction to the comics becomes so pronounced that his son stages an intervention. When Howell is confronted by his son's assertion that "the people in your comics aren't made up" (79), and that, in fact, national news coverage has ceased and that once-newsworthy reports are now being repackaged as low-brow comic book—above all, fictionalized—adventures, he dismisses it as a peculiar conspiracy: "Who'd go to all this trouble just for me?," he asks. Howell's son retorts, "Oh, it's not just you. . . . Thousands and thousands of these [comics] go out to everyone like you. To your whole class, in fact" (80). The ultimate point of it all, of course, is articulated by Howell's son toward the end of their confrontation, when he notes that comic books have taken the place of newspapers so that the American populace "won't be completely uninformed about what's going on, but won't take any of it seriously" (80). The adventures depicted in the comics are American military operations that have taken place in real-world history, and the comic books serve as a form of nationalist propaganda designed to dissimulate the extent of America's military atrocities. Here, newspaper coverage of historical events has been replaced by a series of adventure narratives; history, in this case, has literally come to be fictionalized, re-presented as it is in comic-book narrative form. To Howell and his wealthy, conservative ilk, moreover, history is made unreal (or perhaps unmade altogether), and America's national, ideological agenda is, through the passive receptivity of the comic books' eagerly interpellated readership, tacitly consented to. Carson thus highlights for his readers the (not dissimilar) methods of indoctrination that occur in American mythmaking—or, indeed, any national mythmaking—by which agencies of control exert influence over narrative form, or over the ways in which narrative is constructed, (re)presented, and disseminated. On works of historiographic metafiction, Hutcheon notes that such texts "speculate openly about historical displacement and its ideological consequences, about the way one writes about the past 'real,' about what constitute 'the known fact' of any given event."[26] The ways in which a text or narrative reflects on or categorizes a particular historical moment constitute in its entirety the epistemic response of a culture to that particular moment. History, Carson's novel is at pains to emphasize, is "created by the storyteller, not the historical player."[27] In other words, Carson's reflection on the ideological reification of history (turning news into comic book entertainment) is parodic of both the means by which ideological state apparatuses function in the modern era and the ways in which people have become unaware of their own desubjectification through national metanarratives, but it also invites a readerly interpretation of, rather than a passive submission to, the known past, to that which is understood as "real" history. Carson thus makes explicit the textual nature of history, directing the reader's suspicions of the historical past and calling attention to the means by which agencies of state control position and maintain themselves: through the use and abuse of narrative, of storytelling, and of language.

As if by way of resistance to traditional narrative hegemony, and as a further provocation for the reader to pay attention to the ways in which cultural narratives are constructed, Carson's fifth narrator, Ginger, slowly realizes throughout the course of her chapter in *Gilligan's Wake* that she is a fictional character within a novel, and that she is, herself, a narrative construct. She says, "As for whoever's making all this up about me, well—you go on and enjoy yourself. . . . Believe me, Sprout, I'm used to this. The others aren't, which is why they never spotted you—although Lovey did come closer than she knew one time" (136). The "others" Ginger refers to, here, are the other characters from *Gilligan's Island*—and the other six narrators in *Gilligan's Wake*. Ginger's awareness of her own fictionality, in this context, is further indicative of Carson's counterhegemonic politics. Through her dawning recognition of an implied writer figure (not Carson himself, but the mysterious "Sprout" she refers to), Ginger serves to underline for Carson's readers the notion that narrative of any kind belies authorial intent, and that there is always a "someone" behind the events of narrative who is prescribing, detailing, and controlling it. (Moreover, that Ginger is "used to this" treatment may well suggest that, as the star of adult films, she is not unfamiliar with the misogynistic social and cultural narratives that are often imposed upon beautiful young women.) In other words, Ginger's recognition of the text's fictionality is an implied caution for the reader against a belief in the historicity of cultural metanarratives. Carson does, however, suggest that Ginger has some sort of agency within this narrative-within-the-narrative, and that resistance to such metanarratives is possible. Ginger frequently addresses "Sprout" and snaps back at his attempts to control her story. Her chapter concludes in the following way:

>All right, Sprout. Close me now. Stick me back under the pillow. Toodle-oo and au revoir, and yee-hah. Well finally!—yes, indeed: those *are* my eyes.
>That's really all. I'm not going to show you anything else.
>*Aaaaargh!*
>Enough already.
>Now, scoot.
>Amoose-vay. Scram.
>Beat it, kid. (179)

GILLIGAN'S WAKE AND AMERICAN POPULAR CULTURE

This final exchange—in which Ginger responds orally to the implied prodding and poking at her body ("*Aaaaargh!*") by the silent "Sprout"—is one of tension. Throughout the chapter Ginger exclaims a number of times that her body parts are not her own (perhaps due to the depersonalization she feels as a performer in adult films), or that the implied author of the narrative is in some way adjusting or tampering with her represented body ("Sure would appreciate if you restored me to my natural five eight, though"; 136). Her exclamation in this final scene ("yes, indeed: those *are* my eyes") suggests that she has been restored to some sort of representational wholeness, or that the implied author has concluded his narrative experimentation with her. Moreover, it is also strongly implied that "Sprout" is a juvenile: while "kid" implies a literal youthfulness, the secreting of Ginger herself "back under the pillow" suggests a childish concealment of guilt. Inherent to this scene, and throughout the chapter as a whole, is the strained relations between personal agency and representation, and between the self and those narratives that have been foisted upon the self. In other words, through Ginger's heightened awareness of her own constructivity, and of the ways in which she, as a character, has been conditioned to act and behave, Carson is attempting to redress for the reader the epistemic distance between personal, lived truth and representational experience. Given Carson's focus within the novel on the larger narrative of twentieth-century history, the tension between personal agency and representational narrative—figured here in the conflict between Ginger's actual and represented body—becomes a metonym for the conflict between historical occurrence and historicized (and, thus, culturally memorialized) fictions. Ginger's resistance to the narrative that has been written about her (her continuing addresses to the implied author figure "Sprout") is a resistance to historicization and to the very means by which historical narrative itself does not simply reflect authorized, culturally sanctioned interpretation, but directs and prescribes it. Carson proposes that neither the character (Ginger) nor the reader (the implied reader of *Gilligan's Wake*) is passive within the processes of historicization. Rather, he advocates for his readers a cautiousness and a suspicion toward historicized cultural metanarratives, suggesting to his readership that they question and resist national and political narratives that take for granted the individual's tacit consent and that attempt to elide their own fictionality as narrative.

Suspicion of those narratives peddled by the agencies of state control is well founded, Carson implies, for, in the novel's sixth chapter, narrated by the character of the Professor, Carson pushes to the extreme limits his hypothesis on historicization. In this chapter the mild-mannered, congenial, knowledgeable, but rather generic Professor from *Gilligan's Island* is reenvisioned as a narcotics-addled alcoholic, necrophiliac, pedophile, and rapist who has, in Carson's reimagining, been at the center of some of the most prominent historical moments and government conspiracies in twentieth-century America. For instance, the reader is told that the Professor worked with Robert Oppenheimer in Los Alamos on the Manhattan Project, the development of the first American atomic bomb; that he was responsible for selecting Nagasaki as the second test site for the atomic bombing of Japan; that he oversaw the establishment of both the CIA and the Apollo Program; and that he instigated the Suez Canal Crisis. The reader also learns that the Professor is responsible for a social experiment in the mid-1960s, during which he selected six civilians and marooned them all on an island off the California coast, along with himself. It is heavily implied that this experiment is the inspiration for the television sitcom *Gilligan's Island* and that it was the Professor, not the hapless Gilligan, who was always foiling the castaways' attempts to escape. All of these activities, the Professor tells his readers, were facilitated by a shadowy cabal of agents with sinister designs on the course of world history, and united under the leadership of Franklin Delano Roosevelt—who, the novel implies parodically, was ultimately responsible for manipulating and shaping twentieth-century America's cultural, historical vision of itself. While this all reads as sardonic hyperbole, Carson nevertheless manages in the course of the chapter to deconstruct assumed notions of history and of specific historical events. Indeed, the Professor's chapter promises the reader to explore "what the books don't tell you" (183), a deliberate choice of words and a mocking play on Carson's part on the absence from authorized narratives of American history of the salacious details of some of the most well-respected historical figures. For instance, when it comes to deciding where the second American atomic warhead is to be dropped, the Professor notes that one colonel proffers the suggestion of San Diego, precisely and solely because it was where he "had recently picked up a nasty case of the clap" (187). When a decision cannot be made with logic, the Professor arranges a makeshift game of "Pin the Tail on the Donkey," in which Robert Oppenheimer is blindfolded, spun around rapidly, and instructed to mark with a piece of chalk a location on a hanging wall map. The absurdity of Carson's reinvented twentieth-century America is that historicized events, not inconsiderable in terms of their consequences in the real world, are rendered as nothing more than the product of arbitrary play on the part of those involved; and American cultural history is presented overwhelmingly as a farcical, offensive charade around which narratives of "Americanness" and national pride have been woven. The Professor delights, for instance, at the FBI's "staggering success at hoodwinking the populace" (191), at the cabal's invention and marketing of communism to the American people, and at the ingenuity of initiating America's puppet presidencies. In the Professor's words—perhaps the most telling of the entire novel—"the true story of history isn't what occurs, which is often perfectly haphazard, but how and by whom its events are turned to advantage" (210). This is the point of *Gilligan's Wake*, and the premise upon which Carson builds his fictional rehistoricization of the American twentieth century: history is already a fabrication. That the Professor ends up teaching history at a high school in Virginia after his government career is over is Carson's ultimate indictment of America's schooling in its own national narratives.

However, Carson is not content to leave it there, as the Professor's narrative reaches its overblown and grotesque conclusion: in his sordid quest for pleasure, the Professor travels to Nagasaki and rapes and murders an elderly, disabled survivor of the nuclear blast, before transmorphing into a giant reptile, reminiscent of Godzilla, and destroying downtown Tokyo. Unlike the narrator of the novel's final chapter, Mary Ann, whom Carson identifies as the personification of America (288), here the Professor's monstrous form becomes a far more literal embodiment of America's rampaging globalization. This chapter's final revelation—that the mysterious cabal for whom the Professor worked has now expanded globally, and, it is implied, controls the world in the same sinister fashion—functions as a foil to the narrative's ultimate revelation: the fact that the implied author figure, the narrator of the first chapter who identifies as Krebs, but who is, in reality, the titular Gilligan and the sinister, controlling "Sprout" whom Ginger addresses, is, in fact, a lunatic who has invented the stories of each of the six other characters while he has been sectioned in a mental institution. In other words, the novel's vision of history is being written by a madman. In the final chapter, the reader learns from Mary Ann's roommate, Susan, that the novel *Gilligan's Wake* is the product of one Jack Gil Egan (nicknamed "Gilligan" by his peers, after the eponymous television series), who is Susan's former boyfriend. When Egan discovers that Susan has been having an affair with her history teacher (none other than the priapic Professor), he loses his mind and has to be admitted to the Mayo Clinic for psychiatric treatment. It is there that he begins to come to terms with Susan's perfidiousness, by crafting for himself an invented narrative using the seven characters from the popular television sitcom *Gilligan's Island*. Thus, Egan's reorganized national history of the American twentieth century is actually an attempt to come to terms with his own personal experiences of betrayal, loss, and pain. Carson makes it clear, in Luter's words, that by "bringing received national myths and shared cultural memory into ironic conflict,"[28] historical authenticity is itself deconstructed. Egan's madness is fueled by the conflation of different metanarratives and historical and cultural myths, as well as the multiple, competing guises he has adopted. These different guises, which appear in each of the seven chapters and through which Egan sublimates his own identity (Jack Gil Egan, Maynard

G. Krebs, Algigni, Mr. Gliaglin, Lil Gagni, Mr. Gagilnil, Lili Gang), all coalesce in the novel's final chapter. Through Carson's eyes, history is to be viewed not as a monolithic discourse; rather, by way of Egan's spliced and fractured retelling of twentieth-century American history, and through the competing but interlinked accounts of each of the seven narrators, Carson urges his readers to imagine a thoroughly polyglossic approach to history. That the characters of *Gilligan's Wake* come to understand their own fictionality—in other words, that they are conscious of their appropriation by Egan within the fictional universe of *Gilligan's Wake*—suggests that, helpless though they appear to be, they are nevertheless imbued with a consciousness of their own place in history, and with an awareness of the processes by which their lives have become narrativized.

The novel concludes with several short scenes of the characters from *Gilligan's Island* back on the sitcom's fictional island, where they have been living since the show first aired in the 1960s. When a newspaper in a coffee jar washes ashore onto the island, the seven castaways eagerly pore over it for news of themselves: "Even the non-egotists among us were eager to read about ourselves in no matter how distorted and travestied a version" (332). Here, the characters are conscious of their own reification as characters; they are aware of their own historicization through printed, recorded media. Moreover, they are aware that the narrative in which they have been trapped is a "distorted" and "travestied" one. Rather than a passive acceptance of the overarching metanarrative by which they have been framed, the characters now evince a knowing consciousness of the narrativizing processes of history itself, and of the ways in which historical narratives are often arbitrarily configured to impose upon the disorder of human existence a structural code it does not warrant. While Gilligan, the implied author of Carson's novel, is the text's perverse, oppressive autocrat, that the other characters are each given a voice, and that they voice resistance to their own textual oppression (Ginger and Mary Ann, in particular), suggests that Carson's novel is distinctly democratic in its impulses. While the characters of *Gilligan's Wake* are ultimately unable to escape the text, the reader is left to understand that the apparatuses of control employed by Gilligan within the narrative are resisted, and that those characters about and around whom this particular sordid history of twentieth-century America has been written demonstrate the political import of protesting and resisting culturally sanctioned, seemingly authorized historical narratives. Ultimately, Carson's project in *Gilligan's Wake*—the novel's mélange of high and low cultural art forms, fantasy and invented history—is driven by the postmodernist desire to "close the gap between past and present" and to "rewrite the past in a new context,"[29] and Carson demonstrates the need for a considered interrogation of the role shared cultural memory plays within macropolitical narratives. Much like

Daniel Defoe's *Robinson Crusoe*, then, *Gilligan's Wake* reifies a particular type of cultural history; it exists in the interstice between fiction, history, and cultural memory as a hypertextual mythos. As *Robinson Crusoe* reifies the imagined history of British imperialism, so *Gilligan's Wake* reifies the imperialist and historicizing power of narrative in American national and cultural politics. *Gilligan's Wake* is not *like* a fantastical history of the American twentieth century; it *is* the American twentieth century: a complex web of shared cultural memories, popular texts, and references that have been authenticated in narrative as history.

NOTES

1. Tom Carson, *Gilligan's Wake* (New York: Picador, 2003). Further references are to this edition and are given parenthetically.
2. Matthew Luter, "More Than a Vast Avante-Pop Wasteland: Tom Carson's *Gilligan's Wake*, Television, and American Historical Fiction," *Genre* 42.3/4 (2009): 29.
3. Sherwood Schwartz, *Inside* Gilligan's Island*: From Creation to Syndication* (London: McFarland, 1988), 13.
4. Walter Metz, *Gilligan's Island* (Detroit: Wayne State University Press, 2012), 13.
5. Ian Watt, "Robinson Crusoe as a Myth," *Essays in Criticism* 1.2 (1951): 96.
6. Tim Severin, *In Search of Robinson Crusoe* (New York: Basic Books, 2002), 23–24.
7. Paul Cantor, *Gilligan Unbound: Pop Culture and the Age of Globalization* (New York: Rowman & Littlefield, 2001), xxv.
8. Ibid., x.
9. Luter, "More Than a Vast Avante-Pop Wasteland," 27.
10. Brendan Driscoll, "Gilligan's Wake," *Booklist* 99.8 (2003): 731.
11. Luter, "More Than a Vast Avante-Pop Wasteland," 37.
12. Critics have attempted to read *Gilligan's Island* in a number of different ways. For Laura Morowitz, the show's core political ideology is "the quest for escape from western civilization and the ultimate impossibility of achieving that goal." See Morowitz, "From Gauguin to *Gilligan's Island*," *Journal of Popular Film and Television* 26.1 (1998): 4. For Heidi C. M. Scott, *Gilligan's Island* is very much a show about democracy and about the fantasies of anticapitalism. See Scott, "Havens and Horrors: The Island Landscape," *Interdisciplinary Studies in Literature and Environment* 21.3 (2014): 654. The show's creator, Sherwood Schwartz, envisioned *Gilligan's Island* as "comedy on top and allegory underneath." See Schwartz, *Inside* Gilligan's Island, 9.
13. Tim Cavanagh, "Sucking in the American Century," *Reason*, November 2011, http://reason.com/archives/2011/10/20/sucking-in-the-american-centur
14. Theodor W. Adorno and Max Horkheimer, *Dialectic of Enlightenment: Philosophical Fragments*, ed. Gunzelin Schmid Noerr, trans. Edmund Jephcott (Stanford, CA: Stanford University Press, 2002), 94.
15. Fredric Jameson, *Postmodernism; or, The Cultural Logic of Late Capitalism* (London: Verso, 1991), ix, 22.
16. Linda Hutcheon, *A Poetics of Postmodernism: History, Theory, Fiction* (London: Routledge, 1988), 89.
17. Ibid., 105.
18. Ibid., 89.
19. Luter, "More Than a Vast Avante-Pop Wasteland," 35.
20. Jameson, *Postmodernism*, 25.

21. Louis Gottschalk, *Understanding History: A Primer of Historical Method*, 2nd ed. (New York: Knopf, 1969), 48.
22. Hutcheon, *Poetics of Postmodernism*, 93.
23. Ibid., 110.
24. Luter, "More Than a Vast Avante-Pop Wasteland," 22.
25. Maynard G. Krebs is the beatnik character from the CBS sitcom *The Many Loves of Dobie Gillis* (1959–1963), played by actor Bob Denver. Denver also played the titular role in *Gilligan's Island*.
26. Hutcheon, *Poetics of Postmodernism*, 94.
27. Luter, "More Than a Vast Avante-Pop Wasteland," 32.
28. Ibid., 21.
29. Hutcheon, *Poetics of Postmodernism*, 118.

CODA

Rewriting the Robinsonade

DANIEL COOK

IF YOU PLANNED TO WRITE a Robinsonade for the 2019 tercentenary of the first publication of *The Life and Strange Surprizing Adventures of Robinson Crusoe*, you would have had many precedents to follow.[1] Your Robinsonade might not even be a novel: the principal characters, themes, and settings of *Robinson Crusoe* have always been reworked into nonfictional genres, poems, plays, pantomimes, films, advertisements, and material objects at large. Taking Defoe's own lead, you might have prolonged the eponymous hero's life into "farther adventures." Or you might have written a sort of echoistic story that engages with the original at varying points of divergence. Muriel Spark's *Robinson* (1958), for one, recounts the experiences of a writer stranded on an island named Robinson, which is home to a reclusive Crusoe-like figure also named Robinson. It is quite literally a Robinsonade in name—and, for the most part, it is a Robinsonade in name only. You might have revisited the original novel's origins more directly, and even fictionalized Defoe the author, as we see most famously in J. M. Coetzee's *Foe* or in Gaston Compère's *Robinson '86* (both 1986).

You might have robinsonized other characters. *Krinke Kesmes* (1708) became *Der holländische Robinson* (1721), and *Gil Blas* (1715) became *Der spanische Robinson* (1726). Or you could have recalibrated the power dynamic between Crusoe and Friday. Michel Tournier's *Vendredi, ou les limbes du Pacifique* (typically retitled *Friday, or The Other Island* in English; 1967) and Derek Walcott's *Pantomime* (1979) both reverse the roles of the colonialist and the Carib as a means of writing back to literary colonialism.[2] Once dubbed "a sort of second *Robinson Crusoe*," *The Female American* (1767) is the story of Unca Eliza Winkfield, a woman of mixed race, and therefore a double departure from Defoe's Robinsonade.[3] Recasting remains a popular option. Andrew Lane's "A Crusoe Adventure" trilogy (2016–2018) gives us a teenage Crusoe and a female Friday—of the two, the latter is by far the more common transformation. Few imitators have paid any attention to the fact Defoe killed off Friday in his sequel, *The Farther Adventures of Robinson Crusoe* (1719). But you might have done away with Crusoe and Friday altogether. Rex Gordon's science fiction Robinsonade *No Man Friday* (1956) even turns the

[165]

natives into giant automaton anthropoids on Mars. Other popular subgenres that might have enticed you include the apocalyptic Robinsonade, a label sometimes given to Cormac McCarthy's *The Road* (2006), most famously, or Marlen Haushofer's *Die Wand* (*The Wall*; 1963).[4] A more clearly marked apocalyptic Robinsonade, E. J. Robinson's *Robinson Crusoe 2244* (2014), transposes the isolated adventurer to a twenty-third-century wasteland filled with unspeakable horrors. With a flick of the pen a fear of cannibalism has become a dread of zombiism. But the Robinsonade has long been prone to darker reworking. Edgar Allan Poe's *The Narrative of Arthur Gordon Pym of Nantucket* (1838) conjoins to Defoe's story a litany of Gothic trappings, not least of all a corpse-ridden ghost ship. The pioneering scientific-romance writer, H. G. Wells, spliced the castaway tale with a Frankensteinian vision of humanity's godlike meddling in *The Island of Dr. Moreau* (1896). Or we might consider generic mashups. Ivan Fanti's *Robinson Crusoe on Zombie Island* (2013) imbues the narrative of the marooned man with Lovecraftian horror. (As in Lane's trilogy, Fanti recasts Friday as a young woman—here a cannibal.)

Young adult Robinsonades are especially prevalent and always have been. Frederick Marryat's *Masterman Ready; or, The Wreck of the Pacific* (1841), R. M. Ballantyne's *The Coral Island* (1858), and Robert Louis Stevenson's *Treasure Island* (1882) remain among the most famous of all Robinsonades. Ballantyne alone revisited the Robinsonade over the next twenty-odd years of his career, with *Sunk at Sea* (1869), *Jarwin and Cuffy* (1878), *The Lonely Island* (1880), and *The Island Queen* (1885). That said, Ballantyne's Robinsonades ought to belong to a whole new category, something like "idyllic adventure stories," even if his most direct devotee, Stevenson, returned to the mercantilism of Defoe's Robinsonade in his own take. In order to reach modern audiences, secondary authors have long pushed the story into a more familiar urban environment, as in J. G. Ballard's downbeat novella *Concrete Island* (1973) or James Gould Cozzens's comical *Castaway* (1934), the latter of which is set in a department store. They have also sexed up the original, as we see in *The Sexual Life of Robinson Crusoe* (1971) or *Miss Robinson Crusoe* (1990), a Harlequin romance, as well as in Tournier's *Friday*, where a frustrated Crusoe penetrates a pink grove in the island itself and various inanimate objects. You might have invented a whole new genre. Second only to *Robinson Crusoe* itself, the next most popular Robinsonade in the eighteenth century was Peter Longueville's *The Hermit* (1727). One might reasonably argue that the success of the latter spawned a new alternative to the Robinsonade, the hermit's tale, which became especially popular in America later that century.[5] Equally, Longueville's slight substitutions render it a parallel text of sorts—Philip Quarll, the hermit, has his Friday (a shipmate fulfils the role here) as well as a pet ape (rather than a parrot).

CODA

    The Robinsonade is named after Defoe's lead character, of course. But some Robinson Crusoes are not Robinson Crusoes at all. Despite the title of the novel, the lone protagonist of John Argo's *Robinson Crusoe 1,000,000 A.D.* (2004) is Alex Kirk (a nominal return to Defoe's historical model, Alexander Selkirk, one might suppose), a bullish buccaneer who craves female company. Besides, Crusoe was far from alone: other Crusoe-like characters fronted their own Robinsonades throughout the eighteenth century, including Peter Wilkins, John Daniel, William Bingfield, Drake Morris, and Friga Reveep. Another went by the name of Crusoe Richard Davis, while yet another, Hannah Hewit, was dubbed "the Female Crusoe" in the subtitle of her book. Some titular Crusoes are not the foci of their stories. The eponymous James Dubourdieu is really an ancillary character; the narrator-character Martha Rattenberg leads the account.

    The island need not be an island either. A popular example is the 1964 movie *Robinson Crusoe on Mars*, which, as the title suggests, takes place on the red planet. Despite the title—again, like Argo's novel—the hero is not Robinson Crusoe but rather a modern counterpart named Commander Kit Draper. This time, however, the Crusoe-like character does rename a native man Friday explicitly in homage to Defoe's original. The titular hero of Thomas Berger's *Robert Crews* (1994), whose name echoes that of Robinson Crusoe, is far more Crusoe-like than many so-called "modern Crusoes" (a common if somewhat casually applied label). He even has his own Friday, a woman who has fled from her violent husband.

    If we were to define the Robinsonade as a tale in which the protagonist (the notional "Robinson" after whom the genre is named) is suddenly isolated from the comforts of civilization, usually by being shipwrecked on a secluded island, we would have to discount several works that in name draw a clear line to *Robinson Crusoe*, most obviously William Godwin's 1816 translation of Johann David Wyss's *Der Schweizerische Robinson* (1812), *The Swiss Family Robinson*. Otherwise we would have to find a new category, perhaps the familial Robinsonade. One of the earliest of all Robinsonades, one published in the same year as *Robinson Crusoe*, in fact, Ambrose Evans's *The Adventures, and Surprizing Deliverances, of James Dubourdieu, and His Wife*, would also fall under this new label. One of the most celebrated Robinsonades, Jules Verne's *L'Île mystérieuse* (*The Mysterious Island*; 1874), recounts the resourcefulness of a team of escaped prisoners. The size of their party, and their expertise, mark a clear departure from Defoe's original. Many juvenile Robinsonades center on the adventures and misadventures of at least two youngsters, as we see in Rowland Walker's *Phantom Island: A Modern Crusoe Story* (1925), in which Tom Bevis and Sandy Macky get shipwrecked together. We might also eject one of the earliest Robinsonades, one that predates *Robinson Crusoe*—Henry Neville's *The Isle of Pines* (1668). Far from being a lone survivor, the hero, George

[167]

Pines, has an entourage of women by whom he fathers many children. (Or, more radically, we might rename the mode after this seemingly foundational text—the Pinesade or Pinesiad.) If we were to fixate on the imperiled individual grappling with hostile environments, conversely, we would have to become more accustomed to calling *Gulliver's Travels* (1726) a Robinsonade. To be sure, Swift's satire speaks back to *Robinson Crusoe*, not least of all in the commingled depiction of savagery and civility in the voyage to Houynhmhm-land. Paul Dottin identified a subgenre he calls the "Robinsonade gullivérienne," but I suspect many readers would share the view espoused in an early review of *The Life and Adventures of Peter Wilkins* (1750) in the *Monthly Review*.[6] For the reviewer, *Peter Wilkins* fails precisely because it is the "illegitimate offspring" of a "no very natural conjunction" between *Gulliver's Travels* and *Robinson Crusoe*. Many named Robinsonades have more in common with Swift's work, as Martin Green avers, especially where the comic or excessive fantasy of the adaptation or imitation destroys any illusion of reality.[7]

How might we narrow the reach of the Robinsonade, and therefore make it more viable as a subject of study, or, for my purposes here, more visible as a creative field of secondary authorship? One suitable approach concerns the theory and practice of adaptation: we might consider the different ways in which specific aspects of Defoe's novel have been parodied, pastiched, or otherwise reworked. This means we could look at competing retellings of, say, the iconic scene in which Crusoe stumbles across a lone footprint. A master of motifs, Defoe conveys at once in this image the horror and hope one might feel at such a sudden discovery ("I stood like one Thunder-struck"; 112). Swift rehashes this scene in order to expose Gulliver's disingenuousness: "I saw many Tracks of human Feet," he recalls at the outset of his adventures in the fourth voyage, though he almost immediately insists that the Yahoos are deformed creatures with whom he shares little physical or mental affinity, or so he thinks.[8] Maxine Hong Kingston's *China Men* (1980), a densely woven tale of the lives of Chinese immigrants in America, features a short story about a sailor named Lo Bun Sun. Stumbling across a human footprint on the beach, the sailor suddenly feels "a burning fear up his spine."[9] The experience sends him into a paranoid state ("For days he shivered in his cave, peeked through cracks in every direction, jumped at noises of winds and animals").[10] Even after the wind and rain had worn away the footprint, he thinks about it for many more years—a parable about the ceaseless emotional turmoil of the immigrant's experience, perhaps, or even an ironic take on colonial exclusionism. Alternatively, the scene is replayed for laughs in Willis Hall's *Vampire Island* (1998). Count Alucard, Skopka the wolf, and Peppina the parrot lazily loll on a marooned island—until they discover an unfeasibly large boot print in the sand, which, we eventually learn, belongs to Frankenstein's creature. A potent motif of human hopes and fears here

CODA

sets up a humorous exchange between the vampire, with his entourage of animals, and Baron Frankenstein and his creation. In Jane Gardam's *Crusoe's Daughter* (1985), an obsessive reader of *Robinson Crusoe*, Polly Flint, dismisses the "most famous heart-stopping incident" in the novel as a disappointing experience, somewhat ironically ("Just the print of some quite anonymous foot, probably crunched up on a later occasion around the cannibal fires").[11] The reaction of Alex in *Robinson Crusoe 1,000,000 A.D.* is far more visceral, in keeping with the jeopardy often seen in the science fiction Robinsonade: "As Alex looked down at the footprint, and then around him, his stomach contorted with a mixture of emotions, ranging from fear to elation, back and forth."[12] Gordon Holder, in *No Man Friday*, is far more poised, as befits his training: "I saw it there, the elongated impression, as of a giant's shoe-sole." ("In Crusoe's day," he boasts earlier in the text, "people did not know how skilled they were.")[13] Highly malleable, the motif is one of the most recognizable elements of the Robinsonade.

A writer's study of the Robinsonade would also need to consider extensions of Robinson Crusoe's life (prequels, coquels, sequels, and the like), following Defoe's own lead. But there are far fewer explicit examples in this category, meaning we would have to overlook many inventive reimaginings of *Robinson Crusoe* for little reason beyond mere convenience. To put it another way, works in this category might not necessarily follow Defoe's template, despite appearances. Henry Treece's *The Return of Robinson Crusoe* (1958) opens with a wealthy Crusoe reflecting on his prior exploits overseas. He also fills in blanks left (for want of a better word) in the original. We finally learn that Friday's real name is Tashmaga, for instance. The format of Treece's novel, although written in the first person, bears little resemblance to Defoe's—it has short, sharp chapter breaks, for one thing, as well as a prevalence of reported speech. The hero also ends up knighted and renamed (Sir Robinson Kreutznaer) and eager for fresh adventures—all things we might consider anathema to Defoe's character. An extension, in short, is no more worthy of the name Robinsonade than any other creative engagement with *Robinson Crusoe*. After all, Defoe effectively forbade unofficial sequels. Fearful that other writers would capitalize on the rapid success of *Robinson Crusoe*, Defoe rushed out in the same year, 1719, a continuation that sought to complete the story for good, as the fuller title indicates: *The Farther Adventures of Robinson Crusoe; Being the Second and Last Part of His Life*. In the preface to the latter work, Defoe made clear his thoughts on secondary authors: "The Injury these Men do the Proprietor of this Work, is a Practice all honest Men abhor; and [the Author] believes he may challenge them to shew the Difference between that and Robbing on the Highway, or Breaking open a House."[14] Contrary to Treece's sequel, Defoe's *Farther Adventures* opens with a sixty-one-year-old Crusoe expressing little interest in

[169]

wealth. Heeding Defoe's authoritative words, we would need to discard Treece's sequel. Otherwise, in the democratic spirit of textual pluralism, we could treat them as coexisting sequels; taking a meritocratic view of textual pluralism, though, means we wouldn't *have* to enforce that.

In addition to the reworked motif and the explicit continuation, a third major area of concern in the rewriting of *Robinson Crusoe* might be called, at the risk of redundancy, the authorial Robinsonade. Many books in this category revisit the originary scene of writing, more particularly the explicit figuring of a fictive Defoe as an author, often a dishonest one, in the secondary work of fiction. In Coetzee's *Foe*, Foe (Defoe's real name) is a renegade hack who has stolen the literary property of the "true" heroine of the story and her fellow islanders. By contrast, in Muriel Spark's *Robinson*, the Crusoe-like recluse (a borrowing from a separate genre, the hermit's tale, one might suppose) encourages the narrator of the story to commit her experiences to paper, as fact rather than as the basis of fiction. Like Coetzee's Foe, Spark's Robinson goes missing. In the latter case, this prolonged absence inadvertently upends the genre of the novel itself, moving it from a shipwreck tale to crime fiction. In both novels, the apparent deaths of Foe and Robinson speak to the burdens of authorship and ownership, specifically who has the right to retell a tale and to whom the material belongs. In the case of Defoe's original composition, setting aside the author himself, does it belong to Alexander Selkirk (the real-life model for Crusoe) or Crusoe (as the first-person narrator and subject)? In the case of Coetzee's revisiting, does it belong to Susan Barton (the claimant and subject) or Foe (the hack who writes it up)?

Defoe was the first author to attempt to rewrite the Robinsonade with his own sequels. In what ways have his authorial descendants followed suit? Are they inviting us to redo or, conversely, to redact *Robinson Crusoe* further still? Most Robinsonades are what we might call authorial Robinsonades. The new characters retrace Crusoe's steps either directly or indirectly, in new hostile or paradisiacal places. Often these characters will outwardly invoke the memory of Crusoe as a forebear, as in *Robinson Crusoe 1,000,000 A.D.*, or even read the original book, as in *Crusoe's Daughter*. Even *The Swiss Family Robinson* is an authorial Robinsonade, at least in part, as the shipwrecked family rely upon their edition of *Robinson Crusoe* as a survival guide ("since Heaven has destined us to a similar fate, whom better can we consult?").[15] Another famous children's Robinsonade, Joachim Heinrich Campe's *Robinson der Jüngere* (1779), features a father who retells sanitized versions of Crusoe's exploits to his children at bedtime: he is effectively editing Defoe's story. The authorial Robinsonade even overlaps with a modern subgenre, the mashed-up Robinsonade. A case in point is Peter Clines's *The Eerie Adventures of the Lycanthrope Robinson Crusoe* (2010), which not only introduces a werewolf plot into the Robinson Crusoe story but directly challenges Defoe's authorship: the book purports to be a true version of *Robinson Crusoe* recovered from the papers of the horror writer H. P. Lovecraft and based on the castaway's own journals.

A Robinsonade of a rather different kind, Andrew Lane's *Dawn of Spies* (2016), the first book in his "A Crusoe Adventure" series, has Defoe cameo as an opportunistic writer who recruits Crusoe and Friday as spies in seventeenth-century London. Pooling their respective skills (as a writer and as survivors), Defoe, Crusoe, and Friday work well together in foiling a high-level kidnapping plot. But the islanders are reluctant to trust Defoe: "we do not feel comfortable having you tell our stories, or using what we know as intelligence that can be bartered around like grain," Crusoe says, to which Defoe responds with the offer of "Perhaps more money?"[16] Lane's Defoe is at once a spy, a hack, and a man of business ("I can make a fortune—simply put").[17] But for Crusoe and Friday the new world of espionage offers "an alternative to telling this Defoe our stories."[18] Largely an homage to the real Defoe, Gardam's *Crusoe's Daughter* ends with an elderly Polly Flint conversing with a shadowy figure identified as Crusoe, with whom she discusses the fictionality of *Robinson Crusoe*. "My creator had quite a facility," claims Crusoe, conceding authority to the author; "Stood him in very good stead. Memoirs." "Nonsense," retorts Polly, "he made it all up."[19] The authorial Robinsonade—or the Defoeade, we might say—is not a modern invention, however. Coetzee's *Foe* might be the most famous novel in which a fictive Defoe is pursued by an angry claimant over the material purportedly written by the English author. But it was not the first. In fact, Charles Gildon's *The Life and Strange Surprizing Adventures of Mr. D— De F—, of London, Hosier* (1719) appeared a matter of weeks after the original novel was published. A derisive commentary on *Robinson Crusoe*, it includes a handful of metafictional episodes. In one of the most inventive scenes, Defoe's characters appear to him in a dream vision and lambast him for making them look ludicrous. They wreak savage revenge on the author by making him eat a copy of the book in two volumes ("me will make him swallow his own Vomit," Gildon's Friday warns).[20]

Since then, the written document has taken central place in the most famous authorial Robinsonades, *Foe* and *Robinson*. In Spark's version Robinson enables the narrator's authorship by giving her blue notebooks, which she soon fills up. However, a man whom January Marlow, the narrator, wrongly suspects had killed Robinson, namely Tom Wells, claims to have destroyed the journals out of fear. In Coetzee's novel, Susan Barton thinks to herself that Foe "is like the patient spider who sits at the heart of his web waiting for his prey to come to him. And when we struggle in his grasp . . . he opens his jaws to devour us."[21] Authorship in both books is associated with sabotage—or highway robbery, to adopt Defoe's own complaint about sequelists. Unlike Defoe's Crusoe, Coetzee's Cruso has no interest in writing down his experiences anyway: "Cruso kept no journal, perhaps because he lacked paper and ink, but more likely, I now believe, because he lacked the inclination to keep one."[22] Tongueless and barely literate, Friday cannot repeat his life story, even if Cruso encourages him to write it down. Confidently poised at Foe's bureau in London, by contrast, Barton seeks to usurp the role of the author—or, to her mind, claim it back: "I sat at your bureau this morning (it is afternoon now, I sit at the same bureau, I have sat here all day) and took out a clean sheet of paper and dipped pen in ink—your pen, your ink, I know, but somehow the pen becomes mine while I write with it, as though growing out of my hand—and wrote at the head: 'The Female Castaway. Being a True Account of a Year Spent on a Desert Island. With Many Strange Circumstances Never Hitherto Related.'"[23] Her speech quietly captures many of the concerns shared by the Robinsonade writ large. One is the tension between repetition and prolongation—to what extent must a secondary author stick to the particulars of the original? What would those particulars be? Another is the metafictional debate between telling the "true" story and stolentelling, a hallmark of Defoe's fictional art more generally. Yet another is the endless variety of the Robinsonade, each one newly filling up an inexhaustible supply of clean sheets of paper. A typological study would need to address the vexed issue of what is, or what is *not*, a Robinsonade. But nomenclature would not help: a Crusoe is not always called Crusoe, and often a named Crusoe has little in common with his or her forebear. Instead, as the contributors to the present volume have demonstrated, a case-by-case examination of the creative ways in which a Robinsonade responds to *Robinson Crusoe*, or a shared cultural memory of the text, would better elucidate the *Strange Surprizing* reach of Defoe's story in anything from bleak science fiction reimaginings to young adult pastiches. Not merely a species of the adventure story, the Robinsonade spotlights, playfully or aggressively, and with varying levels of referentiality, the mechanics of authorship in any genre it pursues.

NOTES

1. For a recent survey of scholarly definitions of the Robinsonade, from the eighteenth century to the present, see Artur Blaim, *Robinson Crusoe and His Doubles: The English Robinsonade of the Eighteenth Century* (Frankfurt: Peter Lang, 2016), 35–43. See also Philip Babock Gove, *The Imaginary Voyage in Prose Fiction: A History of Its Criticism and a Guide for Its Study. With an Annotated Check List of 215 Imaginary Voyages from 1700 to 1800* (1941; New York: Octagon Books, 1975), 122–154.
2. For a history of the decolonizing Robinsonade, see Ann Marie Fallon, *Global Crusoe: Comparative Literature, Postcolonial Theory and Transnational Aesthetics* (Farnham: Ashgate, 2011). Carl Fisher discusses different national traditions (British, French, and German) in "The Robinsonade: An Intercultural History of an Idea," in *Approaches to Teaching Defoe's*

Robinson Crusoe, ed. Maximillian E. Novak and Carl Fisher (New York: MLA, 2005), 129–139.
3. *Monthly Review* 36 (1767): 238.
4. See Susanna Layh, "'All Alone in an Empty World': Post-Apocalyptic Robinsonades," in *Yesterday's Tomorrows: On Utopia and Dystopia*, ed. Pere Gallardo and Elizabeth Russell (Newcastle upon Tyne: Cambridge Scholars, 2014), 345–356.
5. See Coby Dowdell, "The American Hermit and the British Castaway: Voluntary Retreat and Deliberative Democracy in Early American Culture," *Early American Literature* 46.1 (2011): 121–156.
6. Quoted after Blaim, *Robinson Crusoe and His Doubles*, 42.
7. Martin Green, *The Robinson Crusoe Story* (University Park: Pennsylvania State University Press, 1990), 26.
8. Jonathan Swift, *Gulliver's Travels*, ed. Claude Rawson and Ian Higgins (Oxford: Oxford University Press, 2008), 209.
9. Maxine Hong Kingston, *China Men* (1980; New York: Vintage, 1989), 229.
10. Ibid., 229.
11. Jane Gardam, *Crusoe's Daughter* (1985; London: Abacus, 2012), 207.
12. John Argo, *Robinson Crusoe 1,000,000 A.D.* (2004; San Diego: Clocktower Books, 2014), 56.
13. Rex Gordon, *No Man Friday* (1956; London: New English Library, 1977), 41.
14. Daniel Defoe, *The Farther Adventures of Robinson Crusoe*, ed. W. R. Owens (1719; London: Routledge, 2017), 3.
15. Johann David Wyss, *The Swiss Family Robinson* (1812; New York: Aladdin Paperbacks, 2007), 260.
16. Andrew Lane, *Dawn of Spies* (Culver City: Adaptive Books, 2016), 39.
17. Ibid., 29.
18. Ibid., 39.
19. Gardam, *Crusoe's Daughter*, 303.
20. Charles Gildon, *The Life and Strange Surprizing Adventures of Mr. D—De F—, of London, Hosier* (London: J. Roberts, 1719), xvii.
21. J. M. Coetzee, *Foe* (1986; London: Penguin, 1987), 120.
22. Ibid., 16.
23. Ibid., 67.

ACKNOWLEDGMENTS

This book would not have materialized without the support and encouragement of Greg Clingham, who believed *Transits* should have its Crusoe at three hundred publication. Sincere thanks are also due to the two anonymous readers for Bucknell University Press, the BUP editorial staff, and the excellent team of contributors—it was a pleasure to work with you all. My own research for this volume was partly facilitated by the NCN grant Miniatura II (2018/02/X/HS2/03216) and the Schwerpunkt Polen fellowship at Mainz University.

BIBLIOGRAPHY

Adorno, Theodor W., and Max Horkheimer. *Dialectic of Enlightenment: Philosophical Fragments.* Edited by Gunzelin Schmid Noerr. Translated by Edmund Jephcott. Stanford, CA: Stanford University Press, 2002.
Anon. *Disputes in China; or, Harlequin and the Hong Kong Merchants.* Coburg, 15 July 1822.
———. *Monkey Island; or, Harlequin and the Loadstone Rock.* Lyceum, 3 July 1824.
———. Playbills 284. British Library Mic. C 12137. *Robinson Crusoe; or, Harlequin Friday.* Stockport, 16 December 1799.
———. Review of *Kaloc* (Sadler's Wells, 3 April 1818). *European Magazine, and London Review* 73 (May 1818): 434.
Arendt, Hannah. *The Human Condition.* Chicago: University of Chicago Press, 1958.
Argo, John. *Robinson Crusoe 1,000,000 A.D.* 2004. San Diego: Clocktower Books, 2014.
Assmann, Jan. "Collective Memory and Cultural Identity." *New German Critique* 65 (1995): 125–133.
Astbury, Katherine. "Le Robinson de l'Ile d'Elbe: The Robinson Crusoe of Elba." www.100days.eu/items/show/2.
Backscheider, Paula. *Daniel Defoe: His Life.* Baltimore: Johns Hopkins University Press, 1989.
Bakhtin, Mikhail. *Problems of Dostoevsky's Poetics.* Edited and translated by Caryl Emerson. Minneapolis: University of Minnesota Press, 1984.
"Ball Rolling on Bougainville Referendum." Radio New Zealand, 23 May 2016. www.radionz.co.nz/international/pacific-news/304534/ball-rolling-on-bougainville-referendum.
Bannet, Eve Tavor. *Transatlantic Stories and the History of Reading, 1720–1810: Migrant Fictions.* Cambridge: Cambridge University Press, 2011.
Barrie, James M. *The Admirable Crichton.* 1902. London: Hodder and Stoughton, 1918.
Barrymore, William. *Philip Quarl! The English Hermit.* Coburg, 14 September 1819.
Bauman, Zygmunt. "From Pilgrim to Tourist—or a Short History of Identity." In *Questions of Cultural Identity*, edited by Stuart Hall and Paul du Gay. London: Sage, 2003. 18–36.
Beasley, Jerry. "Portraits of a Monster: Robert Walpole and Early English Prose Fiction." *Eighteenth-Century Studies* 14.4 (1981): 406–431.
Beck, Ulrich. *Risk Society: Toward a New Modernity.* Translated by Mark Ritter. London: Sage, 1992.
Bertsch, Janet. *Storytelling in the Works of Bunyan, Grimmelshausen, Defoe, and Schnabel.* Rochester, NY: Camden House, 2004.
Bhabha, Homi K. *The Location of Culture.* London: Routledge, 2004.
Birdsall, Virginia Ogden. *Defoe's Perpetual Seekers: A Study of the Major Fiction.* Lewisburg, PA: Bucknell University Press, 1985.
Blaim, Artur. *Robinson Crusoe and His Doubles: The English Robinsonade of the Eighteenth Century.* Frankfurt: Peter Lang, 2016.
Blewett, David. "The Iconic Crusoe: Illustrations and Images of *Robinson Crusoe*." In *The Cambridge Companion to "Robinson Crusoe,"* edited by John Richetti. Cambridge: Cambridge University Press, 2018. 159–190.

BIBLIOGRAPHY

Bogue, Ronald. "Speranza, the Wandering Island." *Deleuze Studies* 3.1 (June 2009): 124–134.

Bohls, Elizabeth. "Age of Peregrination: Travel Writing and the Eighteenth-Century Novel." In *A Companion to the Eighteenth-Century English Novel and Culture*, edited by Paula R. Backscheider and Catherine Ingrassia. Oxford: Blackwell, 2005. 97–116.

Bohuszewicz, Paweł. *Od "romansu" do powieści: Studia o polskiej literaturze narracyjnej (druga połowa XVII wieku—pierwsza połowa XIX wieku)*. Toruń: Wydawnictwo Naukowe Uniwersytetu Mikołaja Kopernika, 2016.

Boudry, Maarten, and Massimo Pigliucci, eds. *Science Unlimited? The Challenges of Scientism*. Chicago: University of Chicago Press, 2017.

Bougainville, Louis de. *A Voyage Round the World Performed by Order of His Most Christian Majesty, in the Years 1766, 1767, 1768, and 1769*. 1772. Translated by John Reinhold Forster. Cambridge: Cambridge University Press, 2011.

"Bougainville Peace Agreement." *United Nations Peacemaker*, 30 August 2001. https://peacemaker.un.org/png-bougainville-agreement2001.

"Bougainville Referendum Process Electoral Process Formally Ends." Radio New Zealand, 23 January 2020. www.rnz.co.nz/international/pacific-news/407953/bougainville-referendum-electoral-process-formally-ends.

Braidotti, Rosi. *The Posthuman*. Cambridge: Polity, 2013.

Brantly, Susan C. "Engaging the Enlightenment: Tournier's *Friday*, Delblanc's *Speranza*, and Unsworth's *Sacred Hunger*." *Comparative Literature* 61.2 (2009): 128–141.

British Library Mic. C 13137. Playbills. 166–377.

Brown, Homer Obed. "The Institution of the English Novel: Defoe's Contribution." *Novel: A Forum on Fiction* 29.3 (1996): 299–318.

Brown, Laura. *Fables of Modernity: Literature and Culture in the English Eighteenth Century*. Ithaca, NY: Cornell University Press, 2003.

Burnett, Paula. "The Ulyssean Crusoe and the Quest for Redemption in J. M. Coetzee's *Foe* and Derek Walcott's *Omeros*." In *Robinson Crusoe: Myths and Metamorphoses*, edited by Lieve Spaas and Brian Stimpson. Houndmills: Macmillan, 1996. 239–255.

Burnham, Michelle. Headnote to "Appendix A: 'English' Sources." In *The Female American*, edited by Michelle Burnham. Peterborough: Broadview Press, 2001. 157.

Burnham, Michelle, and James Freitas. Introduction to *The Female American; or the Adventures of Unca Eliza Winkfield. Compiled by Herself*. Edited by Michelle Burnham and James Freitas. Peterborough: Broadview, 2014. 9–32.

Burwick, Frederick. *British Drama of the Industrial Revolution*. Cambridge: Cambridge University Press, 2015.

Burwick, Frederick, and Manushag Powell. *British Pirates in Print and Performance*. Houndmills: Palgrave Macmillan, 2015.

Butterwick, Richard. *Poland's Last King and English Culture: Stanisław August Poniatowski, 1732–1798*. Oxford: Clarendon, 1998.

Calarco, Matthew. *Thinking through Animals: Identity. Difference. Indistinction*. Stanford, CA: Stanford University Press, 2015.

Campbell, Jill. "Robinsonades for Young People." In *The Cambridge Companion to "Robinson Crusoe,"* edited by John Richetti. Cambridge: Cambridge University Press, 2018. 191–206.

Cantor, Paul. *Gilligan Unbound: Pop Culture and the Age of Globalization*. New York: Rowman & Littlefield, 2001.

Carson, Tom. *Gilligan's Wake*. New York: Picador, 2003.

Cavanagh, Tim. "Sucking in the American Century." *Reason*, November 2011. http://reason.com/archives/2011/10/20/sucking-in-the-american-centur.

Charlton, John. *Hidden Chains: The Slavery Business and North East England*. Newcastle upon Tyne: Tyne Bridge, 2008.

Coetzee, J. M. *Foe*. 1986. London: Penguin, 1987.
Cohen, I. Bernard. "The Compendium Physicae of Charles Morton (1627–1698)." *Isis* 33.6 (June 1942): 657–671.
Coleridge, Samuel Taylor. "Lecture XI." In *The Complete Works of Samuel Taylor Coleridge*, edited by W. G. T. Shedd. New York: Harper, 1853. 309–319.
Cony, Barkham. *The Red Indian; or, Selkirk and His Dog*. Surrey, 26 August 1822.
Cook, Daniel. "On Authorship, Appropriation, and Eighteenth-Century Fiction." In *The Afterlives of Eighteenth-Century Fiction*, edited by Daniel Cook and Nicholas Seager. Cambridge: Cambridge University Press, 2015. 20–42.
Cooke, Edward, Captain. *A Voyage to the South Sea, and round the World, Perform'd in the Years 1708, 1709, 1710, and 1711. Containing a Journal of All Memorable Transactions during the Said Voyage . . . a Description of the American Coasts from Terra del Fuego . . . to California . . . an Historical Account of All Those Countries from the Best Authors . . . Wherein an Account Is Given of Mr. Alexander Selkirk His Manner of Living . . . during the Four Years and Four Months He Liv'd upon the Uninhabited Island of Juan Fernandes. Illustrated with Cuts and Maps*. 2 vols. London: H.M. for B. Lintot & R. Gosling, 1712.
Cormack, James E. *Isle of Solomon*. Washington, DC: Review and Herald, 1944.
Cuddon, J. A. (revised by C. E. Preston). "Desert Island Fiction." In *The Penguin Dictionary of Literary Terms and Literary Theory*. 4th ed. London: Penguin, 1998. 215–216.
Dannenberg, Hilary P. "Divergent Plot Patterns in Narrative Fiction from Sir Philip Sidney to Peter Ackroyd." In *Proceedings of the Conference of the German Association of University Teachers in English*, vol. 21, edited by Bernhard Reitz and Sigrid Rieuwerts. Trier: WVT, 2000. 415–427.
Davis, Emily S. "Teaching Coetzee's *Foe* in an Undergraduate Theory Classroom." In *Approaches to Teaching Coetzee's* Disgrace *and Other Works*, edited by Laura Wright, Jane Poyner, and Elleke Boehmer. New York: MLA, 2014. 180–186.
Davis, Heather, and Etienne Turpin, eds. *Art in the Anthropocene: Encounters among Aesthetics, Politics, Environments and Epistemologies*. London: Open Humanities Press, 2015.
Day, Charles. *Joe Blackburn's A Clown's Log*. 2nd ed. Edited by William Slout. Rockville, MD: Borgo Press, 2007.
Defoe, Daniel. *The Farther Adventures of Robinson Crusoe*. Edited by W. R. Owens. 1719. London: Routledge, 2017.
———. *Moll Flanders*. 1722. Edited by Albert J. Rivero. New York: Norton, 2003.
———. *Przypadki Robinsona Krusoe*. Translated by Jan Chrzciciel Albertrandi. Warszawa: Nakładem Michała Grela, 1769.
———. *Robinson Crusoe*. 1719. 2nd ed. Edited by Michael Shinagel. New York: Norton, 1994.
———. *Roxana*. 1724. Edited by John Mullan. Oxford: Oxford University Press, 1996.
———. *The Storm*. 1704. Edited by Richard Hamblyn. London: Penguin, 2003.
Deleuze, Gilles. "Desert Islands." In *Desert Islands and Other Texts (1953–1974)*, translated by Michael Taormina. New York: Semiotext(e), 2004.
———. "Michel Tournier and the World without Others." In *Logic of Sense*, translated by Mark Lester and Charles Stivale. New York: Columbia University Press, 1990.
Deleuze, Gilles, and Felix Guattari. *A Thousand Plateaus*. Translated by Brian Massumi. Minneapolis: University of Minnesota Press, 1987.
Dibdin, Charles, Jr. *Hannah Hewitt, or the Female Crusoe*. Drury Lane, 7 May 1798. Henry E. Huntington Library; Manuscript: Larpent 1210.
———. *Kaloc; or, The Slave Pirate*. Sadler's Wells, 9 August 1813; 14 August 1815; 3 April 1818. London: Button and Whitaker, 1813.
———. *Sketch of the Serio-comic Pantomime, Philip Quarll; or, The English Hermit*. Sadler's Wells, 9 May 1803. London: Glendenning, 1803.

BIBLIOGRAPHY

Dibdin, Thomas John. *Jocko; or, The Ape of Brazil.* Sadler's Wells, 6 June 1825.
Dickens, Charles. *Memoirs of Joseph Grimaldi.* London: Richard Bentley, 1846.
Dinnen, Sinclair, Ron May, and Anthony J. Regan, eds. *Challenging the State: The Sandline Affair in Papua New Guinea.* Canberra: National Center for Development Studies, 1997.
Doc Ezra. "Robinson Crusoe (2001)." *Needcoffee.com*, 7 December 2003. www.needcoffee.com/2003/12/07/robinson-crusoe-2001-dvd-review/.
Dolphijn, Rick. "Undercurrents and the Desert(ed): Negarestani, Tournier and Deleuze Map the Polytics of a 'New Earth.'" In *Postcolonial Literatures and Deleuze: Colonial Pasts, Differential Futures*, edited by Lorna Burns and Birgit M. Kaiser. Houndmills: Palgrave Macmillan, 2012. 199–216.
Doody, Margaret Anne. *The True History of the Novel.* New Brunswick, NJ: Rutgers University Press, 1996.
Douglas, Clark. "Robinson Crusoe." *365movieguy.com*, 22 March 2015. www.365movieguy.com/review/3/22/robinson-crusoe.
Dowdell, Coby. "The American Hermit and the British Castaway: Voluntary Retreat and Deliberative Democracy in Early American Culture." *Early American Literature* 46.1 (2011): 121–156.
Driscoll, Brendan. "Gilligan's Wake." *Booklist* 99.8 (2003): 731.
Duncan, Ian. Introduction to *Kidnapped* by Robert Louis Stevenson, edited by Ian Duncan. Oxford: Oxford University Press, 2014. ix–xxvi.
Ebert, Roger. "Cast Away." *Rogerebert.com*, 22 December 2000. www.rogerebert.com/reviews/cast-away-2000.
Edis, Taner. "Two Cheers for Scientism." In *Science Unlimited? The Challenges of Scientism*, edited by Maarten Boudry and Massimo Pigliucci. Chicago: University of Chicago Press, 2017. 73–94.
"Editions in French and Some Other Translations." In *Robinson Crusoe at Yale. Yale University Library Gazette* 11.2 (1936): 28–32.
Elmst, Pete. "The Secret Affair in Cast Away: Kelly Frears Should Be Ashamed of Herself." *Applaudience*, 25 November 2016. https://medium.com/applaudience/the-secret-affair-of-cast-away-7b7f9999a303.
Esdaile, Arundell. "Author and Publisher in 1727: 'The English Hermit.'" *The Library (The Transactions of the Bibliographical Society)* 4.2 (3) (1921): 185–192.
Experience Bougainville. Christensen Fund (Palo Alto, CA), 21 January 2014. www.youtube.com/watch?v=_sCxL0oF0rs.
Fallon, Ann Marie. "Anti-Crusoes, Alternative Crusoes: Revisions of the Island Story in the Twentieth Century." In *The Cambridge Companion to "Robinson Crusoe,"* edited by John Richetti. Cambridge: Cambridge University Press, 2018. 207–220.
———. *Global Crusoe: Comparative Literature, Postcolonial Theory and Transnational Aesthetics.* Farnham: Ashgate, 2011.
Farley, Charles. *Aladdin, or the Wonderful Lamp.* Covent Garden, 19 April 1813. London: Printed by J. Barker, 1813.
Fawcett, John. *De la Perouse; or, The Desolate Island.* Covent Garden, 28 February 1801. Newcastle upon Tyne: Printed by Edw. Walker, 1808.
Findlater, Richard. *Grimaldi: King of Clowns.* London: Magibbon & Kee, 1955.
Fisher, Carl. "Innovation and Imitation in the Eighteenth-Century Robinsonade." In *The Cambridge Companion to "Robinson Crusoe,"* edited by John Richetti. Cambridge: Cambridge University Press, 2018. 99–111.
———. "The Robinsonade: An Intercultural History of an Idea." In *Approaches to Teaching Defoe's* Robinson Crusoe, edited by Maximillian E. Novak and Carl Fisher. New York: MLA, 2005. 129–139.

Fleissner, Jennifer. "Henry James's Art of Eating." *English Literary History* 75.1 (2008): 27–62.
Florman, Samuel C. *The Introspective Engineer*. New York: Thomas Dunne, 1996.
Friedman, Emily C. *Reading Smell in Eighteenth-Century Fiction*. Lewisburg, PA: Bucknell University Press, 2016.
Gardam, Jane. *Crusoe's Daughter*. 1985. London: Abacus, 2012.
Genest, John. *Some Account of the London Stage, from the Restoration to 1830*. 10 vols. Bath: H. E. Carrington, 1832.
Genette, Gérard. *The Architext: An Introduction*. Berkeley: University of California Press, 1992.
———. *Palimpsests: Literature in the Second Degree*. Translated by Channa Newman and Claude Doubinsky. Lincoln: University of Nebraska Press, 1997.
Geriguis, Lina Lamanauskaite. "Discovering the Lithuanian Reinscription of *Robinson Crusoe*." *Lituanus: Lithuanian Quarterly Journal of Arts and Sciences* 54.4 (Winter 2008): 61–75.
Geriguis, Lora. "'A Vast Howling Wilderness': The Persistence of Space and Placelessness in Daniel Defoe's *Captain Singleton*." In *Topographies of the Imagination: New Approaches to Daniel Defoe*, edited by Kit Kincaid, Katherine Ellison, and Holly Faith Nelson. New York: AMS Press, 2014. 185–207.
Gigante, Denise. *Taste: A Literary History*. New Haven, CT: Yale University Press, 2005.
Gildon, Charles. *The Life and Strange Surprizing Adventures of Mr. D—De F—, of London, Hosier*. London: J. Roberts, 1719.
Girten, Kirstin. "Mingling with Matter: Tactile Microscopy and the Philosophic Mind in Brobdingnag and Beyond." *Eighteenth-Century Studies* 54.4 (2013): 497–520.
Gold, Jack, dir. *Man Friday*. ABC Entertainment; ITC Films, 1975.
Gołębiowska, Zofia. "British Models and Inspirations in Czartoryskis' Country Residence in Puławy at the Turn of the Eighteenth Century." In *Culture at Global/Local Levels: British and Commonwealth Contribution to World Civilisation*, edited by Krystyna Kujawińska-Courtney. Łódź: Wydawnictwo Biblioteka, 2002. 139–150.
Golinski, Jan. *British Weather and the Climate of Enlightenment*. Chicago: University of Chicago Press, 2007.
Gordon, Rex. *No Man Friday*. 1956. London: New English Library, 1977.
Gottschalk, Louis. *Understanding History: A Primer of Historical Method*. 2nd ed. New York: Knopf, 1969.
Gove, Philip Babcock. *The Imaginary Voyage in Prose Fiction: A History of Its Criticism and a Guide for Its Study. With an Annotated Check List of 215 Imaginary Voyages from 1700 to 1800*. 1941. New York: Octagon Books, 1975.
Graciotti, Sante, and Jadwiga Rudnicka, eds. *Inwentarz biblioteki Ignacego Krasickiego z 1810 r.* Wrocław: Zakład Narodowy im. Ossolińskich, 1973.
Green, Martin. *The Robinson Crusoe Story*. University Park: Pennsylvania State University Press, 1990.
Haill, Catherine. "Animal Performers." East London Theatre Archive. www.deltaproject.org/theme-animal.html.
Halewood, William H. "Religion and Invention in *Robinson Crusoe*." *Essays in Criticism* 14 (1964): 339–351.
Hammond, J. R. *A Robert Louis Stevenson Companion: A Guide to the Novels, Essays, and Short Stories* London: Macmillan, 1984.
Harakas, Rev. Stanley S. "To Clone or Not to Clone?" In *Ethical Issues in Human Cloning: Cross-Disciplinary Perspectives*, edited by Michael C. Brannigan. New York: Seven Bridges Press, 2001. 89–92.
Hardy, Rod, and George T. Miller, dirs. *Daniel Defoe's Robinson Crusoe*. Miramax, 1997.
Havini, Marilyn Taleo, and Josie Tankuanani Sirvi, eds. *As Mothers of the Land: The Birth of Bougainville Women for Peace and Freedom*. Canberra: Pandanus Books, 2003.

Hazlitt, William. *Complete Works of William Hazlitt*. 21 vols. Edited by P. P. Howe after the edition of A. R. Waller and Arnold Glover. London: J. M. Dent and Sons, 1930–1934.

Hofland, Barbara. *The Young Crusoe; or, The Shipwrecked Boy*. London: Printed for A.K. Newman and Co., 1828.

Hong Kingston, Maxine. *China Men*. 1980. New York: Vintage, 1989.

Hunt, John Dixon. *A World of Gardens*. London: Reaktion Books, 2012.

Hunter, J. Paul. *The Reluctant Pilgrim: Defoe's Emblematic Method and Quest for Form in Robinson Crusoe*. Baltimore: Johns Hopkins University Press, 1966.

Hutcheon, Linda. *A Poetics of Postmodernism: History, Theory, Fiction*. London: Routledge, 1988.

Hutchins, Henry. "Some Imitations of Robinson Crusoe—Called Robinsonades." *Yale University Library Gazette* 11.2 (1936): 32–36.

Jaëck, Nathalie. "Kidnapping the Historical Novel in *Kidnapped*: An Act of Literary and Political Resistance." *Journal of Stevenson Studies* 11 (2014): 87–104.

James, Isaac. *Providence Displayed, or, The Remarkable Adventures of Alexander Selkirk of Largo in Scotland: Who Lived Four Years and Four Months by Himself on the Island of Juan Fernandez . . . and on Whose Adventures Was Founded the Celebrated Novel of Robinson Crusoe*. Bristol: Printed by Riggs and Cottle, 1800.

Jameson, Fredric. *Postmodernism; or, The Cultural Logic of Late Capitalism*. London: Versos, 1991.

Janes, Daniela. "The Limits of the Story: Reading the Castaway Narrative in *A Strange Manuscript Found in a Copper Cylinder* and *Life of Pi*." *Mosaic: An Interdisciplinary Critical Journal* 46.4 (December 2013): 109–125.

Johnson, Daniel J. "*Robinson Crusoe* and the Apparitional Eighteenth-Century Novel." *Eighteenth-Century Fiction* 28.2 (Winter 2015–2016): 239–261.

Jones, Duncan, dir. *Moon*. Sony Pictures Classics, 2009.

Joseph, Betty. "Re(playing) Crusoe/Pocahontas: Circum-Atlantic Stagings in 'The Female American.'" *Criticism* 42.3 (Summer 2007): 317–335.

Juda, Maria. "Uprzywilejowane drukarnie we Lwowie doby staropolskiej." *Folia Bibliologica* 55/56 (2013/2014): 11–18.

Kaufman-Scarborough, Carol. "Two Perspectives on the Tyranny of Time: Polychronicity and Monochronicity as Depicted in *Cast Away*." *Journal of American Culture* 26.1 (March 2003): 87–95.

Keiller, Patrick, dir. *London*. BFI Production; Koninck Studios, 1994.

———. *Robinson in Space*. BBC; Koninck Studios, 1997.

Kinane, Ian. *Theorising Literary Islands: The Island Trope in Contemporary Robinsonade Narratives*. London: Rowman & Littlefield, 2017.

Kinnell, Margaret. "Sceptreless, Free, Uncircumscribed? Radicalism, Dissent and Early Children's Books." *British Journal of Educational Studies* 36.1 (1988): 49–71.

Klimowicz, Mieczysław. "Wstęp." In Ignacy Krasicki, *Mikołaja Doświadczyńskiego przypadki*, edited by Mieczysław Klimowicz. Wrocław: Zakład Narodowy im. Ossolińskich, 1975. iii–lxi.

Krasicki, Ignacy. *The Adventures of Mr. Nicholas Wisdom*. Translated by Thomas H. Hoisington. Evanston, IL: Northwestern University Press, 1992.

———. *Historia*. 1779. Kraków: Universitas, 2002.

———. *Mikołaja Doświadczyńskiego przypadki*. 1776. Edited by Mieczysław Klimowicz. Wrocław: Zakład Narodowy im. Ossolińskich, 1975.

Krick, Patrick Vinton, and Jean-Louis Rallu, eds. *The Growth and Collapse of Pacific Island Societies: Archaeological and Demographic Perspectives*. Honolulu: University of Hawaii Press, 2007.

Kvande, Marta. "'Had You No Lands of Your Own?' Seeking Justice in *The Female American* (1767)." *Women's Studies* 45.7 (2016): 684–698.

Lane, Andrew. *Dawn of Spies*. Culver City: Adaptive Books, 2016.

Larpent, John. *Examiner of Plays (1778–1824)*. Catalogue of the John Larpent Plays. San Marino, CA: Huntington Library.

Layh, Susanna. "'All Alone in an Empty World': Post-Apocalyptic Robinsonades." In *Yesterday's Tomorrows: On Utopia and Dystopia*, edited by Pere Gallardo and Elizabeth Russell. Newcastle upon Tyne: Cambridge Scholars, 2014.

Levy, Michelle. "Discovery and the Domestic Affections in Coleridge and Shelley." *Studies in English Literature, 1500–1900* 44.4 (2004): 693–713.

Lipski, Jakub. "Picturing Crusoe's Island: Defoe, Rousseau, Stothard." *Porównania* 25 (2019): 85–99.

Loar, Christopher. "How to Say Things with Guns: Military Technology and the Politics of *Robinson Crusoe*." *Eighteenth-Century Fiction* 19.1–2 (2006): 1–20.

London, April. *The Cambridge Introduction to the Eighteenth-Century Novel*. Cambridge: Cambridge University Press, 2012.

Longueville, Peter. *The Hermit: or, The Unparalleled Sufferings and Surprising Adventures of Mr. Philip Quarll, an Englishman Who Was Lately Discovered by Mr. Dorrington a Bristol Merchant, upon an Uninhabited Island in the South-Sea; Where He Has Lived above Fifty Years, without Any Human Assistance, Still Continues to Reside, and Will Not Come Away*. London: Printed by J. Cluer and A. Campbell for T. Warner in Pater-Noster-Row, and B. Creake at the Bible in Jermyn-Street, St. James's, 1727.

———— [under the pseudonym of Edward Dorrington]. *The Hermit; or, The Unparalleled Sufferings, and Surprising Adventures, of Philip Quarll, an Englishman, Who Was Discovered by Mr. Dorrington, a Bristol-Merchant, upon an Uninhabited Island, in the South-sea, Where He Lived about Fifty Years, without Any Human Assistance*. Gainsborough: Henry Mozley, 1814.

Lovelock, James, and Sidney Epton. "The Quest for Gaia." *New Scientist* 65.935 (6 February 1975): 304–309.

Loxley, Diana. *Problematic Shores: The Literature of Islands*. Houndmills: Palgrave Macmillan, 1990.

Luter, Matthew. "More Than a Vast Avante-Pop Wasteland: Tom Carson's *Gilligan's Wake*, Television, and American Historical Fiction." *Genre* 42.3/4 (2009): 21–40.

Maixner, Paul, ed. *Robert Louis Stevenson: The Critical Heritage*. London: Routledge, 1998.

Marryat, Frederick. *Masterman Ready; or, The Wreck of the Pacific*. 3 vols. London: Longman, Orme, Brown, Green, & Longmans, 1841–1842.

Martel, Yann. *Life of Pi*. 2001. Edinburgh: Canongate, 2002.

Mayer, Robert. "Defoe's Cultural Afterlife, Mainly on Screen." In *Afterlives of Eighteenth-Century Fiction*, edited by Daniel Cook and Nicholas Seager. Cambridge: Cambridge University Press, 2015. 233–252.

————. "*Robinson Crusoe* in Hollywood." In *Approaches to Teaching Defoe's* Robinson Crusoe, edited by Maximillian E. Novak and Carl Fisher. New York: MLA, 2005. 169–174.

————. "Robinson Crusoe in the Screen Age." In *The Cambridge Companion to "Robinson Crusoe,"* edited by John Richetti. Cambridge: Cambridge University Press, 2018. 221–233.

————. "Three Cinematic Robinsonades." In *Eighteenth-Century Fiction on Screen*, edited by Robert Mayer. Cambridge: Cambridge University Press, 2002. 35–51.

McConnell Stott, Andrew. *The Pantomime Life of Joseph Grimaldi*. Edinburgh: Canongate Books, 2009.

McDowell, Paula. *The Invention of the Oral: Print Commerce and Fugitive Voices in Eighteenth-Century Britain*. Chicago: University of Chicago Press, 2017.

McVeagh, John. "*Robinson Crusoe*'s Stage Début: The Sheridan Pantomime of 1781." *Journal of Popular Culture* 24.2 (Fall 1990): 137–152.

Meer, Jan IJ. van der. *Literary Activities and Attitudes in the Stanislavian Age in Poland (1764–1795): A Social System?* Amsterdam: Rodopi, 2002.

Metz, Walter. *Gilligan's Island*. Detroit: Wayne State University Press, 2012.

BIBLIOGRAPHY

Michals, Teresa. *Books for Children, Books for Adults: Age and the Novel from Defoe to James.* Cambridge: Cambridge University Press, 2014.
Miłosz, Czesław. *The History of Polish Literature.* Berkeley: University of California Press, 1983.
Monastersky, Richard. "Anthropocene: The Human Age." *Nature* 519.7542 (2015): 144–147.
Moore, John Robert. "Defoe, Stevenson, and the Pirates." *English Literary History* 10.1 (1943): 35–60.
Morawińska, Agnieszka. "Osiemnastowieczna wizja ogrodu." In August Fryderyk Moszyński, *Rozprawa o ogrodnictwie angielskim, 1774,* edited by Agnieszka Morawińska. Wrocław: Zakład Narodowy im. Ossolińskich, 1977. 15–36.
Morowitz, Laura. "From Gauguin to *Gilligan's Island.*" *Journal of Popular Film and Television* 26.1 (1998): 2–10.
Moszyński, August Fryderyk. *Rozprawa o ogrodnictwie angielskim, 1774.* Edited by Agnieszka Morawińska. Wrocław: Zakład Narodowy im. Ossolińskich, 1977.
Munjin, Margaret. "Farewell Takaku, You Were Truly a Legend." *National,* 7 February 2011. www.thenational.com.pg/farewell-takaku-you-were-truly-a-legend/.
Nayak, Bhagabat. "Magic Realism in Yann Martel's *Life of Pi.*" In *Studies in English Literature,* vol. 11, edited by Mohit K. Ray. New Delhi: Atlantic, 2005. 168–180.
Nicoll, Allardyce. *The Garrick Stage: Theatres and Audience in the Eighteenth Century.* Edited by Sybil Rosenfeld. Manchester: Manchester University Press, 1980.
Nikoleishvili, Sophia. "The Many Faces of Daniel Defore's *Robinson Crusoe*: Examining the Crusoe Myth in Film and on Television." PhD diss., University of Missouri–Columbia, 2007.
Noë, Alva. *Out of Our Heads.* New York: Hill & Wang, 2010.
Novak, Maximillian E. *Daniel Defoe: Master of Fictions, His Life and Ideas.* Oxford: Oxford University Press, 2001.
———. "Ideological Tendencies in Three Crusoe Narratives by British Novelists during the Period Following the French Revolution: Charles Dibdin's *Hannah Hewit, The Female Crusoe,* Maria Edgeworth's *Forester,* and Frances Burney's *The Wanderer.*" *Eighteenth-Century Novel* 9 (2012): 261–280.
———. *Transformations, Ideology, and the Real in Defoe's "Robinson Crusoe" and Other Narratives: Finding "The Thing Itself."* Newark: University of Delaware Press, 2015.
O'Malley, Andrew. *Children's Literature, Popular Culture, and "Robinson Crusoe."* Houndmills: Palgrave Macmillan, 2012.
Ordway, Holly E. "Robinson Crusoe." *Dvdtalk.com,* 17 February 2002. www.dvdtalk.com/reviews/3419/robinson-crusoe/.
Panek, Melissa Barchi. *The Postmodern Mythology of Michel Tournier.* Newcastle upon Tyne: Cambridge Scholars, 2012.
Parsons, Coleman O. "The Mariner and the Albatross." *Virginia Quarterly Review* 26.1 (1950): 102–123.
Pearl, Jason H. "*Peter Wilkins* and the Eighteenth-Century Novel." *SEL Studies in English Literature 1500–1900* 57.3 (2017): 541–559.
Petit, Susan. *Michel Tournier's Metaphysical Fictions.* Amsterdam: John Benjamins, 1991.
Phillips, Richard. *Mapping Men and Empire: A Geography of Adventure.* London: Routledge, 1997.
Pivetti, Kyle. "The King of Mars: *The Martian*'s Scientific Empire and *Robinson Crusoe.*" In *The Cinematic Eighteenth Century: History, Culture, and Adaptation,* edited by Srividhya Swaminathan and Steven W. Thomas. London: Routledge, 2018. 118–138.
Pixerecourt, René-Charles Guilbert de. *Robinson Crusoe.* Paris: Barba, 1805.
———. *The Dog of Montargis or the Forest of Bondy* [*Le chien de Montargis*]. Théâtre de la Gaîté, 18 June 1814.

Pocock, Isaac. *Robinson Crusoe; or, The Bold Buccaniers. A Drama, in Two Acts:* [toy theater] *Adapted to Hodgson's Theatrical Characters and Scenes in the Same*. London: Printed by and for Hodgson & Co., 1822.

———. *Robinson Crusoe; or, The Bold Bucaniers: A Romantic Melo-drama*. London: Printed for J. Miller, 1817.

Poenicke, Klaus. "Engendering Cultural Memory: 'The Legend of Sleepy Hollow' as Text and Intertext." *Amerikastudien/American Studies* 43.1 (1998): 19–32.

Poniewozik, James. "Saving Tom Hanks." *Time Europe* 157.1 (8 January 2001). http://content.time.com/time/world/article/0,8599,2056298,00.html.

Probyn, Clive. "Paradise and Cotton-Mill: Rereading Eighteenth-Century Romance." In *A Companion to Romance: From Classical to Contemporary*, edited by Corinne Saunders. Malden, MA: Blackwell, 2004. 251–268.

Rader, Ralph. "The Concept of Genre and Eighteenth-Century Studies" (1973). In *Fact, Fiction, and Form: Selected Essays*, edited by James Phelan and David H. Richter. Columbus: Ohio State University Press, 2011. 58–81.

Rayman, Paula M. *Beyond the Bottom Line: The Search for Dignity at Work*. New York: Palgrave Macmillan, 2001.

Recarte, Claudia Alonso. "Canine Actors and Melodramatic Effects: The Dog of Montargis Arrives on the English Stage." *Cahiers victoriens et édouardiens* 86 (Automne 2017). http://journals.openedition.org/cve/3345.

Reid, Julia. *Robert Louis Stevenson, Science, and the Fin de Siècle*. Houndmills: Palgrave Macmillan, 2006.

Reilly, Mathew. "'No Eye Has Seen, or Ear Heard': Arabic Sources for Quaker Subjectivity in Unca Eliza Winkfield's *The Female American*." *Eighteenth-Century Studies* 44.2 (Winter 2011): 261–283.

Rex, Cathy. *Anglo-American Women Writers and Representations of Indianness, 1629–1824*. London: Routledge, 2015.

Richetti, John. "Defoe as Narrative Innovator." In *The Cambridge Companion to Daniel Defoe*, edited by John Richetti. Cambridge: Cambridge University Press, 2008. 121–138.

———. *Defoe's Narratives: Situations and Structures*. Oxford: Clarendon, 1975.

Rigney, Ann. *The Afterlives of Walter Scott: Memory on the Move*. Oxford: Oxford University Press, 2012.

Rogers, Pat, ed. *Defoe: The Critical Heritage*. New York: Routledge & Kegan Paul, 1972.

———. *Robinson Crusoe*. London: George Allen & Unwin, 1979.

Rousseau, Jean-Jacques. *Emile, or On Education*. Edited and translated by Christopher Kelly and Allan Bloom. Hanover, NH: University Press of New England, 2010.

Rowley, Charles D. *The Australians in German New Guinea, 1914–1921*. Melbourne: Melbourne University Press, 1959.

Rudnicka, Jadwiga, ed. *Biblioteka Stanisława Augusta na Zamku Warszawskim: Dokumenty*. *Archiwum Literackie* 26 (1988): 1–363.

Ruszała, Jadwiga. *Robinson w literaturze polskiej*. Słupsk: Wydawnictwo Wyższej Szkoły Pedagogicznej w Słupsku, 1998.

———. *Robinsonada w literaturze polskiej*. Słupsk: Wydawnictwo Akademii Pomorskiej w Słupsku, 2000.

Sargent, Lyman Tower. *Utopianism: A Very Short Introduction*. Oxford: Oxford University Press, 2010.

Scheckter, John. *The Isle of Pines, 1668: Henry Neville's Uncertain Utopia*. London: Routledge, 2016.

Schierenbeck, Daniel. "The Adventure Novel." *Encyclopedia of Romanticism*. 3 vols. Edited by Frederick Burwick, Nancy Goslee, and Diane Hoeveler. Oxford: Wiley-Blackwell, 2012. 1:19–27.

BIBLIOGRAPHY

Schmidgen, Wolfram. "The Metaphysics of *Robinson Crusoe.*" *English Literary History* 83.1 (Spring 2016): 101–126.

Schwartz, Sherwood. *Inside* Gilligan's Island: *From Creation to Syndication*. London: McFarland, 1988.

Scott, Heidi C. M. "Havens and Horrors: The Island Landscape." *Interdisciplinary Studies in Literature and Environment* 21.3 (2014): 636–657.

Scott, Ridley, dir. *The Martian*. 20th Century Fox, 2015.

Seidel, Michael. *Robinson Crusoe: Island Myths and the Novel*. Boston: Twayne, 1991.

———. "*Robinson Crusoe*: Varieties of Fictional Experience." In *The Cambridge Companion to Daniel Defoe*, edited by John Richetti. Cambridge: Cambridge University Press, 2008. 182–199.

Severin, Tim. *In Search of Robinson Crusoe*. New York: Basic Books, 2002.

Shakespeare, William. *Richard II*. The New Folger Library Shakespeare. Edited by Barbara A. Mowat and Paul Werstine. New York: Washington Square Press, 1996.

Sheridan, Richard Brinsley. *Robinson Crusoe; or, Harlequin Friday. A Grand Pantomime, in Two Acts, as Performed at the Theatre-Royal, Newcastle upon Tyne, in 1791*. Newcastle upon Tyne: Printed by Hall and Elliot, 1791.

———. *Short Account of the Situations and Incidents Exhibited in the Pantomime of Robinson Crusoe, at the Theatre Royal, Drury-Lane*. London: Printed for T. Becket, 1789.

Shulgasser-Parker, Barbara. "Robinson Crusoe (1997)." www.commonsensemedia.org/movie-reviews/robinson-crusoe-1997.

Sidney, Philip. "The Defence of Poesy." In *Sir Philip Sidney: The Major Works*, edited by Katherine Duncan-Jones. Oxford: Oxford University Press, 1989. 212–251.

Simon, Edward. "Unca Eliza Winkfield and the Fantasy of Non-colonial Conversion in *The Female American*." *Women's Studies* 45.7 (2016): 649–659.

Singer, Jefferson A. *The Proper Pirate: Robert Louis Stevenson's Quest for Identity*. New York: Oxford University Press, 2017.

Sinko, Zofia. *Powieść angielska osiemnastego wieku a powieść polska lat, 1764–1830*. Warszawa: Państwowy Instytut Wydawniczy, 1961.

———. "Powieść zachodnioeuropejska w Polsce stanisławowskiej na podstawie inwentarzy bibliotecznych i katalogów." *Pamiętnik Literacki* 57.4 (1966): 581–624.

Smith, Christopher. "Charles Guilbert de Pixérécourt's *Robinson Crusoé* (1805)." In *Robinson Crusoe: Myths and Metamorphoses*, edited by Lieve Spaas and Brian Stimpson. Houndmills: Macmillan, 1996. 127–140.

Smith, John. *A Generall Historie of Virginia* (1624). In *Captain John Smith's America: Selections from His Writings*, edited by John Lankford. New York: Harper & Row, 1967.

Spaas, Lieve, and Brian Stimpson, eds. *Robinson Crusoe: Myths and Metamorphoses*. Houndmills: Macmillan, 1996.

Spark, Muriel. *Robinson*. London: Macmillan, 1958.

Sproxton, Judy. "The Women of Muriel Spark: Narrative and Faith." *New Blackfriars* 73.863 (September 1992): 432–440.

Squire, Louise. "Circles Unrounded: Sustainability, Subject and Necessity in Yann Martel's *Life of Pi*." In *Literature and Sustainability: Concept, Text and Culture*, edited by John Parham, Adeline Johns-Putra, and Louise Squire. Manchester: Manchester University Press, 2017. 228–245.

Stannard, Martin. *Muriel Spark: The Biography*. London: Weidenfeld and Nicolson, 2009.

Stella, Regis Tove. *Imagining the Other: The Representation of the Papua New Guinean Subject*. Honolulu: University of Hawaii Press, 2007.

Stevenson, Robert Louis. "A Gossip on Romance." In *Memories and Portraits*. London: William Heinemann, 1928. 119–131.

———. *Kidnapped*. 1886. Edited by Ian Duncan. Oxford: Oxford University Press, 2014.
Strickland, Agnes. *The Rival Crusoes*. London: J. Harris, 1826.
Sullivan, Nancy. "Interview with Albert Toro." In *Cultural Producers in Perilous State: Editing Events, Documenting Change*, edited by George E. Marcus. Chicago: University of Chicago Press, 1997. 331–356.
Summers-Bremner, Eluned. "'Another World Than This': Muriel Spark's Postwar Investigations." *Yearbook in English Studies* 42 (2012): 151–167.
Summit, Jennifer, and Blakey Vermeule. *Action versus Contemplation: Why an Ancient Debate Still Matters*. Chicago: University of Chicago Press, 2018.
Swenson, Rivka. "'It Is to Pleasure You': Seeing Things in Mackenzie's *Aretina* (1660), or, Whither Scottish Prose Fiction Before the Novel?" *Studies in Scottish Literature* 43.1 (2017): 22–30.
———. "Optics, Gender, and the Eighteenth-Century Gaze: Looking at Eliza Haywood's *Anti-Pamela*." *Eighteenth Century: Theory and Interpretation* 51.1–2 (2010): 27–43.
———. "The Poet as Man of Feeling." In *Oxford Handbook of British Poetry, 1660–1800*, edited by Jack Lynch. Oxford: Oxford University Press, 2016. 195–209.
———. "*Robinson Crusoe* and the Form of the New Novel." In *The Cambridge Companion to "Robinson Crusoe,"* edited by John Richetti. Cambridge: Cambridge University Press, 2018. 16–31.
Swift, Jonathan. *Gulliver's Travels*. 1726. Edited by Claude Rawson and Ian Higgins. Oxford: Oxford University Press, 2008.
Swindells, Julia. "Abolitionist Theatre." In *Encyclopedia of Romanticism*, 3 vols., edited by Frederick Burwick, Nancy Goslee, and Diane Hoeveler. Oxford: Wiley-Blackwell, 2012. 1:7–14.
Swindells, Julia, and David Francis Taylor, eds. *The Oxford Handbook of the Georgian Theatre, 1737–1832*. Oxford: Oxford University Press, 2014.
Takaku, William, narrator. "Bougainville Reed Festival at Kieta." https://youtu.be/jX2_BinvFNc.
Taylor, Frederick. *Shop Management*. New York: Harper & Brothers, 1912.
Thompson, Helen. "The Crusoe Story: Philosophical and Psychological Implications." In *The Cambridge Companion to "Robinson Crusoe,"* edited by John Richetti. Cambridge: Cambridge University Press, 2018. 112–127.
Tigner, Amy L., and Allison Carruth, eds. *Literature and Food Studies*. Oxford: Routledge, 2017.
Torke, Celia. *Die Robinsonin: Repräsentationen von Weiblichkeit in deutsch- und englischsprachigen Robinsonaden des 20. Jahrhunderts*. Göttingen: V&R unipress, 2011.
Tournier, Michel. *Friday*. Translated by Norman Denny. Baltimore: Johns Hopkins University Press, 1997.
———. *Le vent Paraclet*. Paris: Gallimard, 1977.
"Trivia: *Cast Away* (2000)." *IMDb*. www.imdb.com/title/tt0162222/trivia.
"Trivia: *Robinson Crusoe* (1997)." *IMDb*. www.imdb.com/title/tt0117496/trivia?ref_=tt_trv_trv.
Tytler, Ann Fraser. *Leila; or, The Island*. 1833. London: J. Hatchard and Son, 1839.
United Nations. "The United Nations and Decolonization." http://un.org/en/decolonization/history.shtml.
Van Ghent, Dorothy. *The English Novel: Form and Function*. New York: Harper & Row, 1953. Reprint, 1961.
Veltman, Andrea. *Meaningful Work*. Oxford: Oxford University Press, 2016.
Wall, Cynthia. *The Prose of Things: Transformations of Description in the Eighteenth Century*. Chicago: University of Chicago Press, 2006.
Wampole, Christy. *Rootedness: The Ramifications of a Metaphor*. Chicago: University of Chicago Press, 2016.
Watt, Ian P. *The Rise of the Novel: Studies in Defoe, Richardson, and Fielding*. Berkeley: University of California Press, 1957. Reprint, 2000.
———. "Robinson Crusoe as a Myth." *Essays in Criticism* 1.2 (1951): 96–119.

BIBLIOGRAPHY

Weaver-Hightower, Rebecca. *Empire Islands: Castaways, Cannibals, and Fantasies of Conquest.* Minneapolis: University of Minnesota Press, 2007.
Weir, Andy. *The Martian: A Novel.* 2011. New York: Crown, 2014.
Wheeler, Roxann. "The Complexion of Desire: Racial Ideology and Mid-Eighteenth-Century British Novels." *Eighteenth-Century Studies* 32.3 (Spring 1999): 309–332.
White, Lynn, Jr. "The Historical Roots of Our Ecological Crisis." In *The Ecocriticism Reader: Landmarks in Literary Ecology,* edited by Cheryll Glotfelty and Harold Fromm. Athens: University of Georgia Press, 1996.
Wiggins, Marianne. *John Dollar.* New York: Harper & Row, 1988.
"William Takaku." *Alchetron,* 24 March 2018. https://alchetron.com/William-Takaku.
Wilson, Kathleen. *The Island Race: Englishness, Empire and Gender in the Eighteenth Century.* London: Routledge, 2003.
Winkfield, Unca Eliza. *The Female American.* 1767. Edited by Michelle Burnham and James Freitas. Peterborough: Broadview, 2014.
Woolf, Virginia. "*Robinson Crusoe.*" In *The Second Common Reader,* edited by Andrew McNeillie. 1932. New York: Harcourt Brace, 1986. 51–59.
Worrall, David. *Harlequin Empire: Race, Ethnicity and the Drama of the Popular Enlightenment.* London: Pickering & Chatto, 2007.
Wyss, Johann David. *The Swiss Family Robinson.* 1814. New York: Aladdin Paperbacks, 2007.
Yakham, Henzy. "Stage Set for Referendum on Bougainville's Future." *Papua New Guinea Post-Courier,* 18 January 2019. https://postcourier.com.pg/stage-set-referendum-bougainvilles-future/.
Zemeckis, Robert, dir. *Cast Away.* 20th Century Fox and DreamWorks, 2000.
Żołądź-Strzelczyk, Dorota. "Kilka uwag o znajomości dzieła Jana Jakuba Rousseau *Emil, czyli o wychowaniu* w Polsce przełomu XVIII i XIX wieku." *Problemy wczesnej edukacji* 2.29 (2015): 7–14.

NOTES ON CONTRIBUTORS

FREDERICK BURWICK, professor emeritus at the University of California, Los Angeles, is the author and editor of thirty-four books and one hundred fifty-four essays. He is editor of the *Coleridge's Biographia Literaria: Text and Meaning* (1989) and *The Oxford Handbook of Coleridge* (2009). His recent monographs include *Romanticism: Keywords* (2015), *British Pirates in Print and Performance* (2015), *British Drama of the Industrial Revolution* (2015), and *A History of Romantic Literature* (2019). He has been named Distinguished Scholar by the British Academy (1992) and by the Keats-Shelley Association (1998). The International Conference on Romanticism has presented him with their Lifetime Achievement Award (2013).

DANIEL COOK is the head of English and associate director of the Centre for Scottish Culture at the University of Dundee in Scotland. He has published widely on eighteenth- and nineteenth-century British and Irish literature, with a particular focus on Jonathan Swift and his circle. His books include *Thomas Chatterton and Neglected Genius, 1760–1830* (2013), *Women's Life Writing, 1700–1850: Gender, Genre and Authorship* (2012, with Amy Culley), and *The Afterlives of Eighteenth-Century Fiction* (2015, with Nicholas Seager). His forthcoming titles include *Reading Swift's Poetry* and *Walter Scott and Shorter Fiction*.

LORA E. GERIGUIS is professor of English and associate dean of the College of Arts and Sciences at La Sierra University in Riverside, California, whose research is currently focused on producing ecocritical readings of seventeenth- and eighteenth-century British texts. Her publications include ecocritical analysis of Daniel Defoe's *Captain Singleton (Topographies of Imagination)* and Richard Lewis's poetry (*Early American Literature*, coauthored); studies of Margaret Cavendish as anthologized in the *Norton Anthology of English Literature* (*English Studies*) and her relationship to the library network that supported the early Royal Society (*Pacific Coast Philology*); an explication of the spiritual symbolisms expressed through the grammatical anomalies found in John Donne's poetry (*The Explicator*); and an analysis of the performance of English masculinity on the Restoration and eighteenth-century stage (*Restoration and Eighteenth Century Theatre Research*).

NOTES ON CONTRIBUTORS

PATRICK GILL received his PhD in English literature from Johannes Gutenberg-Universität Mainz, where he is now a senior lecturer. He has published essays on English poetry of all ages, the contemporary novel, and various aspects of British and American popular culture. His teaching and research tend to focus on the efficacy of literary form. Most recently, he was coeditor of *Constructing Coherence in the British Short Story Cycle* (2018).

IAN KINANE is senior lecturer in English literature at the University of Roehampton, London. He is the author of *Theorising Literary Islands* (2016), editor of *Didactics and the Modern Robinsonade* (2019), and coeditor of *Landscapes of Liminality: Between Space and Place* (2016). He is currently writing a monograph provisionally titled *Ambiguity and Resistance in Ian Fleming's Jamaica-Set Works*, and he is the editor of the *International Journal of James Bond Studies*.

JAKUB LIPSKI is associate professor and head of Anglophone Literatures at Kazimierz Wielki University in Bydgoszcz, Poland. He is the author of *In Quest of the Self: Masquerade and Travel in the Eighteenth-Century Novel* (2014) and *Painting the Novel: Pictorial Discourse in Eighteenth-Century English Fiction* (2018). His research interests include eighteenth-century English fiction and culture as well as the correspondences between word and image. He is currently working on a new edition of *Robinson Crusoe* for the Polish National Library series.

ROBERT MAYER is professor emeritus at Oklahoma State University, where he taught British literature and was for many years director of the Screen Studies Program. He is the author of *History and the Early English Novel: Matters of Fact from Bacon to Defoe* (1997) and *Walter Scott and Fame: Authors and Readers in the Romantic Age* (2017) and the editor of *Eighteenth-Century Fiction on Screen* (2002). He lives in New Mexico.

MÁRTA PELLÉRDI is associate professor at the Institute of English and American Studies, Pázmány Péter Catholic University, Budapest, where she has been teaching since 1998. She holds a PhD in American literature from Eötvös Loránd University, Budapest, and teaches courses in nineteenth- and twentieth-century British and American fiction. She is the author of a study on Vladimir Nabokov, *Nabokov's Palace: The American Novels* (2010). She has published on Nabokov, Jane Austen, Washington Irving, and George Moore in various journals and edited volumes.

KRZYSZTOF SKONIECZNY is assistant professor at the Faculty of "Artes Liberales," University of Warsaw. His interests include political philosophy, psychoanalysis, posthumanities, animal studies, and contemporary American literature, which he occasionally translates. He is the author of *Immanence and the Animal: A Concep-*

tual Inquiry (2020) and the co-editor (with Szymon Wróbel) of *Atheism Revisited. Rethinking Modernity and Inventing New Modes of Life* (2020).

RIVKA SWENSON is associate professor of English at Virginia Commonwealth University. Her first book, *Essential Scots and the Idea of Unionism in Anglo-Scottish Literature, 1603–1832*, was published in 2016. Her recent essays have appeared in *Studies in Scottish Literature, Cambridge Companion to British Women's Writing, 1660–1789, The Cambridge Companion to "Robinson Crusoe,"* and *Oxford Handbook of British Poetry, 1660–1800*. Her coedited work includes a special issue of *The Eighteenth Century: Theory and Interpretation* ("Sensational Subjects," with Manushag Powell) and a collection of essays, *Imagining Selves: Essays in Honor of Patricia Meyer Spacks*. She is coediting, with John Richetti, an edition of Daniel Defoe's *Farther Adventures of Robinson Crusoe*. Her other current works in progress are centered upon women and the Robinsonade microgenre and upon optics, gender, and the eighteenth-century gaze.

PRZEMYSŁAW UŚCIŃSKI is assistant professor at the Institute of English Studies, University of Warsaw, and assistant editor of *Anglica: An International Journal of English Studies*. He has published a number of articles on eighteenth-century British literature and culture, the history of the novel, and the aesthetics of parody and translation. His book *Parody, Scriblerian Wit and the Rise of the Novel* was published in 2016. He has taught courses in British literature and culture, literary theory, and cultural studies.

JENNIFER PRESTON WILSON, associate professor of English at Appalachian State University, is coeditor, with Elizabeth Kraft, of *Approaches to Teaching the Novels of Henry Fielding* (2015). Her recent articles include "On Honor and Consequences: The Duel in *The Small House at Allington*" (*Dickens Studies Annual*), "'We Know Only Names, So Far': Samuel Richardson, Shirley Jackson, and Exploration of the Precarious Self" (*Shirley Jackson: Influences and Confluences*), and "'I Have You in My Eye, Sir': The Spectacle of Kingship in *The Madness of King George*" (*The Cinematic Eighteenth Century*).

INDEX

abolitionism, abolitionist movement, 67–68, 69, 71–72, 75
abridgements, 2, 60
agency, 4, 158–159, 122–123
Albertrandi, Jan Chrzciciel (Giovanni Battista), 58–61
allegory, 29, 49, 119, 137, 139, 153, 163n12
Anthropocene, 120–121
apocalyptic Robinsonade, 166
Argo, John, *Robinson Crusoe 1,000,000 A.D.*, 167
authorial Robinsonade, 170

Bakhtin, Mikhail, xi
Ballantyne, R. M., *Coral Island, The*, 5, 80, 166
Ballard, J. G., *Concrete Island*, 166
Barrie, James M., *Admirable Crichton, The*, 73
Bauman, Zygmunt, 39–40
becoming-animal (Deleuze and Guattari), 123, 128
becoming-Earth, 4, 122–123, 125, 128
Behn, Aphra, 50n13
Berger, Thomas, *Robert Crews*, 167
Bhabha, Homi K., 41
Blanchard, Edward L., *Robinson Crusoe*, 65
Bougainville: crisis of, 103, 107, 115nn63–64, 116n77; island of (or Autonomous Region of), 101, 102, 103, 107, 108, 111, 115n55, 115n58; people of, 102, 103, 105, 111, 115n53, 115n56, 115n65
Bougainville, Louis de, 96, 101–102, 103, 104, 105, 110, 113n29, 114n47, 114nn49–50, 114n52, 116n76
Braidotti, Rosi, 4, 122–123, 130
Brosnan, Pierce, 100, 101, 103–107, 108, 114n44
Brown, Laura, 44–45, 49

Campe, Joachim Heinrich, *Robinson der Jüngere*, 5, 57, 170
cannibalism, 25, 30, 36n18, 70, 75

capitalism, 41, 45, 124–127
Carson, Tom, *Gilligan's Wake*, ix, 5, 148–163
Cast Away (film), x, 5, 95, 96, 108–110, 114n45, 115n67, 116nn68–72, 116nn74–75, 135–136, 137, 138–139, 141, 142–143, 144, 145
children's literature, 57, 64n26, 72, 75, 89n12. *See also* young adult Robinsonade
Christianity, 26, 39, 44, 45, 49, 86, 98, 120
Clines, Peter, *Eerie Adventures of the Lycanthrope Robinson Crusoe, The*, 170–171
cloning, 139–140, 141–142
Coetzee, J. M., *Foe*, 2, 3, 29–33, 34, 165
Coleridge, Samuel Taylor, 20n2, 21n8
Colman, George, *Inkle and Yarico*, 72
Colonialism, x, 25n4, 26, 32, 44–45, 47, 65, 80, 82, 126
commedia dell'arte, 66–67
Coral Island, The (Ballantyne), 5, 80, 166
corporations, 5, 135–136, 138, 140, 143, 144
counterfactuals, 3, 23–24, 25, 27–28, 30, 32, 34, 35
counter-Robinsonade, 3, 4, 79, 81–82, 88
Cozzens, James Gould, *Castaway*, 166

Daniel Defoe's Robinson Crusoe (film), 95, 96, 100–107, 108, 110, 114n44
Defoe, Daniel: *Farther Adventures of Robinson Crusoe, The*, 1, 35n4, 106; *A Journal of the Plague Year*, x; *Moll Flanders*, x, 2, 19, 112n4; *Robinson Crusoe*, ix, 1, 24–26, 40, 65, 66, 79, 82, 84, 86–87, 94, 111n1, 112n4, 114n44, 135, 137, 138, 142, 144–145, 149–150, 163; *Roxana*, 112n4; *Serious Reflections*, 1, 64n33; *Storm, The*, 93–94, 111n1, 112nn2–3, 112n6; *Tour thro' the Whole Island of Great Britain*, x
Deleuze, Gilles, 117, 121, 123
description, 9–10, 14–17, 19, 21nn6–9, 102, 105

[193]

INDEX

Dibdin, Charles, *Hannah Hewitt, or the Female Crusoe* (play), 72–73, 75, 76; *Kaloc; or, The Slave Pirate*, 68; *Philip Quarl*, 68, 69, 75, 76
Doyle, Arthur Conan, 80
Dubois-Fontanelle, Jean Gaspard, *Naufrage et aventures de M. Pierre Viaud*, 61

ecological crisis, 120
Eliot, T. S., *Waste Land, The*, 152, 156
engineering, 135, 136–137, 138, 139, 140, 141, 143, 146
Enlightenment, 3, 52, 54–55, 63n12, 64n33, 131n13
Evans, Ambrose, *Adventures, and Surprizing Deliverances, of James Dubourdieu, and His Wife, The*, 2, 167

Fanti, Ivan, *Robinson Crusoe on Zombie Island*, 166
Fawcett, John, *De la Perouse; or, The Desolate Island*, 68–69
Female American, The, 3, 41–50, 95, 96–100, 105, 108, 113n19, 113nn21–22, 113n25, 165
female castaways, 3, 26–27, 29, 31, 41–42, 72–73, 172
Feutry, Joseph, 56, 60, 63n23
Fitzgerald, Francis Scott, *Great Gatsby, The*, 151
Foe (Coetzee), 2, 3, 29–33, 34, 165
Freud, Sigmund, 126
Friday, 4, 23, 29–33, 56, 65, 66, 67, 68, 69, 71–72, 73, 74, 75, 76, 101–107, 108–110, 114n44, 119, 124, 128–129, 141–142, 145–146

Gaia (hypothesis), 122
Gardam, Jane, *Crusoe's Daughter*, 169, 171
Genette, Gérard, 61, 119
Genre, xi, 1–2, 48, 142, 145
Gildon, Charles, *Life and Strange Surprizing Adventures of Mr. D—De F—, of London, Hosier, The*, 171
Gilligan's Island (television show), ix, 5, 148–150, 152–153, 155, 156, 158, 159, 160, 161, 162, 163n12, 164n25
Gilligan's Wake (Carson), ix, 5, 148–163
Gold, Jack, *Man Friday*, x
Golding, William, *Lord of the Flies*, 5
Gordon, Rex, *No Man Friday*, 23, 165–166, 169

Grimaldi, Joseph, 67–69, 71
Gulliver's Travels (Swift), 4, 53, 168

Hall, Willis, *Vampire Island*, 168
Hanks, Tom, 108–109, 115n67, 116n69
harlequinade, 65, 66–67, 68, 69, 71–72, 73, 74, 75, 76
Hazlitt, William, 74
Hermit, The (Longueville), 2, 9–22, 69, 166
hermit's tale, 170
historiographic metafiction, 155, 157. *See also* metafiction
Hutcheon, Linda, 153–154, 155, 157
hybrid, 40, 45–47, 127, 128, 142, 145

identity, 41–42, 45–47, 67, 151, 161
Indians, 42, 70–71, 97. *See also* native(s)

Jacobite Rebellion, 81, 82, 84–85, 88
James, Henry, 88
Jameson, Fredric, 153, 154–155
Jones, Duncan, 146n6; *Moon* (film), ix, 5, 135, 136, 137, 138, 139–140, 141–142, 143–144, 145, 146n20
Joyce, James, 80, 149; *Finnegans Wake*, ix, 149, 153

Keiller, Patrick: *London*, x; *Robinson in Ruins*, x; *Robinson in Space*, x
Kidnapped (Stevenson), 4, 79–90
Kingston, Maxine Hong, *China Men*, 168
Krasicki, Ignacy, 55, 56; *Historia*, 53–54, 61; *Mikołaja Doświadczyńskiego przypadki (The Adventures of Mr. Nicholas Wisdom)*, 52–54, 61

Lane, Andrew, *Dawn of Spies*, 171
Lemon, Mark, *Robinson Crusoe*, 65
Le Sage, Alain-René, *Gil Blas*, 54, 55, 165
Life of Pi (Martel), ix, 2, 33–36
Lockean man, 14
Longueville, Peter, *Hermit, The*, 2, 9–22, 69, 166
Loutherbourg, Philip James de, 67
Lovecraft, H. P., 166, 171

Marryat, Frederick, *Masterman Ready; or, The Wreck in the Pacific*, 73, 166
Martel, Yann, *Life of Pi*, ix, 2, 33–36

[194]

Martian, The (film), x, 5, 135, 136–137, 138, 139, 140–141, 142, 143, 144–145, 145–146
Más a Tierra, 70, 150
McCarthy, Cormac, *Road, The*, 166
melodrama, 65, 66, 68, 69, 71, 73, 74, 76
metafiction, 9, 11, 19, 34, 35, 155, 157. *See also* historiographic metafiction
modernism, 120–121, 152–153, 155
Monitor, 56, 59
Moon (film), ix, 5, 135, 136, 137, 138, 139–140, 141–142, 143–144, 145, 146n20
Morton, Charles, 94, 112n8
Moszyński, August Fryderyk, *Essay sur le jardinage Anglois*, 58
mutiny, 67, 74, 75, 137, 138
myth, 96, 97, 98, 104, 109, 110, 111, 113n23, 118–119, 146

narrator, 24, 26–27, 29, 30, 32, 41, 97, 115n64
NASA, 136–137, 138, 140, 142, 144–145, 146n16
native(s), 42, 69, 71, 72, 75, 97, 98, 101, 110. *See also* Indians
nature, 4, 58, 61, 109, 112n4, 121, 122, 128. *See also* state of nature
Neville, Henry, *Isle of Pines, The*, ix, 167–168
Nietzsche, Friedrich, 40

Oedipus (psychoanalysis), 117, 126, 127, 129, 130
Other(s), ix, x, 4, 33, 49, 95, 109, 110, 114n48, 121, 129, 141

pantomime, 65, 66, 67, 68, 69, 100
Papua New Guinea (PNG), 101, 102, 103, 107, 111, 115n55, 115n57, 115n63, 115n65, 116
Pixérécourt, René-Charles Guilbert, 69, 73–74; *Robinson Crusoe*, 65, 73, 74
Pocahontas, 42, 46, 50n9
Pocock, Isaac, 75; *Robinson Crusoe; or, The Bold Bucaniers*, 65, 73, 74–75, 76
Poe, Edgar Allan, *Arthur Gordon Pym*, 166
postcolonial, 4, 26, 32, 80, 100, 119
postmodernism, 24, 26, 33–34, 120–121, 127, 130, 153, 155
productivity, 135–136, 139, 140
providence, 3, 25, 28, 34, 39–40, 43–50, 53, 94, 95, 111, 145

pseudo-Robinsonade (quasi-Robinsonade), ix, 53
Puck's Pantomime; or, Harlequin and Robinson Crusoe, 65

realism, 24–25, 26, 59, 109, 142
Richardson, Samuel, *Clarissa*, 82
Robinson (Spark), 2, 26–29, 34, 165
Robinsonade gullivérienne, 168
Robinson, E. J., *Robinson Crusoe 2244*, 166
Robinson Crusoe (Defoe), ix, 1, 24–26, 40, 65, 66, 79, 82, 84, 86–87, 94, 111n1, 112n4, 114n44, 135, 137, 138, 142, 144–145, 149–150, 163
Robinson Crusoe on Mars (film), 167
Robinson Crusoe, or Harlequin Friday (Sheridan), 65, 66, 67–68, 71–72, 73, 75, 76
Robinson Crusoe; or, The Bold Bucaniers (Pocock), 65, 73, 74–75, 76
Rogers, Woodes, *A Cruising Voyage round the World*, ix
romance, 52, 59–60, 62n4, 82, 88, 97, 142–143, 147n31
Rousseau, Jean-Jacques, 3, 5, 60, 64n26; *Emile, or On Education*, 53, 56–57, 58
Rousseauvian Robinsonade, 57
Royal Society for the Improvement of Natural Knowledge (also Royal Society), 94, 101, 112n8

Schnabel, Johann Gottfried, *Insel Felsenburg*, ix
science-fiction Robinsonade, 23, 169
scientific management, 136
scientism, 140, 141
Scott, Ridley, *Martian, The* (film), x, 5, 135, 136–137, 138, 139, 140–141, 142, 143, 144–145, 145–146
Scott, Walter, 80, 83, 84
Selkirk, Alexander, 60, 70, 72, 97, 100, 118, 150, 154, 167, 170
setting, 23, 24, 95, 96, 97, 100, 101
Sheridan, Richard Brinsley, 67, 75; *Robinson Crusoe, or Harlequin Friday*, 65, 66, 67–68, 71–72, 73, 75, 76
shipwreck, ix, 5, 33–34, 53, 57, 67, 68, 69, 70, 72, 73, 76, 79, 83, 84, 97, 104, 118, 124, 125, 137, 138

INDEX

Sidney, Philip, *Defense of Poesie, The*, 15, 21n24
slaves (slavery), 31, 43, 47, 65, 67, 68, 71, 72, 73, 76, 103, 105, 106, 107, 121, 125, 129
slave trade, 49, 65, 68, 71, 74, 106
Solomon Islands, 96, 101, 102, 103, 115n55
Spark, Muriel, *Robinson*, 2, 26–29, 34, 165
Spectator, 56
spiritual autobiography, 137, 145
Stanislaus August, King of Poland, 3, 52, 54–55, 58, 61, 63n18
state of nature, 52, 56. *See also* nature
Steele, Richard, 59–60, 61
Stevenson, Robert Louis: "A Gossip on Romance," 79; *Kidnapped*, 4, 79–90; *Treasure Island*, 79, 80, 89n12, 166
Storm of 1703, 93
Swift, Jonathan, *Gulliver's Travels*, 4, 53, 168
Swiss Family Robinson, The (Wyss), 73, 75, 167, 170

Takaku, William, 101–108, 110, 114n44, 115n60
theater, 4, 65–76, 103, 100
theatrical Robinsonade, 4, 65–76
third space, 41, 46, 48
Tournier, Michel, 117, 118–119, 120, 126; Speranza (island), 4, 117, 118–119, 120, 121, 124–130; *Vendredi ou les Limbes du Pacifique (Friday, or The Other Island)*, 4, 117–131, 165, 166; *Vent Paraclet, Le*, 118–119
translation, 41, 45, 54, 56, 58–61, 73, 74, 75, 101, 129
Treasure Island (Stevenson), 79, 80, 89n12, 166

Treece, Henry, *Return of Robinson Crusoe, The*, 169–170
Tytler, Ann Fraser, *Leila*, 72

utopia, 41, 52–53, 56, 61, 62n8, 137, 140, 145

Vendredi ou les Limbes du Pacifique (Friday, or The Other Island) (Tournier), 4, 117–131, 165, 166
Verne, Jules, *Mysterious Island, The*, 167
Victorian Robinsonade, 81, 86, 89n12
Voltaire, *Candide*, 53

Walcott, Derek, *Pantomime*, 165
Walker, Rowland, *Phantom Island*, 167
Watt, Ian P., *Rise of the Novel, The*, 9, 21n12, 62n4
Weber, Max, 40
Weir, Andy, *Martian, The*, ix, 146n8
Wells, H. G., *Island of Dr. Moreau, The*, 166
Wild Life, The (film), 3
Woolf, Virginia, 21n8
workplace, 135–137, 139, 145
Wyss, Johann David, *Swiss Family Robinson, The*, 73, 75, 167, 170

young adult Robinsonade, 5, 166

Zemeckis, Robert, 115n67; *Cast Away* (film), x, 5, 95, 96, 108–110, 114n45, 115n67, 116nn68–72, 116nn74–75, 135–136, 137, 138–139, 141, 142–143, 144, 145; Chuck Noland, 5, 108–110, 116n72, 135–136, 137, 138–139, 141, 142–143, 144, 145; Wilson (the volleyball), 5, 108–110, 116n73, 141